Seneca: *Medea*

COMPANIONS TO GREEK AND ROMAN TRAGEDY

Series Editor: Thomas Harrison

Aeschylus: Agamemnon, Barbara Goward
Aeschylus: Eumenides, Robin Mitchell-Boyask
Aeschylus: Libation Bearers, C.W. Marshall
Aeschylus: Persians, David Rosenbloom
Aeschylus: Prometheus Bound, I.A. Ruffell
Aeschylus: Seven Against Thebes, Isabelle Torrance
Aeschylus: Suppliants, Thalia Papadopoulou
Euripides: Alcestis, Niall W. Slater
Euripides: Bacchae, Sophie Mills
Euripides: Cyclops, Carl A. Shaw
Euripides: Hecuba, Helene P. Foley
Euripides: Heracles, Emma Griffiths
Euripides: Hippolytus, Sophie Mills
Euripides: Ion, Lorna Swift
Euripides: Iphigenia at Aulis, Pantelis Michelakis
Euripides: Medea, William Allan
Euripides: Orestes, Matthew Wright
Euripides: Phoenician Women, Thalia Papadopoulou
Euripides: Suppliant Women, Ian Storey
Euripides: Trojan Women, Barbara Goff
Seneca: Hercules Furens, Neil W. Bernstein
Seneca: Oedipus, Susanna Braund
Seneca: Phaedra, Roland Mayer
Seneca: Thyestes, Peter Davis
Sophocles: Antigone, Douglas Cairns
Sophocles: Ajax, Jon Hesk
Sophocles: Electra, Michael Lloyd
Sophocles: Oedipus at Colonus, Adrian Kelly
Sophocles: Philoctetes, Hanna Roisman
Sophocles: Women of Trachis, Brad Levett

Seneca: *Medea*

Helen Slaney

BLOOMSBURY ACADEMIC
LONDON • NEW YORK • OXFORD • NEW DELHI • SYDNEY

BLOOMSBURY ACADEMIC
Bloomsbury Publishing Plc
50 Bedford Square, London, WC1B 3DP, UK
1385 Broadway, New York, NY 10018, USA

BLOOMSBURY, BLOOMSBURY ACADEMIC and the Diana logo are trademarks of Bloomsbury Publishing Plc

First published in Great Britain 2019

Cover design: Terry Woodley

Cover image © Maria Callas as Medea from the 1969 film. Collection Christophel / Alamy Stock Photo

A catalogue record for this book is available from the British Library.

Library of Congress Cataloging-in-Publication Data
Names: Slaney, Helen, 1981- author.
Title: Seneca: Medea / Helen Slaney.
Description: London : Bloomsbury Academic, 2019. | Series: Companions to Greek and Roman tragedy
Identifiers: LCCN 2018048921 (print) | LCCN 2018052253 (ebook) | ISBN 9781474258623 (epub) | ISBN 9781474258630 (epdf) | ISBN 9781474258616 (hb)
Subjects: LCSH: Seneca, Lucius Annaeus, approximately 4 B.C.-65 A.D. Medea. | Medea, consort of Aegeus, King of Athens (Mythological character)—In literature.
Classification: LCC PA6664.M43 (ebook) | LCC PA6664.M43 S53 2019 (print) | DDC 872/.01—dc23
LC record available at https://lccn.loc.gov/2018048921

ISBN: HB: 978-1-4742-5861-6
ePDF: 978-1-4742-5863-0
eBook: 978-1-4742-5862-3

Series: Companions to Greek and Roman Tragedy

Typeset by RefineCatch Limited, Bungay, Suffolk

To find out more about our authors and books visit www.bloomsbury.com and sign up for our newsletters.

Contents

Figures

Translations are my own unless otherwise indicated.

The account of Lavelli's *Medea* on pp. 131–3 was originally published in *The Senecan Aesthetic: a performance history* by Helen Slaney, and has been reproduced by permission of Oxford University Press.

1

Seneca and Roman Drama

Medea survives. Here you see the seas and land, iron and fire and gods and thunderbolts.[1]

Medea, avenger and infanticide, is one of the iconic figures of classical tragedy, and in her treatment by Roman playwright Seneca she takes on superhuman stature as the avatar of an outraged natural world. Medea the betrayed wife and murderous mother remains, but it is not (or not only) interpersonal conflicts which Seneca's tragedy plays out, but also the global consequences of greed and recklessness. It is a theme with particular significance for Seneca's Rome, and one which distinguishes the reception history of Seneca's *Medea* from that of her ancient Greek counterpart.

The question of performance continues to haunt discussions of Senecan tragedy, recent perspectives ranging from Kohn's 2013 defence of full-scale production to Bexley's 2015 reminder that *recitatio* constitutes performance in its own right. I take the view that while it may never be possible to determine with certainty how *Medea* was staged in antiquity, this represents only one point in its performance history, and that subsequent stagings are equally valid manifestations of the text.[2] As well as situating Seneca's *Medea* in ancient Rome, then, this study also considers pivotal moments in its reception history. Early modern translations such as Studley's (Chapter 4) and Corneille's (Chapter 5) became canonical in their own right, shaping perceptions of the Latin text they impersonate. Whether translations for the stage are regarded as descendants, parasites, surrogates, interlocutors, or acts of violence,[3] they become integral to the meaning it has historically accrued. Instances of reception amplify or bring to the surface particular aspects of the text that might otherwise remain latent, such as the rediscovery of theatre's ritual potential that arose in the mid-twentieth century (see Chapter 6). As a gemstone catches the light on different facets as it turns, so a work of theatre acquires different dimensions in the enactment.

1.1 Personal context

The Roman *Medea* was composed in the mid-first century CE and is commonly attributed to philosopher and courtier Lucius Annaeus Seneca, tutor to the young emperor Nero and later one of his close advisors. In addition to *Medea*, the tragedies transmitted under Seneca's name comprise six other mythological dramas corresponding to extant Greek antecedents, mainly Euripidean – *Phaedra*, *The Madness of Hercules*, *Trojan Women*, *Oedipus*, *Agamemnon*, and the fragmentary *Phoenician Women* – as well as *Thyestes*, of which no Greek equivalent survives.[4] Two further texts, *Hercules on Mt Oeta* and the *fabula praetexta* or history-play *Octavia* are now generally acknowledged to be the work of a later poet or poets, although by medieval and early modern readers they were received as genuine.[5] On the basis of stylometric analysis, *Medea* has been placed at the midpoint of Seneca's career as a tragedian and dated to approximately 50–60 CE.[6] Questions regarding the tragedies' authorship have been raised for example by Frederick Ahl, who attributes them to Seneca's rhetorician father,[7] and by Thomas Kohn, who speculates that the literary dynasty of the Annaeii could have produced more than one 'Seneca' active around the 50s CE, and therefore the centuries-long game of reconciling the worldview of Seneca *philosophus* with that of Seneca *tragicus* may have a simpler solution.[8] The general consensus remains, however, that the same Seneca was responsible both for the tragic corpus and philosophical texts such as *De Clementia* ('On Mercy') as well as a scientific treatise, *Questions of Nature*, and a satire on the death of the emperor Claudius entitled *Apocolocyntosis* (or 'Turning-Into-A-Pumpkin').

Seneca's position within the imperial court, then, provides one crucial context for the historical interpretation of these tragedies, including *Medea*; his philosophical writing and adherence to the principles of Stoicism provides another. This is not to suggest that the plays' meaning is exhausted with reference to authorial biography, but in reading *Medea* against our knowledge of the circumstances in which it was most likely to have been composed enables us to tease out those elements which contribute most vividly to a working conception of its contemporary significance. Assuming that its textual evolution occurred within the decadence, violence, and surveillance culture of the autocratic Julio-Claudian court, *Medea* like all of Seneca's dramas presents an extreme focalization of imperial excesses.

Seneca's career spans almost the entire turbulent Julio-Claudian dynasty. Born in Corduba, Spain, during the final years of Augustus's long reign, he trained at Rome in rhetoric and philosophy while the subsequent emperor, Tiberius, grew increasingly paranoid and vicious. Although spending several years in Egypt, Seneca became sufficiently embroiled in the imperial household that in 41 CE, upon Claudius's accession, he was exiled to Corsica on the pretext of having seduced Caligula's sister. Claudius's actual motive was the political need to purge the court of Caligula's associates.[9] Intercession by Agrippina (Caligula's other sister) transmuted Seneca's sentence from death to exile. When Agrippina married the reigning emperor Claudius in 49 CE, she not only had Seneca recalled, but also appointed him tutor to her twelve-year-old son, now Claudius' successor. In 54, Claudius died – reputedly poisoned – and Agrippina's son ascended the throne, becoming at the age of seventeen the emperor Nero. While remaining his tutor, Seneca also took on the roles of advisor, speechwriter, conscience – and, according to Miriam Griffin – publicist and manager of Nero's public image.[10]

Perhaps the starkest illustration of how Seneca manipulated this image is his composition of the philosophical treatise *De Clementia* ('On Mercy') immediately following the suspicious death of Nero's half-brother Britannicus in 55 CE. Britannicus, Claudius's son by his former wife, had been growing too popular; according to anti-Caesarian historian Tacitus, Nero had him poisoned at a banquet and ordered his body immediately cremated to conceal the traces (*Annals*, 13.15–16). Shortly afterwards, Seneca published *De Clementia*. Ostensibly defining the virtue of clemency and arguing for its utility, it also served the dual public-facing functions of painting a flattering imperial portrait and issuing a warning about the consequences of imperial displeasure. Nero, we are told, possesses the rare virtue of total innocence (*Clem.* 1.1.5), his 'crowning glory' being that he has never shed a drop of citizen blood (*Clem.* 1.11.23). His subjects universally admire his benevolent disposition (*Clem.* 1.1.9). Nevertheless, what makes such self-restraint so admirable is its coexistence with absolute power (*Clem.* 1.7.3, 1.8.5, 1.19.1). The Princeps can easily take vengeance. Nations tremble when he raises his voice. He alone has the capacity to pardon those who have offended (*Clem.* 1.5.4). As Griffin points out, however, the corollary is that this places the emperor above the law:[11] it is no longer legal rights which defend a citizen, but the arbitrary whim of an autocrat. 'Mercy makes all the difference between a king and a tyrant' (*Clem.* 1.12.3), Seneca writes, but the further implication of this statement is that it is only the exercise of *clementia* which distinguishes imperial justice from tyranny. Nero's anger, like that of Medea, is compared to a terrifying thunderstorm (*Clem.* 1.7.2–3; cf. *Med.* 411–14; 579–86). In order to survive, one should perhaps refrain from provoking it, rather than testing the limits of imperial goodwill.

Until Nero's accession, Seneca had been a prominent member of Agrippina's circle, but as relations soured between mother and son he consolidated his position behind the emperor. By 59 CE, Seneca seems to have begun assisting Nero to plot Agrippina's assassination, and after her death he certainly participated in the official cover-up (Tacitus, *Annals* 14.7–10). From this time onwards, however, Seneca's own authority began to fail as Nero became less concerned with governance and more abandoned to hedonism. Many of Seneca's tragedies, including *Medea*, contain a scene in which a clear-headed advisor attempts unsuccessfully to dissuade an impetuous protagonist from a catastrophic course of action. Indeed, the later *fabula praetexta* (toga play) *Octavia* represents Seneca himself struggling to restrain Nero from killing his wife Octavia, sister to the late Britannicus.[12] *Octavia*'s Seneca speaks in the same rapid-fire *sententiae*, or pithy aphorisms, as characters such as *Medea*'s Nutrix: 'Those with more power have all the more to fear' (*Oct.* 450). 'It's more admirable to do what you *ought*, than what you can' (*Oct.* 454). 'Swords keep a ruler safe,' sulks Nero; 'Loyalty's preferable', Seneca parries (*Oct.* 456). The paradigm of the thwarted counsellor was transferred from biography to tragedy, and back again.

In 62 CE, Nero became convinced of Seneca's involvement in a conspiratorial plot and ordered his former advisor to be put to death. Seneca's suicide, described in detail by Tacitus and frequently later depicted in art, has acquired iconic status. As was customary, Seneca was not immediately executed but was granted a brief period in which he might retain his dignity by arranging his own death in a manner of his choosing.[13] The most common method employed by condemned Roman aristocrats at this time was to open a vein in the wrist, in contrast to the soldier's death of falling on the sword. Seneca, like other contemporaries who had fallen victim to Nero's purge, stage-managed his death-scene carefully, although as related by Tacitus it is unclear whether its genre turned out to be tragedy or black comedy.[14]

This type of self-fashioning and self-scrutiny, as I will discuss in more detail below, was integral to the Roman Stoicism practised (and crafted) by Seneca. As James Ker demonstrates, it is likely that Tacitus drew on Seneca's own dramatic and philosophical corpus for the language and motifs employed in the author's death-scene.[15] Although only two of Seneca's dramatic characters actually commit suicide,[16] it is frequently spoken of as a desirable response to intolerable disgrace or pain, and as an attempt to regain a measure of control: even if one's life is in shreds, one still has the right to determine how it is to end, to exercise courage and self-discipline in the only act remaining. What else could Jason have done, Medea asks, when compelled to divorce her by royal decree? 'He should have applied his breast / to the iron blade,' she answers herself (137–38). A true hero should choose death over dishonour, or better still, take her enemies with her: *Mecum omnia abeant*, Medea proposes. 'Let everything perish with me: it's a joy to tear it all down when you die' (*trahere, cum pereas, libet*, 428). In the end, however, Medea does not die; it is Jason who pleads for death (*me dedo morti*, 1005) and begs her to kill him in place of their remaining child (*memet perime*, 1018). As elsewhere in Senecan tragedy, it is survival which is represented as the more painful and difficult path, particularly for the fathers like Hercules, Thyestes, *Phaedra*'s Theseus, and Jason who have become guilty – whether directly or indirectly – of causing their children's death. The motif of suicide serves a number of narrative functions in Senecan tragedy. It may be a refuge, a declaration of defiance, an expiation, a redemption, an obliteration of suffering, but most of all it represents the reinstatement of a compromised autonomy. Mortality might be inescapable, but the ever-present option of suicide empowers every individual to choose how they will face it, and how this ending will shape in retrospect everything that went before. *Quomodo fabula, sic vita*, writes Seneca in one of his philosophical letters. 'Life is just like a dramatic plot: it's not how long it is that matters, but how well acted. It's not important where you stop. Stop wherever you like: just make the ending good'.[17]

1.2 Philosophical context

Seneca's philosophical corpus intersects in unexpected and illuminating ways with his dramatic works. At first glance, the earnest, public-spirited drive for self-improvement of the letters and essays has little in common with the tragedies' violent chaos. The beliefs and practices that make up Roman Stoicism, however, were founded on psychological and cosmological principles as well as ethical ones, and it is these which the tragedies draw upon most readily. Senecan Stoicism involves preparing oneself for the inevitability of death, while at the same time embracing every eventuality of life, whether pleasurable (such as wealth) or painful (such as illness or exile).[18] All such experiences are to be approached with equanimity, the practitioner striving to recognize their transience and become neither overly reliant on pleasure and reward nor overwhelmed by disaster and loss. Many Roman Stoics, like Seneca himself and the second-century emperor Marcus Aurelius, were also statesmen, confronting with disarming confessional honesty the challenge of retaining moral integrity amid the temptations of a high-flying political career. Seneca has been accused of hypocrisy in this respect,[19] but it is precisely in the poignant discrepancy between his ideals and their tarnished realization that he lays bare the human struggle, the failure, and our consciousness of that failure to live in a manner we know to be wholly ethical.

Stoicism encouraged an intensely reflective attitude, reviewing one's choices and actions daily in light of the synonymous goals of *ratio* (reason, rationality) and *virtus* (often translated as 'virtue', but perhaps better in this context as 'integrity').[20] In defining *virtus*, and thereby what makes an action morally 'good' or 'bad', Stoics appeal to *Natura*, or Nature, a principle of cosmic order. 'Virtue is in accordance with Nature; vices are that which conflicts with and disrupts it' (*Virtus secundum naturam est, vitia inimica et infesta sunt*, *Ep.* 50.8). The individual is an embodiment of the whole, a microcosmic manifestation of the *pneuma* that holds the universe together. To improve one's behaviour, one should check whether it is aligned with or contrary to Nature: for instance, eating to satisfy hunger is rational, but eating until you are sick is a perversion.[21] Feeling angry cannot be helped, but nurturing murderous rage is indicative of worldly attachments gone awry.[22]

One theory about how Stoicism informed Seneca's tragedies is that they function as cautionary *exempla*.[23] Over-indulging destructive passions such as anger, for instance, is shown to cause devastation, as in the final act of *Medea*. Advice on moderation, meanwhile, is delivered in easily digestible sententiae by characters such as the Nurse and Chorus: 'Courage is admirable in its proper place' (160); 'It is sensible to adapt to your circumstances' (175); 'There's no great risk in the well-trodden path' (603). The problem with this reading is what Rosenmeyer calls 'the theatricality, the sparkling rhetoric, and the proud vitality of the Senecan villain.'[24] Hell-bent on revenge, Medea succeeds in her plotting, and shows no remorse. Her enemies, Creon and Jason, treat her abominably, and get what they deserve. Heartbreaking in her anguish, she is breathtaking in her triumph; there is nothing pusillanimous in this all-out rampage. Moreover, as in other tragedies such as *Thyestes*, it is Medea's design which directs the course of the action, the plot of the protagonist-villain aligned with the plot of the drama.[25] Medea is Seneca's *artifex scelerum*, the architect of his crimes, responsible for setting events in motion and carrying them through to their spectacular finale, acting as the playwright's agent on the inside of the drama. While Seneca's Medea may be repellent as well as attractive, it is this fascinating ambiguity which frustrates her utility as a negative *exemplum*.[26] Unsettlingly, Medea's universe offers no alternative, no character where *virtus* reposes. Medea implores Jupiter to hurl down indiscriminate thunderbolts: 'Whichever of us falls, / a guilty party dies; you can't go wrong' (535–7).

One of Seneca's most well-known philosophical essays, and one which is especially relevant for *Medea*, is *De Ira* ('On Anger'). This essay is remedial, arguing that anger (*ira*) is the worst of all the passions and to be avoided in all circumstances. It investigates the causes of *ira* and suggests strategies for preventing its onset or mitigating its symptoms. Seneca argues that anger is useless; it is discipline which prevails in battle, and punishment should be exercised as a social remedy, not a species of personal revenge. The tendency to anger can be reduced by accepting criticism gracefully, and showing lenience to the errors of others. A fully rational mind should not admit hurt, because nothing should matter so much that it causes distress. Injuries can be borne without the desire for retaliation, and indeed, dissembling calm may under some circumstances be necessary for survival.[27] When asked how he attained old age at Caesar's court, one courtier replied, *iniurias accipiendo et gratias agendo* (by accepting injustice and giving thanks for it), like the knight Pastor, who pretended to feast while his son was condemned, because he had a second son to consider; and the mythological *exemplum* of Priam petitioning Achilles, kneeling before him and kissing the hand still reeking with his son's blood.

In Stoic thought, the passions are regarded as a form of disease, a disturbance in the natural equilibrium of body and soul.[28] Seneca writes in *De Ira* that it is easier not to allow the passions any access at all, rather than to attempt to channel or control them once they are 'in possession' (7.2). If you can put a limit or a check on what you are feeling, it can no longer be called '*ira*', because '*ira*' by its very nature is uncontrollable (*effrenatam*, 9.3). The same word, *effrena*, is used by the Chorus to describe the wild and 'untameable' Medea (*Med.* 103). Seneca spends a considerable proportion of *De Ira*'s second book addressing the question of whether anger arises *sua sponte*, of its own accord, or whether the mind must first assent to its inception. He concludes that anger is not a reflex, that it does not necessarily have to follow upon the initial perception of an injury. In order for *ira* to take hold, it must be consciously invited to proceed. 'Emotion (*adfectus*) does not occur when you are moved by the immediate appearance of things, but when you surrender yourself and pursue (*prosequi*) this chance movement' (*De Ira* 2.3). This is precisely Medea's condition: she allows the *motus*, the agitations of *ira* to overwhelm her, and even frames this decision as a pursuit, using the same vocabulary: *ira, quo ducis, sequor* ('Anger, where you lead, I follow', *Med.* 953). In this way, Seneca can represent her impassioned state as both purposeful and submissive, a voluntary abdication of self-control.

Medea is driven by anger (*ira*) and by mad rage or frenzy (*furor*). 'I see the face of *furor*', shudders her Nurse (*Med.* 396), as her mistress paces frantically to and fro exhibiting all the signs of someone gripped by fury. Medea is *furor* personified. One of Seneca's contentions in *De Ira* is that strong passions such as anger may be diagnosed, like disease, by means of visible physical symptoms. The signs which he lists as indicative of the *furens* (*De Ira* 1.1.3–5) are identical to those which are listed by Medea's Nurse (*Med.* 380–96): a threatening expression and glowering frown, rapid steps, a face changing colour, deep panting breaths; the signs of the *irascens* are equally legible, and equally applicable to the stage Medea: her flashing eyes, flaming cheeks, grinding teeth, and the audible hiss of her breath. The *irascens* performs passion out loud, stamping and groaning, her whole body moving violently, *totum concitum corpus.*[29] It is an intensely theatrical emotion. Seneca writes that if Ira were a goddess, she could be pictured personified like the Furies, the *inferna monstra* which (dramatic) poets (like him) describe elsewhere:

> Flaming eyes burning, with hiss and bellow and groan and shriek and – if such a voice can be imagined – a commotion worse than any of these, brandishing weapons in both hands (she takes no care even to protect herself), vicious and bloody and scarred and bruised from her own blows, reeling madly, wrapped in darkness, charging wildly, spreading destruction and devastation, oppressed by hatred of everything – herself above all. If she cannot otherwise cause harm, she wants to wreck the whole earth, the seas, the heavens, and is hated in proportion to her hostility.
>
> *De Ira* 2.35[30]

We can easily imagine Seneca's Medea in such a guise, and indeed she expresses precisely the same desire for universal devastation. 'I will attack the gods, / and shake everything apart', she threatens. 'I will not rest / until everything is ruined along with me, / until I see it all destroyed' (424–8). Self-harm is also integral to Seneca's portrayal of Medea, not only the figurative harm caused by bereavement but also made literal, as she strikes at her own arms with the knife and sheds her 'own dear blood' (810) in sacrificial preparation for the greater bloodshed to come. Unusual in Seneca's vivid personification of Ira is the factor of self-loathing, not generally associated with either the Furies or the vengeful tragic characters they motivate and assist. Ira's own flesh is livid and scarred with self-inflicted pain, and with acute diagnostic perceptiveness, Seneca casts Ira herself as the prime target as well as the author of her boiling hatred and the indiscriminate damage it causes. Although this self-destructive aspect of anger is not explored explicitly elsewhere in *De Ira* (except insofar as anger is figured as debilitating), it is central to understanding the conflict at the heart of Seneca's *Medea*.

The danger of succumbing to strong emotion, then, is one strand of Stoic psychology evident in *Medea*. Another is the Stoic commitment to self-fashioning, or the idea that integrity or *virtus* can be cultivated through a constant process of monitoring and evaluating one's behaviour. Several scholars have pointed out that Medea exhibits exactly this process,[31] using similar techniques of self-address and visualization en route to becoming her ideal self; but in her case, this ideal self is a pitiless killer, not an enlightened *sapiens*. As Shadi Bartsch has argued,[32] Seneca shows how, in the absence of a reliable ethical framework, the Stoic practice of *meditatio* can be warped such that one crafts oneself into the perfect monster. Medea's ferocious dialogues with herself replicate the structure and purpose of the nocturnal reflections which are described in Book 3 of *De Ira* (3.36).[33] The aspiring philosopher should interrogate himself daily and scrutinize where he has failed to live up to self-imposed standards, exhorting himself to keep improving despite the difficulty of maintaining them. In her logic of revenge, Medea repeatedly exhorts herself in a similar manner to maintain her constancy, carry out her intentions, overcome weaknesses such as maternal affection, and in doing so realize her true potential. *Medea nunc sum*, she exults once the first child is dead. 'Now I am [really, properly, actually] Medea!' (910). She has successfully attained the Stoic philosopher's goals of consistency and integrity, but their efficacy is wilfully misdirected.

Bartsch also shows how Seneca has Medea pervert what she terms 'the ethical force of the gaze'.[34] Pointing out that 'a large part of the *meditatio* is given to the idea that we should live as if we could be seen by an ideal viewer', Bartsch argues that Medea, instead of performing for the imagined judgement of a philosophical exemplar such as Cato or Socrates, sets up her own mythological identity as the aspirational part of herself.[35] Moreover, the lack of a witness makes her revenge incomplete. It is only when Jason arrives, the ideal and indeed the only appropriate spectator for her final *coup de théâtre*, that Medea's enactment of her role can be definitive. Utilizing both its dialogic method and its dependence on spectatorship, then, Seneca's Medea turns Stoic philosophy against nature.[36]

Or does she? In a study of the ways in which Stoic cosmology infuses Seneca's tragedies, Thomas G. Rosenmeyer argues for the predominance of the principle of *sympatheia*. A cosmological version of the pathetic fallacy, *sympatheia* proposes an intimate correspondence between internal and external conditions, between the macrocosm of the natural world and the microcosm of human affairs, even down to the fabric of the human soul – a corporeal substance, in Stoic metaphysics. In the blighted setting of tragedies such as Seneca's *Oedipus*, it appears that *natura versa est* (*Oed.* 371): Oedipus's guilt has caused the unnatural plague that has settled on Thebes. Rosenmeyer's most striking insight, however, is that 'there is, in Seneca's frightening world, no uninfected, unimpaired nature to be inverted'.[37] We could go further: in *Medea*, Seneca explores the possibility unthinkable to orthodox Stoicism that *Natura* itself might be inherently hostile, or at any rate inimical to humanity. As Christopher Star remarks, 'Senecan drama is the tragic double to his philosophy'.[38] Or alternatively, in David Wray's formulation, 'Seneca's tragic theatre stages the repressed content of his Stoicism'.[39] Wray deems this formulation unsophisticated, but while Stoicism is certainly much more than a specious veneer of rationality, *Medea* does permit its very foundations to be questioned.

Through what John Henderson calls 'the iconography of Medea', Seneca relates his protagonist metaphorically to powerful forces of nature, especially fire and flood.[40] Although her magic reverses natural order, causing the ocean to recede and fruit to sprout in winter (754–69), in other respects she appears entirely consonant with elemental energies which, albeit wild and inhuman, are part of seasonal cycles or meteorological phenomena. The danger posed by her rage, for example, is compared by the Chorus to the blizzards borne in on the winter gales (583–4), to a flood that sweeps away human constructions in its path (584–6), and to the force of a river swollen by the spring thaw (588–90). Her power, her *vis* (579) is that of fire and hurricane: not unnatural, yet still fearsomely destructive in human terms. 'Here you see the sea and the land, / iron and fire and gods and thunderbolts' (166–7), Medea retorts when the Nurse suggests she may have nothing left. Hers are geodynamic weapons, ranged against the puny darts that Jason commands. Her *furor*, rationalized, operates in alignment with *Natura*:

> While the earth holds the heavens in perfect equilibrium
> and the shining world turns through predictable changes,
> while grains of sand are countless, and the sun
> attends the day, the stars the night, while the constellation of the Bear
> orbits the pole, and rivers run to the sea,
> my rage to punish [Jason] will never cease
> and will grow forever.
>
> 401–7

As noted above, acting with Stoic *virtus* or integrity consists in aligning one's behaviour with *Natura*, and Medea's rage is here represented as a force as natural and irresistible as the turning earth.

Indeed, it is Jason's quest for the Golden Fleece, rather than Medea's elemental *furor*, which Seneca represents as disruptive or contrary to *Natura*.[41] The voyage of the Argo – according to Roman mythology, the first ship[42] – artificially 'dragged' together disparate parts of the world, violently thrashing the sea with its oars and rendering this previously untouched domain a source of new fears (335–9). The gods, suggest the Chorus, have been consigning the Argo's crew to terrible punishments one by one for this violation (605–15), for daring to break the *sancta foedera mundi*, the sacred 'contract' implicit in the world's very structure: that men should be content with their immediate surroundings and not seek to plunder foreign riches. The merchandise or cargo (*merces*) with which the Argo returned to Thessaly did include the Golden Fleece, but it also included Medea as part of the bargain, 'an evil worse than the sea', *merces prima digna carina*, a cargo suitable, fitting, and worthy (in all senses) for the first ship (362–3). She is the Argo's consequence. Men must now forever after fear the sea, which their own actions have made into a source of avarice and conflict, and the concentrated personification of this new threat, the gods' avenger, Medea.

1.3 Political context

For first-century Rome, and for adherents to Stoic moderation in particular, greed had a strong conceptual link to imperial expansion. The increasing availability of imported consumer goods fed an insatiable demand for products designated as luxurious, or sensorially appealing without practical purpose: incense, amber, coloured marbles, delicacies such as flamingos' tongues,[43] exotic spices, silk. As Emily Wilson comments, 'Seneca's Stoicism is the philosophical response to an elite society that has grown increasingly consumerist and materialistic as a result of the vast growth of the Roman empire.'[44] In his *Naturales Quaestiones*, for example, Seneca depicts his compatriots as enslaved by 'a *furor* of delectation' (*NQ.* 3.18). In winter, the dining room is heated like a sauna, while the sweating gourmands swallow ice in an effort to soothe their heartburn and stimulate their failing appetites. 'You call this thirst?' demands Seneca. 'This is a fever (*febris*) … *luxuria* is an incurable disease.'[45] Like *ira*, *luxuria* by its very nature cannot be satiated.

In the tragedy *Octavia*, written by an unknown author after Seneca's death and set in the reign of Nero,[46] Seneca himself appears as a character, deploring a regime in which *vitia* (vices) are overflowing: criminality is in power and libido dominates, while 'victorious Luxuria has long since been raking in the world's immense resources (*opes*) / with her greedy hands, and wasting them' (*Oct.* 433–4). *Octavia*'s Seneca compares his own time unfavourably with an imagined distant past when human beings were content with the earth's natural bounty, before the onset of the *maximum malum*, the greatest of curses, the 'seductive pestilence', *luxuria* (*Oct.* 426–7). *Octavia*'s author may be referencing here the second chorus of *Medea*, in which a golden age of peace and satisfaction is located in the time before the technology of sailing allowed our ancestors to aspire for more: 'Rich in their poverty, / they knew no resources (*opes*) other than those of their native soil' (*Med.* 333–4).[47] The speech assigned to Seneca in *Octavia* may also be citing the sentiments expressed in another passage from *Naturales Quaestiones*.

Here, it is the winds which have enabled *commercium* between all peoples, and brought together the inhabitants of diverse places. In *Medea*'s second chorus, as a result of sea travel, 'All boundaries have been removed … Nothing remains where it once was / as the world is traversed. A man from India drinks from the freezing Araxes river, / and Persians drink from the Rhine' (*Med.* 369–74). This, according to *Naturales Quaestiones*, would be one of Nature's greatest blessings, if human *furor* had not turned it into a way of doing injury to ourselves. We travel not benignly, but either for the purposes of war and invasion or in search of wealth and profit, serving our *avaritia*, our greed. Gold lures us on, 'defying gods and thunderbolts, despite divine and human wrath', Seneca continues:

> Not without reason has it been said that things would actually have been better for us if Nature had forbidden the winds to blow at all, and by curtailing their freedom to rage had compelled each of us to remain in our own territory … No land is so remote that it cannot export some of its vices … It would be a great source of peace to humankind if the seas were closed.
>
> *NQ.* 5.18.3–12

It could be suggested that Seneca's aversion to open borders is xenophobic. Unlike other Roman authors such as Sallust,[48] however, his dismay is provoked not by immigration but rather by outward expansion and commerce, in particular the consumerist ideology that reduces foreign territory to a resource (*opes*) exploited to feed an insatiable desire for novelty, profit, and sensory gratification. Behind *Medea*'s Argonautic odes we should be aware of this implicit line of criticism, cloaked in poetic idiom, directed at contemporary Rome.

The spread of empire, then, and imperialism in the sense of state expansion, is one aspect of socio-political critique embedded in *Medea*. The other major critique, prominent in all of Seneca's work, is that of imperialism in the sense of autocracy, or the investment of authority in a single individual. Seneca's proximity to the Julio-Claudian dynasty gave him an insider's perspective on the ruling family of Rome, and the mythological settings of his tragedies provided an opportunity to explore in relative safety the negative implications of absolute power. Greek tragedy, Seneca's main generic model, is populated by aristocratic characters, its plots likewise concerned with the cursed kings and queens of Argos and Thebes. Athens in the fifth century BCE, however, was a democratic state, proudly and emphatically opposed to monarchic government. Whereas tragedy on one level depicted family feuds to which any citizen could relate, on another level it reinforced the ideological superiority of democracy as the kings and heroes of the past were repeatedly depicted as matricides, madmen, adulterers, despotic tyrants, and moral cowards. This cast of undesirables was inherited by Seneca and other Roman playwrights, but acquired a different complexion when composed and received not only under an empire, but in the heart of its imperial court.

Seneca wrote tragedy about conflicts within ruling dynasties while the current ruling dynasty was consuming itself. Within Seneca's lifetime, Augustus Caesar had family members exiled for supposed moral delinquency; Tiberius had them executed on suspicion of plotting. Caligula by all accounts (including Seneca's own) took fiendish and arbitrary delight in terrorizing everyone around him, and was assassinated after only four years by his own bodyguard. 'At the court of Caligula', Seneca relates, 'I saw torture and fire. I knew that under him, human life had deteriorated to such an extent that those who were killed were held up as examples of his mercy' (*NQ*. 4.17). Caligula's successor Claudius had his third wife put to death for her infidelity; his fourth wife, Agrippina, reputedly poisoned him to put her son on the throne. Nero, the emperor with whom Seneca had the closest association, allegedly assassinated his half-brother Britannicus, followed soon afterwards by the much more public murder of Agrippina herself. For Seneca, then, the public damage inflicted by the private scandals of a ruling house was not just an abstraction but an everyday reality. The threat posed by a ruler susceptible to *furor* was more than just a stage fantasy.

Just as Seneca's own posthumous representation was influenced by his plays, however, it has been suggested that the characteristics of 'bad emperors' in historiographic texts may likewise draw on those of stage tyrants.[49] Creon in Seneca's *Medea* is a good example: he is cowardly, paranoid, and suspicious, irascible, stubborn, oppressive, prejudiced, and deeply selfish. Medea can neither appease nor reason with him. 'Just or unjust, you have to do what a king commands', he tells her (*aequum atque iniquum regis imperium feras*, 195). Her plea comes too late; he has already made his decision (*constituto decreto*, 198). He will teach her how to obey royal authority (*regium imperium*, 189). He calls her a monster, an infection, and calls on his attendants to prevent her from touching or even approaching him (183–90). Having chosen Jason for his son-in-law, he refuses to hear Medea's counter-arguments. She has killed a king before, and this, in Creon's eyes, condemns her without trial. It is no use Medea insisting that her crimes were committed at Jason's instigation, because Creon would prefer to ascribe the guilt to a woman, a foreigner, and an inconvenient impediment to uniting his own kingdom with Jason's homeland of Thessaly.[50]

In some respects, Medea herself also exhibits the abuse of power, or in any case the catastrophe that ensues when a powerful individual is driven to retaliate against those who have wounded her. Medea's capabilities are superhuman; although unable, ironically, to persuade Jason to return to her or Creon to surrender him, her supernatural command over the forces of nature enables her to concoct a diabolical revenge. Having exhausted her rhetorical resources, Medea turns to enchantment, exerting her will to invoke the witch-goddess Hecate, summon the great Serpents of the sky, and infuse Promethean fire into a golden circlet. Despite social disempowerment due to her status as exile and outcast, Medea nevertheless retains attributes and abilities that mean she still controls the seas, the stars, the spirit world. She is a superpower, and as such, her capacity for doing harm is almost limitless.

Medea's power is not political. It is not consensually or systemically conferred, but rather personal and charismatic, acquired through birthright and maintained through force. In this it resembles the power wielded by the Julio-Claudian emperors under whose regime Seneca developed his career. Although Rome was still nominally ruled by the

Senate, an executive body comprising mature, freeborn male citizens who belonged to the highest income category, Tacitus's political history of the first century CE shows how in practice the Senate's authority had been progressively eroded. By the end of Augustus's long reign, Tacitus comments, almost nobody alive had seen a functioning Republic: 'The state had been overthrown, and nothing remained intact of our former values. Stripped of equality, everyone looked to the emperor for orders' (*Annals*, 1.4). One of Seneca's contemporaries, the senator and practising Stoic Thrasea Paetus, made a point of arguing for the independence of the Senate as a decision-making body. His commitment to the outmoded value of *libertas* or free speech drew Nero's resentment, accusations of sedition, and as a consequence, sentence of death (*Ann.* 16.22).

The concentration of power into a single figure and the adverse consequences of this imbalance may be seen in the structure of many of Seneca's tragedies. Unlike their Greek antecedents, which proceed through dialogue and (often inconclusive) agonistic debate, their choral collectives for the most part playing an integral role, Seneca exploits the monologue. He creates soloists larger than life whose actions have global repercussions. Nero commissioned a statue of himself a hundred feet high to be erected outside his palace (Suet. *Nero* 31); the monstrous egotism of the Caesars found its equivalent in the centripetal colossi populating Senecan drama.

Nero also enjoyed appearing as a performer himself, especially in public musical competitions. His preferred event was to sing tragic arias while accompanying himself on the cithara. Imperial biographer Suetonius reports that he took his preparations and stage appearances very seriously, pampering his voice with a regime of exercise, purges, and a special diet. His favourite roles included 'Oedipus Blinded' and 'Hercules *Furens*', subjects also treated in tragedies by Seneca, along with tragic heroines such as the bereaved Niobe and incestuous Canace (Suet. *Nero* 21). As his parallel career as head of the Roman state progressed, however, Nero became less self-effacing, and began to appear in extended command performances which audiences were forced to attend if they wished to retain the emperor's favour. As Shadi Bartsch has argued,[51] audience members themselves in this scenario became the spectacle or object of scrutiny, their reactions observed both by covert informers and openly by one another. Meanwhile, the emperor onstage – ostensibly the focus of a collective gaze – made his dramatic performances an occasion instead for his subjects to display their loyalty. To survive in the Julio-Claudian court, as Seneca makes clear in *De Ira*, duplicity was necessary. The emperor appeared literally masked as a repertoire of tragic characters, but courtiers and senators alike were required to cultivate a sycophantic façade both inside and outside the theatre.

1.4 Performance context

While theatricality was thus a prevailing condition of Julio-Claudian Rome in the sense of pretence, disguise, and pervasive surveillance, and the emperor encouraged the permeability of stage and public life by taking on tragic personae, Roman 'theatre' in fact consisted of multiple coexisting art-forms. When discussing theatricality or metatheatre in relation to Seneca's tragedies,[52] it is important to consider the performance context in which they first appeared. We should not think of *Medea* as arising in a milieu where tragedy could only be performed in one way.[53] Contemporary performance genres which evidently influenced *Medea*'s dramaturgy, regardless of how the text was eventually staged, include recitation and oratory; pantomime dance, or *orchēsis*; *tragoedia cantata*, or competitive singing; and arena culture, including gladiatorial combat. When these forms are taken into account, Medea's structural departures from classical Greek tragic convention may be understood as responses to a very different theatrical marketplace.

For much of the twentieth century, however, it was assumed that Seneca was simply a bad playwright, and/or that he could not have intended his plays for performance. At most, they could be recited;

some scholars rejected even this in favour of private reading.[54] Not all critics, it is true, regarded Seneca as unstageable,[55] but this is certainly the narrative that prevailed. The basis for rejecting Senecan performance was in the first instance aesthetic, scholarly justification following after the fact. In 1927, T.S. Eliot suggested that Seneca's plays were 'intended for recitation.' According to Eliot, this was a result of their stylistic flaws: in the plays of Seneca, 'the drama is all in the word, and the word has no further reality behind it. His characters all seem to speak in the same voice, and at the top of it; they recite in turn.'[56] A similarly derogatory opinion was expressed in the 1940s by C.W. Mendell, who complains of Seneca's 'failure' to 'properly' motivate his characters or respect what Mendell calls 'the dramatic illusion'.[57] Senecan tragedy was held up against standards of verisimilitude derived from an alien tradition, theatrical naturalism, and not surprisingly found not to conform.

Instead of recognizing the inapplicability of such criteria, mid-century critics became ever more entrenched in their conviction that Seneca's flagrant disregard for 'the dramatic illusion', that is, for psychologically consistent characters whose interactions were portrayed through believable dialogue, vitiated performance. This trend culminated in Otto Zwierlein's magisterial 1966 study *Die Rezitationsdramen Senecas*, which systematically detailed all the inconsistencies, continuity errors, jumps in location, lapses in character, and unrealistic scenes such as the onstage bull sacrifice in *Oedipus* that made staging Seneca impossible. Once again, however, it is the demands of naturalism that give rise to this impossibility: 'in a continuous plot without interruptions, such [inconsistency] would be unthinkable,' Zwierlein states.[58] A well-made play should seem 'lifelike' (*lebensvoll*) and not proceed through rambling monologues and disjointed set-pieces (*Prunkstücken*) while characters appear and vanish unannounced, sometimes unidentified, occasionally seeming unaware of preceding events in which they themselves have participated.[59] These apparent defects, however, become trivial if naturalistic preoccupations are laid aside and Senecan tragedy is read as embedded in a distinctively Roman set of theatrical practices. By the late 1960s, the tide was turning in Senecan scholarship: absurdism, Theatre of Cruelty, Tanztheater, and the performance theory of avant-garde directors such as Jerzy Grotowski and Peter Brook had begun tearing up the dramaturgical rulebook dominating two hundred years of European theatre, and it became possible to reimagine Seneca on a stage of his own making.

Roman public theatres had grown large by the mid-first century CE, their decoration lavish. They were permanent and prominent buildings, constructed from stone and faced in marble. A theatre, according to Augustan architect Vitruvius, was one of the essential components of urban planning (*De Arch.* 5.3). The *cavea*, or auditorium of a Roman theatre was semicircular, with concentric rows of seating rising from the flat area still known as the *orchēstra* but no longer used for dancing; instead, it contained the seats for magistrates, sponsors, and other VIPs. Seating elsewhere in the auditorium was also divided hierarchically, separating spectators into their various social ranks.[60] As in the eighteenth-century opera house, attending the theatre could be as much a form of display as the ostensible performance itself. It not only exhibited the prestige of individuals but also reinforced the imagined authority of a traditional class system which by this time had in practice been seriously eroded.

Unlike a Greek theatre, which is open like a hillside, the *cavea* of a Roman theatre curves round to meet the edges of the *scaenae frons* or stage façade, creating a sealed, almost interior space.[61] Awnings could be extended over the *cavea*, further enclosing it. The stage itself was a relatively narrow platform dividing the crowded terraces of the *cavea* from the architectural extravagance of the *scaenae frons*. The *scaenae frons* supplied a permanent backdrop that could be up to three storeys high, each level constructed of alternating columns and niches and resplendent with coloured marbles and gilding.[62] The niches were occupied by bronze or marble statues, which could also be painted. The actors would enter the stage, the *scaena*, through doorways built into the lower storey of the *scaenae frons*, pausing to declare their presence to the audience and then descending three or four steps to the stage itself. Even before the performance began, the space announced that it would be spectacular.

Visually, there was a lot of competition for a performer stepping down onto the stage. The layer-cake of pilasters and lifelike statues behind him presented a compelling backdrop, but one which did not refer explicitly to the action of the drama. Instead, the set referenced the artifice of the theatre itself, and the power, wealth, taste, and prestige of its patron.[63] Commensurate with this architectural extravagance, however, tragic costume had also evolved into something more elaborate than was customary in classical Greek or even Hellenistic Italian theatre, as far as we can judge from images in vase-paintings and other visual representations.[64] Robes were expensively dyed and richly embroidered,[65] and padded to increase the girth and stature of the actor. His height was also enhanced by boots with platform soles called *cothurnoi* or 'buskins'. Literally larger than life, the Roman tragic actor wore an exaggerated full-face mask with a high forehead, wide eyes, and gaping mouth, the features painted clearly in order to stand out at a distance and the mouth left open as an aperture through which the actor could speak or sing.

Like other forms of poetic performance, tragic vocalization was typically referred to as song (*cantus*) or singing (*canere*, or *cantare*). Just as the actor's visual appearance was highly stylized, so was his vocal delivery. Roman tragic language is a heightened poetic form, and as such implies a delivery that is correspondingly heightened. Its vocabulary, syntactic formality, and the structure of its spoken interactions all signify a departure from everyday speech patterns; this is not the discourse of the bath-house or the Forum. Most distinctively, Roman tragedy (like ancient Greek drama) is a verse form. It is composed in a regular meter, each line employing a characteristic rhythm of alternating long and short beats. The meter of *Medea*'s monologues and dialogue, typical of most solo dramatic speech, is iambic trimeter, a pattern which looks like this:

> ĭncērtă vāecŏrs mēntĕ vāesănā fĕrōr.
>
> *Med.* 123

Similar to Shakespearean iambic pentameter, with its five iambs or two-syllable pulses – Shall Í ı compáre ı thee tó ı a súm ı mer's dáy – the iambic trimeter of classical tragedy contains three sets of double iambs, or three 'feet':

> ĭncērtă vāe ı cŏrs mēntĕ vāe ı sănā fĕrōr.

Whereas English poetic meter is based on where the stress in each word falls ('súmmer'), however, Latin and Greek meters depend on the arrangement of long and short vowel-sounds ('ĭncērtă').

Tragic choral meters can be much more diverse. Each of *Medea*'s choruses uses a different meter, although unlike Greek tragedy they do not employ responsion, or the repetition of complex rhythmic combinations across strophes (stanzas). Instead, they follow a single, internally consistent metrical pattern throughout. The second chorus, for example, uses a flexible four-footed meter called the anapaestic dimeter:[66]

> Aūdāx | nĭmĭūm | quī frĕtă | prīmūs
> rătĕ tām | frăgĭlī | pērfĭdă | rūpīt.
>
> *Med.* 301–2

The third chorus makes use of a different metrical pattern, sapphic hendecasyllables, so called because it has eleven syllables (in Greek, *hendeka*) and was common in the work of the lyric poet Sappho. Note that it is not divided into feet, but forms a continuous line:

> Ēxĭgīt pōenās mārĕ prōvŏcātŭm.
>
> *Med.* 616

While these are the basic rhythms underlying the play's vocal delivery, metrical variation creates aural texture and allows the performer some latitude in interpretation and musicality. It may be helpful to think of Roman tragedy as operatic, with the monologues corresponding to arias and the choral passages sung by many massed voices. Tragic performance was also accompanied by instrumental music, which further increased its emotional intensity and set it sensorially apart from more prosaic modes of verbal and vocal interaction. I reiterate this point because much of the criticism levelled at Seneca's style condemns it as 'excessive', 'bombastic', or otherwise embarrassing in its overstatement. It is worth recalling that Roman theatre in all its permutations was an overstated form, a form for which *Medea*'s extravagance of diction and action is perfectly suited.

Tragedy, however, did not have to be performed in a public theatre, nor with a full cast. One probable option for the performance of Seneca's tragedies was as private or coterie theatre,[67] whether professional or amateur. Many first-century aristocrats, particularly those in favour with the theatre-obsessed Neronian court, had small private *odea* constructed in their own villas or townhouses, suitable for music and poetry readings as well as for drama. It was also common to keep entertainers and professional readers on staff, although the entire companies of mimes kept by satirical character Trimalchio and in real life by the eccentric Ummidia Quadratilla would have been more unusual.[68] In the absence of a purpose-built theatre space, performances of tragic or comic scenes, interspersed with dance, mimes, or philosophical dialogues, could also be given as interludes during the multi-course banquets which moralists and satirists depict as lasting till dawn.

Especially thrilling passages could also be excerpted for solo concert performance as part of musical competitions. This was Nero's preferred mode of singing tragedy, not in costume but as a musical performance only, accompanying himself on the cithara, a large stringed instrument resembling the lyre but heavier and more complex in design. Tacitus makes explicit the contrast between these types of tragic performance, comparing Nero to his political and artistic rival Gaius Piso, remarking that *ut Nero cithara, ita Piso tragico ornatu canebat* (Tac. *Ann.* 16.65): 'while Nero sung to the cithara, Piso did it in full tragic array' (i.e. mask, buskins, padding, the works). Neither, however, is likely to have performed in a complete staging of the play, but rather the aria was rehearsed as a solo highlight and performed either as part of a musical compilation, or certainly in Nero's case in competition with other professional singers. While the public festival stage remained one venue for Roman tragedy, then, the private theatre and *triclinium* (dining room) were equally influential on Senecan dramaturgy. Similarly, the anticipation of musical excerpting has clearly left its stamp on the plays' segmented structure and virtuosic arias.

The one contemporary medium in which Senecan tragedy is attested as having been performed is *recitatio*, or delivery as performance poetry, either declaimed from memory or read aloud. The evidence is scanty: in his handbook on oratory, Quintilian mentions a discussion on tragic language taking place between Seneca and another author, Pomponius Secundus, through their *praefationes* or 'introductory remarks'. The term *praefatio*, however, does not apply to a written preface, but rather to the apologia preceding a reading of the text: elsewhere, the *recitator* 'speaks' his *praefationem* (Pliny, *Ep*. 1.13.2).[69] It appears from this that Seneca was involved in readings of his dramatic works, although it is not clear whether the *recitator* or *lector* (reader) would have been the playwright himself, a professional engaged for the purpose, or even (as is attested by the Greek historian Plutarch) a small troupe of slave-actors.[70] There is certainly a precedent for poets presenting their own work. The Augustan state poet Virgil recited sections of his epic masterpiece, the *Aeneid*, to Augustus and his household (Suet. *Vita* 27–33), and the satirist Juvenal opens his collection of diatribes against modern Roman life by complaining about the number of amateur poetry readings he is obliged to attend (*Sat*. 1). Seneca was an accomplished public speaker who had studied oratory, and indeed his father had been an acclaimed teacher of rhetoric, so if Seneca had chosen a surrogate *recitator* it would not be for want of skill; and delivering a poetic work in progress to an invited audience had none of the infamy associated with performing as an actor.

The links and the tensions between acting and oratory ran deep in Roman culture.[71] Fully aware of the resemblance, orators took great pains to distinguish their profession and its skill-set from the lewd, boisterous, exaggerated antics of stage performers. Their discomfort was based partly on issues of gender – orators should present a figure of exemplary masculinity, whereas actors could slip with disconcerting ease into a feminine persona – and partly class. Orators defined the metropolitan elite, but actors' bodies were frequently those of slaves.[72] Nevertheless, because of the density of rhetorical tropes and techniques in Seneca's dramatic writing, the plays bring oratory into a tragic setting. Medea's supplication to Creon, for example, has a forensic frame: if Creon is to judge her, he should consider the evidence on both sides (*Med.* 194, 199–200). Literary devices such as ecphrasis (verbal description of a scene) and prosopopoeia (temporary occupation of a character) are common to both Roman rhetorical prose and dramatic poetry, and in the performance of such passages the generic distinction between declamation and enactment becomes blurred.

A less conventional performance medium, but one which scholars are now beginning to consider more seriously in association with Senecan tragedy, is the dance form known as *orchēsis* or tragic pantomime.[73] Pantomime was the pre-eminent performance genre in imperial Rome and across the eastern empire between the first and fifth centuries CE. It was enormously popular in both public and private settings. A solo dancer, the *pantomimos*, enacted a mythological narrative, dancing each role in succession, while the libretto was sung alongside by a *cantor* or chorus. The virtuosity of *pantomimoi*, their ability to shape-shift and represent with their metamorphic bodies a huge range of scenarios, characters, and emotions without speaking, was legendary.[74]

Central among the main dramaturgical factors which incline Senecan tragedy towards pantomimic representation is the use of concurrent commentary describing onstage action.[75] Unlike the reportage of a messenger-speech, these passages refer to actions that are occurring simultaneously in full view of the spectators, so their verbal rendition would otherwise appear redundant. In the medium of pantomime, however, in which dance is accompanied by sung libretto, this conjunction is entirely appropriate. One example in *Medea* is the Nurse's commentary on Medea's agitation as she prepares to confront Jason:

Like a maenad possessed, taking tottering steps
as she raves with the onset of the god
on the snowy heights of Pindus or the ridge of Nysa,
she plunges here and there with wild movements
and the signs of frenzied madness in her looks.
Her face is flaming, she draws deep breaths,
she cries out, bathes her eyes in flowing tears,
and smiles again. All kinds of emotions grip her.
She pauses, threatens, burns, laments, groans.

383–90

In particular, the final line in this passage (*haeret minatur aestuat queritur gemit*) can be compared to a syntactically similar line from an epigram praising a pantomime dancer's skill: *pugnat ludit amat bacchatur vertitur adstat* ('He fights, he fools, he loves, he raves, he spins, he halts', *Anth. Lat.* 100.7). Both show a rapid sequence of contrasting states, resembling the sudden extreme transitions for which *pantomimoi* were famed. Medea's passions, as Alessandra Zanobi points out,[76] are here externalized; she does not merely feel them affecting her, but displays them as physical actions. The first half of the passage compares Medea to a maenad or bacchante, an ecstatic follower of the god Dionysus. It includes a specific reference to her movements, characterizing them as 'wild' (*effero*) and 'plunging' (*recursat*). The tears and the flushed face would be invisible behind the dancer's mask, but as Seneca elsewhere remarks, a blush is the one emotional sign impossible for an actor to produce on cue (*Ep.* 11.7). Instead, we may envisage the flowing (*fletu*) gesture for weeping followed immediately by the expansive gesture of beaming; the shaken fist of threat transforming in a moment to the beaten breast of lamentation.

Staged violence is another notorious feature of Senecan tragedy. While less extreme in this respect than some of Seneca's other works, Medea does murder her sons onstage, as opposed to the offstage killing in Euripides' Greek version. It has been suggested that by including scenes of spectacular violence in his tragedies, such as the bull sacrifice in *Oedipus* or the reassembly of Hippolytus's corpse in *Phaedra*, Seneca is responding to the same taste for gore that drove the popularity of the amphitheatre.[77] Medea applies expressions borrowed from the arena to the murder of her children. *Bene est, tenetur*,[78] she remarks, aside, when she identifies this as Jason's weak spot: 'Good, I've got him' (550), and when her second child is dead, *Bene est, peractum est*, ('Good, it's all over', 1019).[79] Although the Colosseum was yet to be constructed, gladiatorial combat and other amphitheatrical spectacles were an intrinsic part of Roman entertainment culture. Not restricted to fights between trained gladiators, the arena's programme also included executions, staged beast-hunts or clashes between wild animals, and according to some ancient authors, a kind of 'snuff' play in which the condemned were killed as part of the plot of a drama.[80]

The connections between Senecan drama and the Roman amphitheatre are perhaps not as direct as they appear, however. In one of his *Moral Letters*, Seneca deplores the bloodthirsty pleasure taken by the crowd attending the gladiatorial Games, from which he returns feeling 'greedier, vainer, more self-indulgent (*luxuriosus*), crueller, and more inhumane', having witnessed the slaughter of unarmed criminals. Many people, he reports, actually prefer this 'sheer butchery' to the more protracted displays by paired gladiators, whose weapons and skill (*artes*) only delay the anticipated deaths. 'Kill him, beat him, brand him!' bawl Seneca's mob, insisting that the carnage should continue throughout the midday intermission to prevent them growing bored (*Ep*. 7.3–5). It was not simply gratuitous bloodshed, then, which interested Seneca.

The gladiator plays a significant metaphorical role in Senecan Stoicism.[81] The fortitude with which a gladiator faced the certainty of his approaching death is comparable to how the *sapiens* or wise man should regard his own condemnation to mortality: life is an arena with only one way out (*Ep*. 37). Just as in his comparison of a life fulfilled to a well-acted play, Seneca stresses the nobility of a gladiator who sees the death-blow falling and does not flinch. Daily confrontation with the possibility – and ultimately, the certainty – of death is at the heart of Stoic practice as outlined by Seneca. His use of the gladiator as an exemplary model accords with the intense ambivalence exhibited elsewhere in Roman culture towards these figures at once exalted and reviled.

*

Seneca's *Medea* is a distinctively Roman take on a myth with its roots in ancient Greece. Imperial Roman tragedy was composed within an eclectic marketplace of venues and performance modes, each of which has left traces in the text. We may not be able to ascertain precisely how, if at all, the play was staged in antiquity, but its performative validity – the ways in which it conforms stylistically to pantomime dance, oratorical *recitatio*, and operatic *tragoedia cantata* – indicates the playwright's responsiveness to contemporary theatrical forms. Medea's characterization as all-powerful yet subject to all-consuming *furor* and erotic frustration recalls that of the Julio-Claudian emperors (and empresses) to whom Seneca had the closest personal ties. Her development over the course of the play follows a Roman Stoic method of self-improvement, albeit arriving at a perverted destination. The *Natura* with which she is aligned is a world which has been traversed and transgressed, like Seneca's own, by the globalizing sprawl of consumer-based imperialism; the first ship is emblematic of Roman expansion abroad. By recombining pre-existing elements of Medea's story and the story of the *Argonautica*, Seneca created a distinct amalgam that spoke to his own socio-cultural conditions. The following chapter will examine some of these pre-existing resources and how they have been woven into *Medea*.

2

The Myth of Medea

Having established the context in which Seneca's tragedy was composed, and before analysing its relationship to prior texts, it may be useful to review the action and structure of the play.

Act 1

Opening with an inverted wedding hymn, Medea invokes several deities, including witch-goddess Hecate and the avenging Furies along with the more conventional gods of marriage and childbirth, to curse the union of Jason and his new bride (1–18). She calls on the sun-god to lend her his fiery chariot, in which she proposes to swoop down on Corinth and annihilate the city in an inferno (28–36). In a sense, although not granted immediately, this prayer will be fulfilled in the play's closing lines. Two important themes are then articulated as Medea turns her imprecations inwards (40–55). Addressing herself, or her *animus*, her spirit,[1] she urges herself to repeat crimes previously performed (wounding, slaughter, and limbs stiffening in death, 47–8) and also to surpass them (her pain is now more intense, so greater crimes are correspondingly more suitable, 49–50). Repetition and return, specifically the replay of Medea's marriage in her revenge, will recur throughout the play and form a cornerstone of Seneca's tragic structure. Likewise, the amplification of crimes when they are repeated and the need to build on what has gone before – by making it even more brutal, even more outrageous – is another structural feature. It also has a metapoetic or metatheatrical dimension;[2] that is, Medea refers in this way to her status as a well-known tragic figure, a literary motif, even a celebrity:

Seneca's *Medea* will both repeat and surpass previous treatments of the same material.

First Chorus

In antithetical contrast to Medea's curse, Seneca's first chorus is an actual epithalamion, a wedding hymn for Jason and his new bride Creusa.[3] The Chorus appear in this stasimon as loyal citizens of Corinth, an extended wedding party for the royal couple. Their invocations mirror Medea's. Although likewise calling on Lucina, goddess of the marriage-bed, they counter Medea's malevolence with an accompanying line-up of propitious deities: Venus for conjugal love, Hymenaeus garlanded and tipsy, and Hesperus, the evening star so congenial to lovers (56–74). They praise the outstanding beauty of the happy couple, especially of Creusa, who is compared above all to the full moon or the goddess Phoebe, beside whose light the stars appear dim (95–101). Like a typical Roman wedding party, the Chorus revel in the license granted them by the occasion to make ribald jokes and rhymes about their *domini* or rulers (107–9);[4] however, their references to the bride and bridegroom are entirely complimentary, and their contemptuous insults are reserved instead for Medea (who may be envisaged as still onstage throughout). She is barbaric, bedding Jason in 'horrid Phasis';[5] the epithet *horridus* here may also be transferred to imply a physical slur, meaning 'bristling' or 'hairy' as opposed to Creusa's blushing smoothness. She is untamed (*effrena*) and Jason only ever touches her reluctantly, with nervous distaste (103–4). These are the celebratory wedding 'jokes' (*iocos*, 114) of the Corinthians: turning on Medea, jeering at the fugitive who 'ran off with a foreigner' (114–15), they condemn her to darkness, silence, and solitude.

Act 2

This act falls into two halves: Medea's dialogue with her Nurse (116–78) and her dialogue with Creon (179–300). Interrupting her deliberations as to who should be the primary target of her vengeance (116–49), the Nurse attempts to calm Medea's frenzied *ira* (rage) on the grounds that dissembling patience will give her more opportunity for plotting against her enemies in secret (150–4). Medea refuses to yield, insisting in a rapid exchange of half-lines or *stichomythia* that she does not fear confrontation. Although prepared to die in taking revenge, she intends to get away with it (170, 173). This type of dialogue between an enraged protagonist and a subordinate who attempts unsuccessfully to dissuade them is typical of Seneca (compare *Phaedra* 129–273, *Agamemnon* 108–225, *Thyestes* 204–335). 'Medea –' pleads the Nurse. '*Fiam*,' Medea responds: I will become [her] (171). She has not yet fulfilled her potential, and must proceed on the course of action pre-ordained by her narrative arc.

Permitted by the Corinthian king Creon to defend herself, Medea's main argument is that her only 'crime' was to have ensured the Argo's safe return to Greece (237–8). As it is Jason and not herself who has profited from her actions, he should share her guilt and be exiled alongside her (272–80). Creon, however, responds with the political sophistry that he has decreed Medea's exile to appease King Acastus of Thessaly, whose father Pelias was another victim of the Argo's return (252–71).[6] It is Medea who was the 'engineer of evils' (*malorum machinatrix*, 266; cf. *scelerum artifex*, 734) and as such she has been made the scapegoat. Creon does, however, magnanimously grant her a single day to say farewell to her children before her departure.

Second Chorus

The voyage of the Argo (301–79) is key to the way in which Seneca incorporates Medea's mythological past. This chorus opens with the literary leitmotif of the *audax ratis*, the 'daring' or 'audacious' first ship, a concept which blends mythology with prehistory. Dissatisfied with their ancestral lands, human beings ventured to cross the sea, eliminating the natural boundary that separated them from distant places and forcibly stitching or 'dragging' disparate parts of the world together

(329–39). The Argonauts endured dangerous adventures on their mission (340–60), passing through the Clashing Rocks and surviving encounters with monsters such as Scylla and the Sirens. These two female monsters can be read as echoing Medea's own monstrosity; Creon referred to her as a *monstrum* in the preceding scene (191; cf. 674–5). The 'spoil' brought back by the Argonauts is twofold. They obtain the Golden Fleece, but they also import 'an evil even worse than the sea', Medea herself: 'a worthy cargo for the first ship' (361–3). Seneca goes on to explicate the ideological ramifications of these mythological events (364–79).[7] In the contemporary world, as a result of the Argo's long-ago audacity, there are no longer any limits to humanity's expansion across the globe: Indians, from the far south of Seneca's world-map, now drink from northern rivers like the Araxes (in modern Armenia), and eastern Persians drink from the western Rhine. In the future, Seneca's Chorus speculate, new lands may be discovered – discovered, that is, from a Roman perspective – even, unthinkably, further away than Britain.[8]

Act 3

In a scene which forms the centrepiece and turning point of the tragedy, Medea confronts Jason. Her anger has escalated to superhuman proportions: more powerful than storms, whirlpools, wildfire or volcanic eruption (407–14), she vows to overthrow the world and shake the cosmos, and if she is to be destroyed, she will take everything down along with her (424–8). She approaches Jason, however, with two final offers of reconciliation, both of which he rejects. First, she attempts to persuade him to acknowledge their mutual guilt (447–505) and confess his ingratitude (465). Employing similar arguments to those she presented to Creon, Medea reminds him that he owes everything to her treasonous betrayal of her father and gruesome murder of her brother. Give back what it rightfully mine, she challenges Jason: return to me my family, my homeland, my innocence (488–9). Jason's defence is that he only cleaved to Creon and repudiated Medea in order to save the lives of their sons (437–9), and she should thank him for mitigating her sentence to exile (490–1). Faced with Jason's moral intransigence, Medea changes tack. If he will flee again alongside her into exile, she will protect them both, prevailing over the armies of Corinth, Colchis, and Thessaly combined (521–8). Jason is tempted, but protests that he is too afraid of royal power. 'Or perhaps you desire it too much,' Medea retorts (529). Her final persuasive gambit has failed, and now nothing stands in the way of her revenge. When Jason reveals how much he loves his sons (544–9), it exposes his greatest vulnerability, and from that point onwards he is lost.

Third Chorus

Picking up and developing the subject matter of the previous chorus, this stasimon falls metrically and thematically into two halves. The Chorus's initial comparison of wildfire, storms, floods, and hurricanes to the fury of a wife betrayed recalls Medea's representation of her own rage in the preceding scene (579–90; cf. 407–14). They ask the gods to pardon Jason for his transgressive (*audax*) voyage, and again Medea is positioned as the instrument of divine or natural retribution: it is Neptune, the sea-god, who is enraged (*furit*) by the Argo's 'conquest' of his domain (597–8).[9] This prompts a choral *sententia*, or statement of generalized advice, that it is better to stay within established boundaries and not risk overextending oneself. The second half of the stasimon (607–79) catalogues the deaths of the other Argonauts, all of which are figured as punishment for their participation in the expedition (614–16), regardless of whether they are causally related. Tiphys, the helmsman, dies *en route* (616–24), but Orpheus is dismembered by maenads many years later (625–33), Hercules inadvertently poisoned by his wife (634–42), and Meleager murdered by his mother in a family feud (644–6). Nevertheless, the gods are implored to stop their persecution of the Argonauts and at least spare Jason, who did not embark of his own free will but on the orders of King Pelias.

Act 4

Medea uses a combination of toxins and enchantments to poison the gifts she will have her children convey to Creusa. As a preamble, the Nurse describes how she has summoned not only venomous serpents from all parts of the world (681–90) but also their mythological and astrological counterparts: the Hydra, the Delphic Python, her own Colchian dragon, and the constellation Draco, earthly poisons being insufficient for her purposes (690–704). She then laces her concoction with a cocktail of deadly plants which she herself has gathered from as far afield as the Danube and the Tigris (705–30). To the poisonous brew now prepared, she adds the verbal potency of incantation (737–42). The spell she casts invokes the dead, in particular the shades of mythological villains suffering the punishments of Tartarus, and the infernal Hecate, goddess of the dark moon (740–51). She describes the rituals performed for Hecate and their unnatural effects on the cosmos as they disrupt the seasons and turn rivers back in their course (752–86). The rhythm of her chanting becomes more rapid as the goddess responds, and as the ritual reaches its climax, Medea slashes her arm and spills her own (*caros*) blood (787–810). This foreshadows how the same knife will be used in the following scene to spill the blood of her own children; it may, indeed, also be the one that previously spilt the blood of her own brother. Hecate's intervention transforms the merely mortal poisons into a supernatural invisible contagion that will consume Creusa from within (833–8).

Fourth Chorus

Much shorter than the other choruses (849–79), this perfunctory interlude allows for the passage of time between the departure of Medea's children with the poisoned gifts and the entry of the messenger reporting Creusa's death. The Chorus reiterate Medea's ferocity, comparing her in an ironic simile to a tiger bereaved of her young (858–65). They describe her movement and appearance: how she paces back and forth, tossing her head violently, her cheeks alternately pallid and flaming. She can restrain neither her love nor her rage; and now both passions are driving her together, the evils she will commit must surely cause the sun to set in haste and night to fall before its time.

Act 5

In a terse exchange with the Chorus (879–90), the messenger informs us that Creusa and Creon are dead, and the citadel in flames. Medea rejoices in her success, but feels that now she has become truly 'Medea', she must exercise her capacity to commit some further, unthinkable atrocity in order to be suitably revenged. She wishes that Jason and Creusa had children together … but Jason's only offspring are also Medea's own. Horrified by where her thoughts have taken her, she vacillates wildly (926–44), and begs her anger to surrender to maternal tenderness (944). She embraces her sons, and almost yields, but then recalls that she cannot take them with her into exile; if they are to be lost to her, she will make sure they are also lost to their father (950–1). At this critical juncture, she is confronted by a vision of her brother's ghost, flanked by Furies, seeking a reparation that can only be made with Medea's own flesh and blood. To appease him, she kills one of her sons. Jason arrives (978), and Medea, taunting him from the rooftop, realizes that his witnessing is what will complete her act of vengeance (992–3). The first child's death was a sacrifice; the second will be a spectacle. 'Do you recognize your wife?' she asks Jason, as she mounts her flying chariot, drawn by twin dragons, and leaves him floundering in the carnage she has made. 'This is how I usually escape' (1021–2).

2.1 Ovid's Medea

Roman audiences did not come to Seneca's *Medea* unaware of how its general plot would unfold. Many existing versions in diverse media had laid the groundwork for Seneca's manipulation of what 'becoming Medea' entailed.[10] Perhaps the most prominent treatment of the previous generation, and a text unavoidably referenced by Seneca, would have been Ovid's tragedy, also entitled *Medea*; however, as this play is lost, it is possible only to conjecture the relationship.[11] Fortunately, Ovid also wrote on Medea in his mythological epic *Metamorphoses* and in his elegiac epistles from famous fictional women to their lovers, the *Heroides*.[12]

Heroides 12 is addressed by Medea to Jason at the point when she discovers the extent of his treachery. His wedding procession to Creusa has just passed her by (*Her*. 12.137–52), and she writes to reproach him with all the past favours she has performed, begging him to reconsider. The majority of the epistle is taken up by an account of Jason's arrival in Colchis and how she fell in love with him, a reminder of the pledge he made to her, and the assistance she provided. She pours out her grief at being abandoned and how it has left her prostrated, unable to call on the magical powers which served her in the past (*Her*. 12.167–8). It is only towards the end of the epistle that Ovid allows her a brief flash of *ira* (anger), threatening Creusa and intimating that Jason will come to regret his infidelity. Some of the terms in which she expresses these threats recur in Seneca's Medea. 'She will weep', Ovid's Medea predicts, 'and burn more fiercely (*vincet adusta*) / than my own flaming passion' (*Her*. 12.180);[13] Seneca's rather more visceral twist on this conceit is that Creusa will burn more fiercely than her own wedding torches (*vincatque suas flagrante . . . / faces*, *Med*. 838–9). Ovid's Medea, like Seneca's, is unsure what form her final revenge will take, only that it will be something unthinkable, something worse than ever before: *nescio quid certe mens mea maius agit* ('I don't know what, but my thoughts are certainly tending towards some great act', *Her*. 12.212).[14] For Seneca, the term *nescioquid* becomes a particularly potent index of the unthinkable, in the same way as *nefas* refers to the unspeakable, acts so appalling they cannot be named or even conceived. *Nescioquid ferox / decrevit animus intus*, realizes Seneca's Medea, after the deaths of Creon and Creusa but before she has decided what will follow. 'Some unthinkable atrocity / has been determined by my inner self' (*Med*. 917–18). *Ira, qua ducis, sequor* ('Anger, where you lead, I follow', *Med*. 953), she continues, almost exactly echoing Ovid's Medea at a similar juncture: *Quo feret ira, sequar* ('Where anger takes me, I will follow', *Her.* 12.209).

These verbal similarities are accompanied by thematic ones, such as Medea's desire for Jason to acknowledge his culpability and in doing so exonerate her. 'Let others condemn me – you have to praise me', argues Ovid's Medea, 'you by/for whom I have so often been forced to do harm (*nocens*)' (*Her.* 12.131–2). Seneca repeats this argument in almost identical terms: 'When everyone condemns your wife / you alone should defend me, call me innocent; / you should regard as innocent one who has done harm (*nocens*) on your behalf' (*Med.* 501–3). The principle of restitution or repayment is also present in Ovid, Seneca retaining the image of the Argo's safe return as the 'dowry' (*dos*) which Medea brought with her from Colchis:

> You ask where my dowry is? Let's count it, on that battlefield
>   which you had to plough before plundering the Fleece.
> That golden ram, famous for its luxurious wool
>   was my dowry, and if I were to say 'Return it!' you'd refuse.
> My dowry is your safety; my dowry is the young heroes of Greece!
>
> *Her.* 12.199–203

Similarly, Seneca has his Medea remind Jason at length of the favours she has done for him, including murder and desecration. *Hac <u>dote</u> nupsi* ('with this dowry, I married [you]', *Med.* 489), recalling also her previous point to Creon that the Argonauts were the *munus*, the 'gift' she brought to Greece.

A rather different Medea came down to Seneca via the legacy of Ovid's *Metamorphoses*.[15] Although comprising over 400 verses and spanning Medea's entire mythological career, from her first glimpse of Jason to her post-tragic exploits in Athens, the action covered in the tragedy is compressed into a mere four lines; something of a literary joke, perhaps, by an author who had himself written a whole play on the subject. The episode from the *Metamorphoses* which has most traction for Seneca is the scene which shows Medea in her capacity as sorceress. Medea's magic is somewhat played down in other literature, but Ovid takes her step by step through a complex ritual which Seneca references in his own Act 4 spell-casting scene. The magic performed by Ovid's Medea has the benign purpose of restoring Jason's father Aeson to youth and health, but Seneca retains components of her ritual while transposing it into something more sinister.

One point of similarity is Medea's appearance. In the *Metamorphoses*, she dresses for the ritual in 'an ungirdled robe, / barefoot (*nuda pedem*), unbound hair flowing over her bare shoulders' (*Met.* 7.182–3). Seneca's costume likewise includes 'hair loosed from its bonds', while she pours libations barefoot (*nudo . . . pede*) in the sacred grove (*Med.* 753). Seneca compares her ecstatic state to that of a maenad (*Med.* 806), the maddened followers of the god Bacchus, while Ovid refers to her circling Hecate's altar with her loose hair flying 'as in the rite of the bacchantes' (*Met.* 7.257–8). The abilities she possesses are also similar:

> When I wanted it, their banks astonished, rivers
> returned to their sources. I calmed the crashing waves,
> and when they were still, I stirred them with my song. I banished clouds
> and summoned clouds, sent winds away and called them back.
> I split the throats of serpents with magic words and charms,
> brought rocks alive and shook the solid earth itself,
> moved forests, and ordered the mountains to tremble,
> the earth to groan, and the shades of the dead to leave their tombs.
> You too, Moon, I have drawn down.
>
> *Met.* 7.199–206

For Seneca's Medea, reversing natural processes is also characteristic of her magic, as is the use of verbal incantations to produce such reversals. She has summoned (*evocavi*) rain out of cloudless skies and caused tides to turn; she has confounded day and night, and with her chanting (*cantu meo*) has conjured frost at midsummer and harvest in winter. She turns rivers back to their sources and raises storms when there is no wind, and her songs (*nostris cantibus*) strip ancient woods of their foliage (754–67). We do not see her raising the dead, but it is the deities and denizens of the Underworld whom she repeatedly invokes. She also calls on the moon, *noctium sidus* (750) to show herself in a 'threatening' light, summoning her with an imperative (*adesse*, 770) to which the goddess responds favourably (785–6, 787–96, 839–42).

Medea in both texts also needs to prepare a potion. Ovid has her collect the plants which are her ingredients from all over northern Greece; Seneca follows this precedent but sends her further afield, harvesting deadly herbs from Arabia, Mesopotamia, and the snowy forests of Europe. Her empire has expanded. In both cases, the plants she assembles are blended with other ingredients, but whereas Ovid's Medea chooses long-lived creatures to represent Aeson's increased lifespan, Seneca's are representatives of burning: the centaur's blood that poisoned Hercules, the ash of his funeral pyre, the firebrand that tortured Meleager, the remains of Phaethon's charred corpse and the Chimaera's fiery breath. In its outline, then, Ovid's spell-casting can be discerned behind Seneca's, but Seneca reformulates it for tragedy.

Unmentioned in the *Metamorphoses*, and passed over as unmentionable by the Medea of the *Heroides* (*Her*. 12.113–15), Medea's murder of her brother Absyrtus was not unknown to Ovid. It forms the subject of one of his elegiac poems of exile, *Tristia* 3.9. The poem ostensibly provides an etymology for the place name Tomis, the Black Sea town to which Ovid was exiled. According to this etymology, the name 'Tomis' was derived from the Greek *temnō*, 'I cut'. Ovid traces the name's mythological origin back to the incident in which Medea kills her brother in order to thwart pursuit by the Colchians, enabling the Argo to escape. Having crossed the Black Sea from east to west, the Argo has moored in this harbour, when the lookout sees Colchian sails approaching (*Trist*. 3.9.7–12). The Argonauts quickly cast off, while Medea strikes her breast with the guilty hand 'which had dared and was yet to dare so many unspeakable things' (*ausa atque ausura multa nefanda manu*, 3.9.16). She determines to delay her father by means of a trick (*fraude*, 3.9.20), and her eyes fall upon her brother, who in this version appears to have accompanied the Argo rather than intercepting them. Before he is aware of her intention,

> She stabbed his innocent side with a sharp blade,
> then cut him up, and scattered his severed limbs
> across the countryside, to be found in several places.

In case her father was unaware, she placed on a high outcrop
his pale hands and bloody head.
So her father was detained by fresh grief, and while he gathered
the lifeless limbs, his sad (*triste*) journey was delayed.

Trist. 3.9.26–32

Absyrtus's murder is central to Seneca's *Medea*, and it is quite likely that its treatment in Ovid's *Tristia* contributed along with the *Heroides*, *Metamorphoses*, and lost tragedy to this reimagining of the myth.

2.2 Epic and lyric

As far as the Argonautic backstory is concerned, the most comprehensive coverage is to be found in the Greek *Argonautica* by Apollonius of Rhodes. Apollonius, a scholar-poet writing in the Egyptian metropolis of Alexandria, composed his *Argonautica* in the mid-third century BCE. Although an epic poem in scope, meter, and other generic conventions such as divine intervention and the inclusion of battle-scenes, it also contains features which place it in the category of romance, that is, a wandering, episodic quest-narrative which includes magic and marvels, monstrous creatures, erotic interludes, and geographical dispersal. Books 1 and 2 concern the Argo's outward voyage, Book 3 Jason's exploits in Colchis, and Book 4 the return to Greece via a circuitous route that takes them (among other places) to Sicily, Libya, and Crete.[16]

While not explicitly an account of conquest or colonization, it should be noted that the *Argonautica* (not unlike Homer's *Odyssey*) participates in a discourse legitimizing Greek expansion and settlement. Greek colonies in the Black Sea region had been established, primarily for trading purposes, since the seventh century BCE.[17] As Apollonius's Argonauts pass among islands and along coastlines, they are at once accumulating and disseminating geographical knowledge, particularly in the first two books of the epic. As Mary Frances Williams has shown, aetiology is also a major theme, Apollonius making his Argonauts repeatedly responsible for the foundation of shrines and the naming of landmarks, leaving a Greek stamp on the local landscape.[18] Such fabrications of shared mythological ancestry typically played an important role in legitimating the foundation of Greek colonies abroad.[19]

Apollonius's Book 3 opens with a rather mischievous invocation addressed to Erato, the Muse not of epic poetry but of erotic lyric, appropriate inspiration for a book which focuses on Medea's agonized infatuation with the leader of the Greek invasion.[20] Still a teenage girl (*kourē*), Medea is introduced as Hecate's priestess (ARh. *Arg.* 3.251–2), skilled in *pharmaka* (spells and drugs, 3.528–30). The goddess Hera engineers her passion in order to ensure Jason's success, and immediately Eros's arrow burns within her 'like a flame . . . and her fast-beating heart / panted painfully in her breast, and nor could she recall / anything other than the sweet wound melting away her soul' (*Arg.* 3.287–90). This Medea is innocent, indecisive, and afraid; she weeps and trembles her way aboard the Argo, and although it is her idea to ambush Absyrtus, it is Jason who kills him (4.414–81).[21] Jason himself, meanwhile, is characterized throughout Apollonius as *amēchanos*, 'clueless' or 'incompetent' (e.g. 1.460). Although nominally leader of the expedition, he is only elected because Herakles steps aside (1.341–52). His future betrayal of Medea is foreshadowed by his liaison with Hypsipyle, queen of the island of Lemnos, whom he impregnates and leaves behind mid-voyage. 'Remember Hypsipyle,' she admonishes him, as he departs; more pragmatic than Medea, however, she does not necessarily expect him to return (1.888–98). The epic tradition, then, forms an important counterpoint to the representation of Medea in tragedy.

In Latin literature, the Argo assumes a greater significance, exploited by Seneca, as the *prima ratis*, the first ship ever to set sail. The trope may have existed earlier, but it is first explicitly attested in an epyllion (mini-epic) by the lyric poet Catullus in the 50s BCE (*Carmen* 64). The epyllion concerns the wedding-feast of mortal hero Peleus and the sea-nymph Thetis, parents of Achilles, and an ecphrasis of the myths embroidered on their nuptial bedspread, primarily Ariadne's rescue from Naxos. The Argo's maiden voyage opens the poem as the occasion on which Peleus first glimpsed his future bride (*Carm.* 64.19–21). Playfully alluding to the opening lines of Euripides' *Medea* and those of its Latin translation by Ennius, Catullus begins with the Argo itself, 'pine-trees grown once upon a time on the hilltops of Pelion', which proceed unnaturally to 'swim through Neptune's liquid waters'. The paradox is then explained: it is Athena who fashioned this vessel and the Argonauts who now propel it across the 'sea-green plain' with pinewood oars, 'the first to accustom [sea-goddess] Amphitrite to their passage' (*Carm.* 64.1–11). The Nereids or sea-nymphs rise from the foam, *monstrum* ... *admirantes*, marvelling at the strange new arrival in their element (*Carm.* 64.15). For Catullus, this incursion signifies a loss of human innocence, and as the motif of the first ship develops, it acquires the additional taint of imperial corruption.

The Argo's next port of call in Latin lyric is Horace's *Carmen* 1.3, published in 23 BCE. The reign of Augustus, Rome's first Princeps, was well-established, and Horace a member of the same circle of court poets that included Virgil. The ode is addressed to Virgil, ostensibly as he sets out on a sea voyage to Greece, or more figuratively as he embarks on the equally demanding venture of his state epic and *magnum opus*, the *Aeneid*.[22] 'That man had oak and three layers of bronze / around his heart, who entrusted a fragile / craft to the violent sea / for the first time', Horace exclaims (Hor. *Carm.* 1.3.9–12). This first fragile craft is not identified as the Argo, but coming after Catullus it may be assumed that this is the case. Horace goes on to condemn the audacity of humanity:

> In vain did a sensible god
> separate the lands with intervening
> Ocean, if impious ships
> skip regardless over waves that shouldn't be touched.
> Reckless (*audax*), daring anything,
> the human race charged into forbidden evil (*nefas*).

Hor. *Carm.* 1.3.21–6

Here, the Argo's voyage acquires (im)moral significance. The sea, and by extension, foreign lands, were forbidden territory until this first transgressive expedition. Horace's *audax* Argo taps into a growing

Roman anxiety over the consequences of conquest, the idea that foreign, especially Eastern nations and the luxury goods they exported had an enervating and deliquescent effect on Roman consumers.[23] *Luxuria*, or decadence, resulted from commerce, commerce depended on seafaring, and seafaring was initiated by this first, unnatural, *audax* voyage abroad.

We find the full realization of the trope a generation after Seneca in the Roman *Argonautica* of Valerius Flaccus. This is a song of imperialism dedicated to the emperor Vespasian, who is flattered in the proem as conquering the 'Caledonian ocean' (VF. *Arg.* 1.8–9) and under whose protection trading vessels now sail from Asia Minor, Egypt, and the Levant (VF. *Arg.* 1.17–20). Presiding gods Neptune and Jupiter both foresee that the Argo's precedent will enable global commerce (1.246; cf. 1.644), although whether this is to be regarded as a desirable or regrettable outcome is left ambiguous. It is certainly regrettable to the sun-god Sol, whose descendent Aeetes rules in Colchis. Sol complains that Jupiter's masterplan is being accomplished at the Colchians' expense (*vulnere nostro*, 1.525), and that he settled his people in this inhospitable region deliberately to deter Mediterranean invaders (1.509–27). Although Jason does not settle where he plunders, the vocabulary pertaining to his divinely ordained mission is littered with terms of conquest: he will be 'victor over the sea and the Scythian king' (1.345–6), the Colchian shores are 'conquered' (*domitis . . . Colchidos oris*, 2.423) along with the sea itself (*domat aequora*, 1.600) and the waters of the Bosphoros (*domitis . . . Symplegados undis*, 5.299).[24] Valerius's *Argonautica* postdates *Medea*, but articulates with useful clarity the supposed lineage of *translatio imperii* that places the Argo at the origin of Roman expansion, a concept which appears already to have had currency for Seneca.

2.3 Medea in tragedy

The most direct comparandum for Seneca's *Medea*, however, is the Greek tragedy by Euripides on the same subject. Superficially, the two plays are very similar. Both cover the same mythological episode, commencing at the point of Jason's new marriage and ending with Medea's escape by flying chariot after murdering her sons. Structurally and dramaturgically, however, their differences are profound. Euripides' *Medea* was first performed at the Athenian Dionysia in 431 BCE. Like all Greek tragedies, it is an intervention into public discourse, a dramatic commentary on the city-state's political and civic life and ideology. It has been suggested that Euripides was the first to have Medea murder her own children.[25] These two factors alone – the play's embeddedness in contemporary Athenian concerns, and the shocking innovation of infanticide – distinguish it considerably from Seneca. One potent similarity, however, should be remarked at the outset, and this is Medea's theatricality, her talent for dissembling. While showing her true face and soliciting the complicity of the Chorus (and audience), she grovels artfully to Creon (Eur. *Med.* 368–9) and later successfully pretends to have forgiven Jason, exploiting his assumptions of female inferiority. Seneca's Medea takes no such measures – 'Bearable is the pain that can conceal itself,' as she tells the Nurse, 'great misfortunes do not hide' (155–6) – but like the Athenian heroine, she makes use of her medium, conscious both of her spectators and her role.

Euripides employs a larger cast of characters, and much more of his action is conveyed through dialogue. The opening scene is a prime example. Whereas Seneca opens the floodgates immediately with a furious tirade delivered by Medea herself, Euripides introduces her predicament indirectly via a conversation between two nameless servants, the Nurse and the children's Tutor. Although her lamentations are heard within the house, Medea does not appear onstage until well after the choral parodos and the Chorus's own exchange with the Nurse. Euripides' Chorus is far more interactive overall, a point to which we shall return below. Perhaps the most prominent Euripidean character absent from Seneca is the Athenian ruler, Aegeus. Aegeus serves two functions, both irrelevant to Seneca. In terms of plot, he provides Medea with a place of refuge after her departure from Corinth, and in terms of ideology he provides a connection between the action of the play and the context of its performance. His appearance gives occasion for the Chorus to sing an exquisite ode in praise of Athens, at the same time questioning the values of a city willing to embrace a polluted child-killer in return for services rendered.[26] The onward destination of Seneca's Medea is never specified, her main concern being her inability to return to Colchis. Her ties to Athens are eliminated, Seneca sending her instead on a voyage 'aloft through the deep space of the skies' (*per alta vade spatia sublime aetheris*, 1026), giving a cosmic dimension to her future travels rather than pinning her down to another earthly home.

The other character who does not play a major role in Seneca's treatment is Euripides' messenger. The messenger-speech is a crucial element of Greek tragedy, and indeed features in most of Seneca's other plays as well. The messenger's show-stopping rendition of the bloody events which have occurred offstage elsewhere provides the Roman dramatist with an ideal mechanism for displaying the rhetorical flamboyance that is his stylistic trademark; in *Medea*, however, Seneca foregoes this opportunity. Euripides, in contrast, makes the most of it, presenting the double death of Creon and his daughter in a virtuoso monologue notorious as one of the most gruesome in the Greek tragic corpus. Suspense is created as the princess arrays herself in Medea's poisoned gifts and admires her reflection. Suddenly, she collapses, falling into violent convulsions. The dress begins to eat away her flesh, and the crown to burn, until 'down from her head dripped blood mingled with flame; her flesh / Attacked by invisible fangs of poison, melted / From the bare bone, like sap from a pine-tree's bark' (Eur. *Med.* 1198–1202, trans. Vellacott). But the horror is not yet over: Creon arrives and embraces his daughter's corpse, but when he tries to rise, it holds him fast 'as ivy sticks to laurel branches' (Eur. *Med.* 1213), and the poison consumes him in turn. Seneca's messenger merely announces what we already know, in a single line: 'Daughter and father lie with their ashes mixed together' (880). The verbal description of Creusa's death is transferred instead to Medea herself, who prays during her spell-casting that 'heat shall enter her breast and her veins, / her limbs shall melt and her bones smoke / and with her hair flaming, may this bride / burn brighter than her wedding torches' (Sen. *Med.* 836–9). Medea's spell, absent from Euripides, forms the climax of Seneca's version, substituting in a sense for the conventional *mise-en-abîme* of the messenger. Both are intensely theatrical devices that draw attention to their own artifice, and both celebrate the verbal potency of the tragic medium.

As mentioned above, Euripides' Chorus play a much greater role in the action. Moreover, whereas Seneca's are actively hostile to Medea, taunting her with their wedding-song for Creusa, the sympathies of Euripides' Corinthian women are firmly aligned with his protagonist. They act as her confidantes and supporters, describing themselves as her friends (*phila*, Eur. *Med.* 181) and agreeing to keep silent about her plots. As women themselves, they take her side in solidarity, informing Jason directly that they disapprove of his behaviour (it is *ou dikaia*, unjust, 578). They pity her situation and pledge to keep her secrets, as this is the obligation of a loyal friend (559–62). Even when Medea divulges her intention to kill the children, they attempt to dissuade rather than denouncing her. Their sympathy makes a substantial contribution to the way in which Euripides' Medea is presented to the audience, and how Euripides' audience are encouraged to take her side, at least initially. The Nurse, too, directs our attitude, calling her mistress 'unfortunate' (*dystēnos*), 'miserable' (*talaina*), and 'wretched' (*tlēmon*) as she lies weeping indoors, refusing to eat and wishing to die. Medea also refers to herself as *dystanos* (Eur. *Med.* 96), as do the Chorus, addressing her as 'poor woman' (*dystane*, 357, cf. 132). The emphasis in Euripides' opening scene is firmly on her suffering; it is not until she emerges onstage in person that she begins to develop another side. The affective journey of Euripides' heroine, from pitiable to admirable to despicable, covers an extraordinarily diverse terrain. Seneca, on the other hand, begins at fever pitch and does not relent.

The point at which Euripides' Medea ceases to command the audience's pity and begins inspiring fear may, of course, be unique to any individual spectator. While it is difficult not to respond to the stricken cries that issue from the *skēnē* (backstage) in the opening scene,

Medea may lose the sympathy of some with her duplicity, and others with her implacable bitterness towards Jason (although Jason's evident callousness and self-interest leave little doubt that he is morally in the wrong);[27] others may stay with her as she bids the boys a tearful farewell (1069–80), and share her desire for a graphic messenger-speech (1134–5). Most will be unable keep condoning Medea's actions once she turns on her own children, although Euripides does provide the exonerative rationale that as they are doomed anyway, it is better for them to die by their mother's loving hand (1240–1).[28] To the last, Medea insists that she is the victim (*dystychēs d'egō gynē*, 'I am such an unlucky/accursed woman', 1250), leaving room for those who still wish to rejoice in her escape. There is no prescribed moment for the transition, but nonetheless a large proportion of the emotional interest in Euripides' drama derives from the precise extent to which we are prepared to defend Medea, and the precise point, if it comes, at which our endorsement is withdrawn.

For the play's original audience, this process would have been even more confronting, as they may have been unaware of Euripides' innovative decision to have Medea kill her own children. Prior to this production, it seems that according to the generally accepted version of the myth, the children were lynched by the Corinthians after delivering the poisoned gifts to Creusa. If this was the case, Euripides' audience would be expecting Medea to take bloodthirsty revenge on the Corinthian royal house, but certainly not to turn on her own flesh and blood. Even her stated intention of killing the children could, under these circumstances, be interpreted as tragic irony, if the audience supposed that the Corinthians and not Medea herself would ultimately be responsible.[29] This competing version also makes sense of Medea's determination that she alone will end her sons' lives (Eur. *Med.* 1236–50). The shock of our complicity in these deaths is unavailable to all subsequent Medeas, including Seneca's. The twist was a sensational *coup de théâtre* reserved for Euripides alone, because once it entered the tradition, it became canonical. There is never any question that Seneca's Medea will not carry out her characteristic crime; indeed, as she is aware, it is only in doing so that she will fully become 'Medea'.

Seneca was not the first Latin tragedian to take on Medea as a subject. Prior to Ovid's lost *Medea*, mentioned above, two Roman Republican playwrights also composed *Medea*s of which fragments survive. The first of these was Ennius, himself an immigrant to Rome from Magna Graeca (South Italy), writing between approximately 200 and 170 BCE. Among the numerous tragedies attributed to Ennius is at least one entitled *Medea Exul* (*Medea Exiled*), and possibly another *Medea* as well, although these may be the same play.[30] *Medea Exul* appears to be a translation of Euripides. Some fifteen fragments of the tragedy are extant, transmitted mainly through their quotation in later handbooks of oratory as examples of diction to be imitated. The largest fragment comes from the start of the play.

> Would that in the grove of Pelion, struck by the axe,
> the ship-building boughs had never fallen to the earth,
> and would indeed that there had never been an original beginning (*exordium*)
> for that ship which is now known by the name
> Argo, because men chosen from among the Argives
> sailed in her, seeking the golden fleece of the Colchian
> ram, ordered by King Pelias, by means of a trick (*dolum*).
> For then my errant mistress would never have left her home:
> Medea, sick at heart, wounded by cruel love.
>
> CIII 208–16[31]

As in Euripides, Medea's Nurse sets the scene with her regret that the Argo ever set sail, retrojecting the play's beginning (*exordium*) back to the pines which were felled on the ridge at Pelion. She stresses that the Argonauts obtained the Fleece *per dolum*, by stealth or deceit, which serves the dual purpose of prefiguring Jason's predilection for treachery and recalling the part which Medea herself played in betraying her own people.[32] Three other brief passages indicate how closely Ennius follows his Greek source-text. The Chorus are addressed as 'Wealthy noblewomen (*matronae opulentae optumates*) who dwell in the high citadel of Corinth' (Frag. CV),[33] unambiguously identifying them, and giving them a Roman cast with the local vocabulary of *matronae* (respectable wives) and *optumates* (members of the Roman social elite). Ennius's Medea also repeats the famous sentiment of her Euripidean counterpart that 'I would rather risk my life three times in battle / than give birth just once' (CIX 232–3). Finally, she puts on the same ingratiating act in front of Creon before showing off her calculated duplicity to the Chorus: 'For would I have crawled to him with such flattering words (*blandiloquentia*) / unless to some purpose? When you know what you want, you do whatever's necessary to get a result' (CVIII 225–8).[34]

As one of the earliest translations of Greek drama in to Latin, Ennius retained both the structure and the dialogue of his Euripidean model. A couple of generations later, writing somewhere between 140 and 100 BCE, the prolific Roman tragedian Accius also composed a *Medea* (or *Argonautae*, if as seems likely these are to be understood as two titles for the same play). This appears to have taken as its subject not Medea's Corinthian infanticide but rather the Argonautic component of her story; Mario Erasmo suggests it may have ended with her brother's murder.[35] A lengthy fragment is preserved in Cicero's treatise *On the Nature of the Gods* (*ND*. 2.89):

Tanta moles labitur
fremibunda ex alto ingenti sonitu et spiritu.
prae se undas volvit, vortices vi suscitat;
ruit prolapsa, pelagus respergit, reflat,
dum quod sublime ventis expulsum rapi
saxum aut procellis, vel globosos turbines
existere ictos undis concursantibus;
nisi quas terrestres pontus strages conciet;
aut forte Triton, fuscina evertens specus
subter radices penitus, undanti in freto
molem ex profundo saxeam ad caelum eruit.

Accius, Frag. I, 1–12

Such a great mass glides
roaring from the deep, huge in sound and exhalation.
It rolls waves ahead, its force creates whirlpools;
it dashes forth, plunging; the sea splashes and spumes,

as if some high cliff had been seized and torn asunder
by winds or gales, or tornadoes had been hammered
into solidity by conflicting waves;
or the sea had wreaked destruction on the lands;
or maybe Triton with his trident, turning out a cave
by its inmost roots, amidst the surging strait
had cast a rocky mass from the depths to the skies.

While not necessarily providing evidence for the existence of the *prima ratis* motif prior to Catullus, Accius is evidently playing here on the novelty of the Argo. The speaker is a shepherd who has never seen a ship before, and who struggles to encompass the phenomenon in words. He attempts to assimilate it to various aspects of the natural world such as a cloud, a rock, a waterspout, or a new island, and to describe it in terms of the sound and motion it produces. In this way, Accius playfully defamiliarizes an everyday object, the ship, in order to present it as something marvellous and strange, relaying it in terms of the sensations associated with its passage uncoupled from standard terminology: the great 'mass' (*moles*) has no mast, oars, hull, and so on, but instead it approaches in a surge of displaced water like a living thing. It certainly does not appear man-made, but like a wild epiphany. Its focalization through the *faux-naivité* of Accius's viewer gives the ecphrasis a striking blend of irony – given our superior knowledge of what the *moles* portends – and surrealism, if we allow ourselves to participate in marvelling at the commonplace. Even if Accius's Argo is not identified literally as the *prima ratis*, this passage captures with extraordinary vividness the impact of such a moment; it is this which confronts Catullus's Nereids as they rise from the sea-foam *monstrum ... admirantes* (Cat. *Carm.* 64.15).

2.4 Medea in visual art

As well as the textual evidence for the background to Seneca's *Medea*, we can also consider her representation in the visual arts, including vase paintings, frescoes, and sculpture. Images such as these surrounded Roman theatre-goers, who may also variously have been readers, viewers, and consumers. Mythological narratives were part of the fabric of everyday life, both public and domestic. Although by Seneca's time figured pottery of the type discussed here was no longer manufactured, it marked the emergence of motifs which became central to Medea's mythological tradition, and moreover represents an important phase of transmission in its own right. On fourth-century BCE South Italian funerary vessels such as that in Figure 2.1, Medea appears aloft in a chariot drawn by two dragons or serpents. As Oliver Taplin points out, dragons are not in fact mentioned at all at the end of Euripides' *Medea*; if indeed anything drew the chariot of the Sun on the Athenian stage, it was most probably horses.[36] Seneca, however, is quite explicit that 'Twin serpents bend their scaly necks / in submission to my yoke' (1023–4), an innovation first attested on red-figure ceramics, where Medea's flight seems to have been a popular theme.[37]

In Figure 2.1, Medea is shown surrounded by a solar halo, as if framed against the sun. She wears Eastern costume, with long diamond-patterned sleeves visible beneath her richly embroidered garment and a peaked headdress with flowing ribbons. To either side are gloating Erinyes or Furies, goddesses of vengeance, with grotesque mask-like faces. Beneath her, a white-haired female figure – probably the Nurse – grieves over the bodies of Medea's sons, which are sprawled across an altar, giving their deaths the sacrificial overtone also present in Seneca. Jason approaches from the left, but he is too late.

If the *coup de théâtre* of Medea's escape was favoured for depiction on fourth-century pottery,[38] later artists in other media preferred to focus on the dramatic excitement of the moment just prior to her sons' murder. A number of frescoes from Pompeii, Herculaneum, and Stabiae take this highly suspenseful point in the narrative as their subject.[39] In a study of the relationship between Senecan tragedy and fourth-style frescoes, Eric Varner shows how theatricality pervaded Roman domestic space. Interior walls were painted with mythological scenes set in illusionistic architecture, often decorated with theatre masks or

Figure 2.1 Lucanian Calyx-Krater, *c.* 400 BC. Attributed to Policoro Painter (Italian). © The Cleveland Museum of Art, Leonard C. Hanna, Jr. Fund 1991.1.

observed by painted figures in order to reinforce the dynamics of spectatorship.[40] In Figure 2.2, from the House of the Dioscuri in Pompeii, a conflicted Medea can hardly bear to look at her two boys as they play obliviously on the very altar which will later be a platform for their corpses. The male figure behind them in the doorway is the children's Tutor, stroking his beard in concern as he watches them. In her left hand, Medea holds a knife, although it is not yet unsheathed, and with her right she pushes it down as if at once restraining herself

Figure 2.2 House of the Dioscuri, Pompeii. © Museo Archeologico Nazionale di Napoli, inv. 8977.

and concealing the weapon. Her body corkscrews: while her stance is turned away from the boys, her torso yearns towards them, but her gaze is directed *past* them to focus on something terrible only she can see. The tension of her deliberation is palpable. In a comparable scene from the House of Jason (Figure 2.3), Medea is addressed by one of her sons as she sits dejected, head resting on one hand in an attitude of sorrow

Figure 2.3 House of Jason, Pompeii. © Museo Archeologico Nazionale di Napoli, inv. 114321.

while her sheathed sword hangs heavy in the other. Once again, the Tutor observes them, this time from an inner window. The fresco's composition is reminiscent of the central doorway of a stage-set, supplemented by *trompe-l'oeil* painted architecture.

These domestic frescoes may have been referencing a particular painting by the artist Timomachus, reputedly on display in Rome from the mid-first century BCE.[41] It is celebrated in a number of epigrams, short, witty poems by various authors now gathered together in the *Palatine Anthology*. The epigrams all concur that Timomachus painted Medea just prior to killing her sons, holding a sword and weeping. Several praise his restraint in not showing the actual murder (e.g. 136, 140). Epigram 135 is a good example of antithesis used to indicate both the inner turmoil Medea is experiencing, and the artist's skill in depicting contradictory emotions:

> The craftsmanship of Timomachus mingles Medea's love and jealousy
> as she condemns her children to death.
> In part she seems to assent to the sword, but in part declines
> planning both to spare her children and to kill them.
>
> *Anth. Pal.* 135

Similar oppositions – erotic and maternal love, anger and pity, tears and rage – inform the structure of the other ecphrastic epigrams. *Anth. Pal.* 136, for example, has her 'dragged in two directions' (*antimethelkomenan*) by her jealousy on the one hand, and her children on the other; Timomachus has taken pains to depict her 'double/twofold character(s)' (*ēthea dissa*), one composed of anger (*orgē*) and the other of pity (*eleos*). Both are intermingled, however: there are tears (*dakrou*) infiltrating her anger, and passion (*thumos*) infecting her pity. *Anth. Pal.* 137 specifies that as in the Pompeiian frescoes, she holds a sword in her hand. In *Anth. Pal.* 139, she likewise 'appears to our eyes pulled in two directions (*antimethelkomenan*), the repetition of this verb indicating how powerful was the impression of an individual divided against herself. These ecphrastic epigrams enter into dialogue with the artwork they purport to describe, rather than communicating its appearance impartially – they do not, for example, pay any attention to colours, nor to overall composition – but it is evident from this poetic series in conjunction with the frescoes how canonical Timomachus's iconography became. Like the frescoes, the epigrams are unique works drawing inspiration from diverse sources; they are transpositions, not imitations.

The same critical moment in Medea's dramatic narrative was also represented in sculpture, although the evidence for this is somewhat later than Seneca. The sophist Callistratus, writing in the 200s CE, includes a Macedonian sculpture of Medea among his prose *Ekphrases* or *Descriptions of Statues*. It is uncertain whether the pieces rendered by Callistratus were based on actual artworks, and as in the Timomachus epigrams their emotional and kinetic detail makes his rhetorical display performative rather than descriptive. It has been suggested by Isemene Lada-Richards that the way in which Callistratus's Medea shifts from one *pathos* (emotion) to another may in fact reflect the way in which a pantomime dancer might enact the role. The iconic poses of pantomimes were frequently compared to paintings or statues, and embodiment of contrasting emotional states was one of their notable skills.[42] Callistratus writes that in this statue's simultaneous representation of reasoning (*logismos*), passion (*thumos*), and grief (*lupē*) one could see 'an exegesis of the entire drama' (Call. *DS*. 13.1). He states explicitly that 'as well as the body, the sculpture imitated/enacted (*emimeito*, from the same root as *mimēsis*) the *pathē*' and that it seemed thereby to express 'all the action of the drama by Euripides' (13.3), Medea's frozen moment of passion recalling the reasoning that preceded it and the grief which was to follow. Three visual details are also mentioned: the figure held a sword, her hair was disordered, and she was dressed in mourning, 'befitting her state of mind' (13.4).

Medea was not a common sculptural subject, but a late second-century funeral monument from Arles (Figure 2.4) shows her in the very act of drawing her sword. Her face is truculent, her eyes deep-set under a heavily-moulded scowl, and while the two infants pull playfully at her robe she turns her head and gaze sharply away as if trying to dissociate herself from the crime her hands are performing. On a sarcophagus now held in Berlin (Figure 2.5), Creusa is caught in a desperate *dans macabre*, fire streaming upwards from her forehead while Creon looks on in despair and Medea gloats impassively. Two

Figure 2.4 Funeral relief, *c.* 200 CE. Statue de Médée. Musée Départementale Arles Antique. FAN.92.00.445, MDAA © R. Bénali, L. Roux.

Figure 2.5 Roman sarcophagus (Medeasarkophag), second century CE. Berlin Altesmuseum 00011191. © BPK-Bildagentur / Antikesammlung, SMB / Johannes Laurentius.

infants play in the foreground, oblivious of the unsheathed sword that would have hung above them; the sword itself is now lost, but the empty scabbard remains in Medea's left hand. In the next 'frame' of the image, Medea is shown again, brandishing the sword aloft, about to escape in her dragon chariot. The visual arts do not 'illustrate' texts, nor reproduce theatrical performances. Rather, along with epic and lyric, they participate in the circulation of motifs across and within diverse media which inform and enrich one another at each point of reception.

3

Themes

The Roman *Medea* may be distinguished from its Ancient Greek counterpart not only through variations in plot, but also through Seneca's treatment of the themes which dominate his action. These themes are not absent altogether from Euripides, but their relative prominence in Seneca situates the Roman tragedy within a different matrix of concepts and ideas. What Seneca's Medea explicitly represents, and what she embodies, are both more wide-ranging and less human than the woman whose dilemma and motives are explored in such harrowing detail by the Athenian dramatist. Whereas Euripides' heroine plays out her myth as if for the first time, the Roman Medea is haunted throughout by her personal and literary history. Even the revenge she seeks is not exclusively her own, but rather a consequence of the elemental forces that are acting through her, as *furor* (rage) instrumentalizes her body as a dehumanized mechanism of retribution.

This chapter will trace three key themes operative in Seneca's text. The first of these is the idea of repetition, or return; the second is Medea's identification with the natural world, particularly the sea; and the third is her self-conscious self-dramatization, her metatheatrical positioning as internal *auctor* (author) as well as actor.[1] The three themes are interrelated, intersecting at the play's motivational heart, namely revenge, and the irrational logic of revenge: the premise that one act of violence may overwrite and cancel out another.[2] Seneca's Medea enacts her infanticide reluctantly, despite herself, with an *invitam manum* (an 'unwilling hand', 952). She feels herself driven by *ira* (anger), *dolor* (pain), and *odium* (hatred), as though these passions possessed an independent existence. In order to be Medea, these are the acts, however repugnant, which as a character she must perforce perform. Similarly, it is her former crimes, specifically fratricide, which have prepared her to carry out what would otherwise be unthinkable (*nescioquid*) and unspeakable (*nefas*).[3] Her revenge on Jason is figured throughout the play as a repetition and indeed an amplification of murders previously committed, and as their inescapable result. In addition, although Medea exerts magical control over the winds and the tides (and other natural phenomena), she also serves as agent of their retaliation: as well as being punished for breaking his marriage vows, Jason must also answer for breaking the global 'treaty' (*foedera*, 335) which kept the oceans inviolate. The common feature of these three thematic vectors – Medea's personal past, her literary identity, and her personification of avenging *Natura* – is that they all place Medea herself at their mercy. Overdetermined by this perfect storm, Seneca's Medea struggles self-consciously to resist her scripting, but comes in the end to embrace the paradoxical empowerment of surrender.

3.1 It's all coming back to me (*cuncta redeant*)

As we have seen, the Argo's voyage had a distinct place in Latin literature of the early empire. To briefly recapitulate: when dispatched by King Pelias on a seemingly hopeless quest for the Golden Fleece – an artefact originally from Thessaly, but now located in Colchis on the far side of the Black Sea – Jason assembles a heroic crew for the mission, including Orpheus and Hercules. After an eventful voyage, the Argonauts pass through the Symplegades or Clashing Rocks at the mouth of the Bosphorus, and travel along the Black Sea coast to Colchis. Here Medea, daughter of the Colchian King Aeetes, falls in love with Jason and uses her magical skill to assist him in the challenges set by Aeetes: facing a fire-breathing bull, defeating an army that sprung from the earth, and finally vanquishing the dragon which guards the Golden Fleece itself. Jason then successfully absconds with his ship, his crew, the Fleece, and Medea, whose price for betraying her father is marriage to Jason and passage back to Greece. Medea kidnaps her brother Absyrtus as a hostage, and when they are pursued she kills him and scatters his dismembered corpse behind them piece by piece in order to delay the king. Having arrived back in Thessaly, Medea performs a further service for Jason: she tricks the daughters of the usurping King Pelias into boiling their father alive, in the belief that it will confer on him eternal youth. Unable then to remain in Thessaly, Jason and Medea seek asylum together as exiles in Corinth.

Euripides makes relatively little of Medea's Argonautic background. As is usual in Greek tragedy, especially for Euripides, the opening monologue – delivered by the Nurse – provides a sketch of the relevant mythology prior to the action of the play. In this sense, the Argo is present behind Euripides' *Medea* from its very first line; however, the Argo's outward voyage and its purpose are not mentioned again, and it has none of the symbolic resonance that has accrued to Seneca's *prima ratis* (first ship). The Argo is subsequently mentioned as the means by which Medea made her way from Colchis to Greece, but as Euripides' primary spatial axis is the perceived dichotomy between 'barbarian' and Greek,[4] its traffic is made to appear one-way. It figures in Medea's own past as the vessel which transported her from her homeland, but its initial launch and quest and crew play no part in her story as related by Euripides. Similarly, although Euripides' Medea reproaches Jason with some instances of her assistance – protecting him from the bull(s), dispatching the dragon, and deceiving Pelias's daughters – fratricide is not among them. Absyrtus's murder is mentioned twice in passing (Eur. *Med.* 167, 1334), but it has none of the prominence given by Seneca to what becomes for the Roman tragedian a parallel act of slaughter, a criminal impiety for which the death of Medea's children is made to atone with uncanny reciprocity.

For Seneca, on the other hand, the Argo's backstory supplies a counterpoint integral to the fabric of the drama, a warp to the weft of the present-day plot. The Argo's voyage is recounted in detail over the two choral episodes that flank the body of the drama, comprising some 150 lines in total. In addition, Medea recalls her part in the Argo's mission to herself (118–36), to Creon (203–46), and to Jason

(447–89) – representing a further 100 lines or so, a quarter of the play devoted to this history – finally asserting that she is 'pleased, delighted' (*iuvat, iuvat*, 911) to have decapitated her brother and hacked apart his limbs, pleased to have desecrated her father's shrine and caused Pelias's death, because this murderous apprenticeship has made her capable of anything (915). Euripides' Medea expresses scant remorse for her past betrayals and atrocities; Seneca's is racked by it. Her brother's murder, as we shall see, is key to the perpetrator's trauma experienced by Seneca's Medea. Absyrtus's literal reappearance (958–71) marks the climax of her guilt and expiation. As Seneca makes clear, however, the success of the Argonautic expedition was predicated on the kindred blood shed by Medea. Medea's crimes are the filthy, necessary secret propping up the Argonautic narrative of heroic (that is, colonial) accomplishment.

Medea, as she states to both Creon and Jason, is owed repayment of a considerable debt. For Creon, she paints a nostalgic picture of the power and prestige she sacrificed in departing from Colchis: 'I used to shine,' she repeats, 'I shone' (*fulsi* . . . *fulsi*, 209 and 218), reminding him of her illustrious ancestry, her direct descent from the sun-god. Courted by suitors, resplendent in her royal finery, she was once heir to a kingdom that stretched from the River Phasis to the River Thermodon, encompassing the entire southeast quadrant of Pontus, the Black Sea. Although she relates tactfully that it was 'fickle Fortune' which snatched her headlong from her birthright and bore her into exile (*levis / praecepsque regno eripuit, exilio dedit*, 219–20), it is evident from this description that 'Fortune' bears an undeniable resemblance to Jason. 'I brought just one thing away from my Colchian kingdom,' she continues, 'and it was this: that I preserved the lives of Greece's finest – her renowned young nobility, / foremost of the Achaeans, sons of gods' (225–7). The 'gift' she brought, the *munus* (228, 230) or dowry, was the safe return of the Argo and its crew, some of whose names she catalogues to illustrate the extent of her munificence. Ostentatiously employing the rhetorical trope of praeteritio, she concludes by drawing Creon's attention to the one name missing from her list: she has not mentioned Jason because, as she explains, he is not included in this debt. 'I brought the rest of them back for the rest of you,' she tells Creon, 'but him alone for me' (*vobis revexi ceteros, unum mihi*, 235).

None of this should be news to the Corinthian king. He was fully aware of Medea's guilt when he granted them asylum, and she denies nothing. However, if framed differently, the single crime with which she can be charged is that the Argo came back in one piece (*obici crimen hoc solum potest, / Argo reversa*, 237–8). It is not Medea herself who has profited from her sacrifice of homeland, property, innocence, decency, and loyalty (*pudor*, 238), but rather Creon and the rest of the people of Greece. She is perfectly willing to take on the blame and the stigma of treachery, provided she is also permitted to retain the *praemium* (244), the little something, the cut of the profits which she had reserved for herself: Jason. 'Condemn the criminal,' she concludes, 'but give me back my crime' (*redde crimen*, 246). If Creon would condemn and punish Medea for her 'savagery', he must also acknowledge that it was responsible for the Argo's success and therefore he, along with the rest of Greece, is deeply in her debt, a debt which she is prepared to cancel upon return of her stolen *praemium*. Medea has been carefully and rhetorically knotting together her actions and their consequences – the Argo was her 'gift', its safe return to Greece with all its passengers her 'only crime'[5] – and therefore when she identifies Jason himself as her *crimen* and demands that Creon relinquish him, the result is a masterpiece of sophistic reasoning. Its adhesive motif is repayment and return: Jason is 'owed' to Medea and must be returned to her as recompense for her costly investment in returning his ship and companions to Greece.

Medea also emphasizes her role as Argonautic protector in her exchange with Jason. Here, the idea of returning takes on a somewhat different complexion as Medea declares its impossibility. The repetition of her situation is underscored by her contrastive repetition of the verb *fugīmus* – I have fled, past tense – and *fugĭmus*, I am on the run again, now in the present (447). Changing her residence is nothing new to her. She has fled before from Colchis and from Thessaly after killing for Jason's sake, and all that has changed this time is that Jason is refusing to flee with her. *Ad quos remittis*? she asks him. 'Where are you sending me back to?' (451). She points out that she can return neither to Colchis nor to Thessaly, as she has become a wanted criminal in both kingdoms: 'Wherever I opened a way for you, I closed it to myself' (458). *Quo me remittis*? she asks again (459). The world may have infinite other destinations, but Medea (or Seneca) chooses not to refer to exile as a passage into the unknown, but rather as a blocked route back to the scenes of former crimes.

As before, Medea makes no attempt to deny her culpability. 'Consign me to deadly punishment,' she invites Jason. 'It's what I deserve' (461–2). Again, however, she is attempting to correlate the magnitude of her guilt with the corresponding magnitude of Jason's debt. *Redde vicem*, she demands: give me my compensation, my due return (482). She has supplied her husband with wealth, status, safety, and children, committing despicable acts so that he might prosper. Like Euripides' heroine, she enumerates occasions when she acted on Jason's behalf, but in greater detail and with no omissions. Indeed, she lingers on the two gory deaths which she procured, that of Absyrtus and that of Pelias. In both instances, the victim is dismembered, her brother somewhat euphemistically ('an evil deed performed not all at once, but many times over', 474), and Pelias butchered quite explicitly, his daughters persuaded to *secare membra*, to 'chop up his limbs' (476). When confronting Creon, Medea's claim was that all she brought with her from Colchis was the Argo and its captain. She revises this for Jason, rebuking him instead that 'I brought nothing into exile / but parts of my brother's body; and even these I cast away for you' (486–7). Like a divorced Roman matron,[6] she presents him with the reasonable request that he return her 'dowry' (*dota*, 489), but in the same breath renders this request impossible. Medea's dowry, the 'gift' that accompanied her marriage, was void in the transfer: *patria . . . pater, frater, pudor*: homeland, father, brother, and innocence (488). When Medea orders her estranged husband to 'return to this fugitive what is/was hers, her own [family]' (*redde fugiente sua*, 489), she knows full well that he cannot comply, and therefore his attempt at legitimate divorce is invalid.

The two types of return – return as (re)payment (in Latin, *reddere*, to give back) and return as homecoming or retracing one's steps (in Latin, *redire*, to go back) are cunningly interwoven in both of these scenes.[7] The refusal of Creon and Jason to pay their respective debts for the crimes that have resulted in Medea's perpetual exile, her inability to retreat, receives another kind of payback: the equally calculated 'return' of revenge. Ideally, Medea would wish to recover what she gave up for Jason's benefit; as this is not possible, she desires the adequate recompense of Jason himself; but if this will not be forthcoming, she will find another method of redemption.

Alongside return, repetition is the other important structural principle in Seneca's representation of Medea.[8] Parallels between past and current events are made apparent from her opening monologue onwards. Medea exhorts herself to reactivate her former vigour, 'if you're still alive in there, if anything of the old / zeal (*antiqui vigoris*) remains' (41–2). She must shake off her acquired timidity and assume again the harsh mentality of the steppes where she was born, where she first established herself as killer and sorceress.

> Every unspeakable (*nefas*) thing that Phasis saw, or Pontus,
> Corinth will see too. Savage, unknown, terrifying
> evils to shock both heaven and earth
> are stirring in my mind: wounding, slaughter, and limbs
> stiffening in death. These memories are too trivial;
> things I did as an unmarried girl. More severe now, my pain needs to
> gather its strength. Greater crimes now suit me, after childbirth.
>
> 44–50

Although at this point Seneca's Medea has not yet, it seems, decided on infanticide as a means of revenge, she nevertheless touches upon the possibility in the contrast she draws between the petty crimes that suit (*decent*) a *virgo*, and those she does not name which will suit her better in her full maternal maturity. She will not only repeat her previous atrocities before the horrified gaze of Corinth, but will find a way to outdo them. Nevertheless, her new crimes will not be unrelated, but rather will replicate the originals. 'They will say your divorce was equal match to your wedding,' she declares. 'How will you leave your husband? / In the same way you married him … / Your household must be dissolved through the same crime that established it' (52–5). These equivalences are carefully drawn out by Medea herself, enabling Seneca to set up from the beginning a principle of reciprocity underlying his protagonist's destructiveness.

It must at the same time in some sense surpass these crimes in order to cancel them out.[9] As she perceives it, fratricide has to appear 'trivial' in comparison to the loss she shall inflict on *ingratus* Jason. She wishes to show him that this was merely a 'rehearsal' (*prolusit*, 907), that a young girl's 'inexperienced hands' (*manus rudes*, 908) could accomplish nothing significant. Her *dolor* needs to find more suitable material (*materiam*, 914) to work on, now that she can bring 'the dexterity of experience' to the task (*non rudem dextram*, 915). Other characters are fully aware of the lethal potential to which Jason himself seems oblivious. 'Your deceitfulness is well-known', Creon tells her, 'and well-known your handiwork' (181); it is because of this infamy that he prudently cannot allow her to remain in his kingdom to fume and scheme. The Nurse recognizes the familiar signs of her rage, but is afraid that this time it is a wave that has overflowed, a flood, and in its grip she will surpass herself (*se vincet*, 392–4). The magical force she is preparing to unleash is greater than anything she has practised before: as her pain (*dolor*, again) gathers momentum, it 'renews its former energy', which increases in proportion. Medea has often (*saepe*) performed incredible feats, has often menaced the gods and bent the heavens to her will (673–4), but in repeating her customary rites, on this occasion she is preparing 'something even greater, greater than this, / something monstrous' (674–5). Uncertainty over the precise nature of the *monstrum* remains even after Creusa and Creon have perished. 'My spirit has settled / on some unknown atrocity (*nescioquid ferox*)', Medea reports, 'but I don't dare / admit it to myself' (917–19). *Nescioquid*, 'unknown thing', is an important word for Seneca,[10] occurring at key moments and indicative of one of his recurrent tropes, the supposed existence of acts so terrible they are resistant to speech or contemplation. They typically echo what has gone before, but exceed it in the process: Oedipus's incest, Thyestes' cannibalism, or here Medea's infanticide. *Nescioquid* encapsulates the idea of something unthinkable about to be realized or revealed.

At this point, her past returns to haunt Medea in a very literal way. As she wavers between love for her children and the compulsion for retaliation, she has a dreadful vision: the Furies, underworld goddesses who persecute murderers, are approaching her, their torches dripping blood, cracking venomous snakes like whips, hunting her down. And as if this were not enough, 'Whose ghost comes here, unrecognisable, / dismembered, limbs undone? It is my brother. He wants justice. / We will dispense it . . .' (963–5). She begs Absyrtus to make use of her hand (*manu*) in exacting retribution for his death. The first child's sacrifice, then, is a blow which punishes both Jason and Medea herself for Absyrtus's murder.

The motif of a ghost who seeks reparation from beyond the grave is not unknown in earlier tragedy, occurring most notably in Aeschylus's *Eumenides* and indirectly in Euripides' *Hecuba*,[11] but it is through this moment in Seneca's *Medea* that it finds firm coalescence. It becomes conventional for Elizabethan drama, operating in the background of Hamlet's father and Hieronymo's murdered son in *The Spanish Tragedy*, spawning at the same time the figure of the guilty murderer haunted by their victim(s). In Medea, Seneca has combined both roles. Polydorus's apparition inspires Hecuba to seek revenge, although he does not demand it; Clytemnestra sets the Furies on her matricidal son. Both precedents are active in Seneca's Absyrtus, and although his appearance is brief, it marks the climax of a relationship that has been steadily intensifying throughout the play. Absyrtus, as we have seen, is much more integral to Seneca's representation of Medea than to Euripides'. Euripides makes sense of the child-killing with reference to the expectation that if Medea does not do it, the Corinthians will. Seneca, on the other hand, makes sense of it by introducing a logic of retribution and reciprocity. The return of Absyrtus at this crucial juncture provides the material explanation (if albeit not an excuse) for Medea's act.

But does it work? If we are to believe Medea's triumphant cry upon the death of her first son, it certainly seems to have had the desired effect. She has succeeded in the symbolic restoration of her innocence:

> Now, now I have recovered (*recepi*) my inheritance, brother, father,
> and the Colchians their stolen Golden Fleece.
> My homeland returns (*rediere*), my raped virginity returns (*redit*).
> Oh gods who are finally appeased, oh festive day,
> oh, wedding day!
>
> 982–6

While in one sense undeniably figurative, what this rapture figures is the consummation of a deal that has been struck much earlier. Medea has discharged her obligation, paid her brother's blood-debt, and is momentarily released from guilt. Her jubilation is expressed in terms of return and recovery, bringing back everything she lost in leaving Colchis and cancelling out her crimes. This apparent recovery, however, follows hard upon the actual return of Absyrtus, not as a living person but as a still-dismembered ghost. What comes back to Medea is not quite the reinstatement she yearns for. Instead, it is Absyrtus's compulsion which finally forces her hand to infanticide: 'Leave me alone, and use this hand, brother, / which has drawn a blade' (*quae strinxit ensem*), or, 'which drew the blade [on you]'; the Latin leaves it nicely ambiguous (969–70). She has become her brother's avenger. He has indeed returned to her, but in the form of a crime reiterated, the shedding of kindred blood (*caros cruores*, 810).

3.2 The angry sea (*mare provocatum*)

As touched upon briefly in Chapter 1, Medea is closely identified throughout the play with the natural world, in particular the sea. Through metaphorical association,[12] she comes to represent or personify entities which cannot otherwise be represented onstage. Personification featured centrally in Roman religion, which not only worshipped anthropomorphic Olympian deities such as Venus (love), Vulcan (technology) and Mars (war), but also an almost infinite cast of concepts including Consus (storage), Robigo (mildew), and the city-goddess Roma herself.[13] Coins frequently depicted emperors in the virtuous feminine company of Victory or Liberty;[14] every boundary gave rise to its guardian god, Priapus. Rivers each had their own avatar, usually male – such as the Capitoline Nile, or the defeated Danube on Trajan's Column – although springs and pools such as Arethusa, Egeria, or Salmacis were embodied by nymphs. Partly an artistic conceit, but partly the product of an animist worldview, the practice of personification means nevertheless that human figures could commonly be perceived as standing for something non-human.

When Seneca's protagonist asserts, 'Medea remains! Here you see the sea and land, / iron and fire and gods and thunderbolts' (166–7), this should be understood not merely as defiant bragging but rather as a fundamental statement regarding 'Medea's' constituent elements. Most frequently it is Medea's defining emotional state, her *furor*, which attracts similes taken from nature. While fire also features (e.g. 387, 412, 591), Seneca repeatedly draws a less conventional comparison between her raging emotions and water: a turbulent ocean, a flood, a river in spate. *Exundat furor*, comments Medea's sympathetic Nurse: her rage 'overflows'. *Ubi se iste fluctus franget*? 'Where will this wave break?' (392). A *fluctus* flows and fluctuates, an *unda* undulating like the pull of the tide, both of these words typically used of the sea. Medea herself, as she is struck in turn by the desperate thought of killing her children and by equally powerful surges of maternal love, articulates these feelings in terms of conflicting ocean currents: 'As when high winds declare savage war / and each stirs up the swell into clashing waves / and the sea boils in confusion – this is how / my heart wavers' (*fluctuatur*), 940–3. She compares herself not to a human swimmer caught in the rip, but rather to the very waters over which the winds contend. Her heart or mind (*cor*) is as helpless – and destructive – as the waves that are driven before the hurricane to shatter ships and batter coastlines.[15] Earlier, Medea threatened that the solar flare of her rage would burn the entire Corinthian isthmus away to ash (*cremata*), allowing the seas on each side to pour through the resulting crater and merge (33–6), an image not dissimilar to the waves she now envisages crashing in her own breast.

Generally when Medea is compared to natural phenomena, she is represented as surpassing them in violence. The chorus regard her as *maiusque mare Medea malum*, 'more accursed than the sea' (362).[16] The preceding stanzas of this ode detail the terrors (*timores*) encountered by the Argo on its voyage to Colchis. Three in particular are singled out: the Clashing Rocks at the neck of the Bosphorus, and two female monsters located on the Italian coastline, the Sirens and Scylla. Scylla inhabits the coast of Sicily, where sailors must famously pass between her rocky jaws and the equally feminine threat of the whirlpool Charybdis. Like Medea, Scylla was a *virgo* (350) who betrayed her father and homeland for love of a foreign invader; her grotesque punishment was to be transformed from the waist down into a pack of savage dogs (Virgil, *Ecl.* 6.74–7).[17] Seneca describes her as *rabidos utero succincta canes*, having 'rabid dogs surrounding her womb' (351), the word *utero* anticipating Medea's weapon of choice. The Sirens are associated with the region around Naples, their seductive voices typically luring ships and sailors to their death, although in Seneca's formulation Orpheus overpowers them with his own lyrical music. Medea shares with the Sirens their uncanny vocal powers. Just as the Sirens soothe the sea with their song (<u>*voce canora*</u> *mare mulcerent*, 356) and halt ships (<u>*cantu*</u> *retinere rates*, 359) so Medea likewise uses her voice to raise and suppress the tides (<u>*vocis*</u> *imperio meae*, 767) and lull the Colchian dragon to sleep (*sopite . . .* <u>*cantibus*</u> *meis*, 703–4). The perils of seafaring are concentrated into two vivid images, two personifications, both of them female entities who share distinctive characteristics with Medea.

Medea also compares herself to Scylla when seeking correlatives for the extent of her fury. Rabid Scylla, Charybdis's gaping vortex, and the magma roiling up from Mt Etna are all insufficiently extreme (408–10). Each of these figures – Scylla, Charybdis, and Typhon, the legendary Titan imprisoned beneath Etna – personifies a natural feature of the Sicilian landscape: the cliffs, the dangerous whirlpool, the volcano with its liquid fire. In this way, Medea aligns herself rhetorically with the forces they represent, claiming indeed to surpass them. In Medea's soliloquy at 401–14, Seneca takes three different approaches to constructing this alignment. First (401–6), she reels off a list of stable, reliable, unchanging phenomena – day follows night, the earth keeps turning, the constellations hold their course, and grains of sand are innumerable – to show, with a surprising rhetorical twist, that she is equally steadfast, equally predictable … in her insatiable, ever-increasing lust for revenge. As if mentioning her *furor* aloud brings it surging back to the surface, the second movement of Medea's monologue (407–10) claims the inadequacy of Scylla, Charybdis, and Typhon as comparanda. Finally (411–14), she sets her *ira* in competitive conflict with another catalogue of extreme weather events, none of which, she claims, could contain (*inhibere*) its magnitude. Like her preceding tricolon of Sicilian personifications, two of these events involve water – the rushing river and the stormy sea – and one wildfire, the flames fanned by the wind. Her anger occupies the same register as these phenomena, its effects allegedly comparable, or even more powerfully destructive.

The same conceit recurs when the Chorus repeat their conviction that Medea's burning hatred (*ardet et odit*, 582) exerts a *vis* (force) greater than fire, wind, or weapons. The subsequent two stanzas (583–90) expand on this sentiment:

> Nor when the cloudy south wind brings
> the winter rains, and the torrential Hister
> rushes down, preventing bridges from crossing it,
>   bursting its banks;
>
> Nor when the Rhodanus thrusts deep into the sea;
> nor when into streams, as melting snow

is warmed by the strong spring sun,
 Haemus dissolves.

583–90

Both employ images of uncontrollable water, one flood resulting from torrential winter rains (583–6) and the other from the spring thaw (588–90). Between them, a third river, the Rhone (Rhodanus) spills out into the deep sea, burying itself (*impellit*) in the ocean's breast like the spear cast above in line 580. Again, Medea's irresistible rage is aligned with the inevitability of seasonal change. Puny human bridges will be washed away when winter downpour swells the river Hister (Danube); in spring, the snowmelt comes cascading down the Thracian Haemus as the sun grows stronger. Just as when Medea describes the waves of her mind as driven by opposing winds, so here too the rivers' destructive force results from external factors: the south wind brings the rainclouds, the spring sun melts the ice. From a human point of view, it is the river that is responsible for destroying their bridges, the waves that wreck their ships, but Seneca subtly subverts this impression of direct causality. The river and the waves do not act of their own volition, but instead are set in motion by forces beyond their control.

The idea that Medea is instrumental, rather than personally responsible for the carnage she causes is articulated by the Chorus in this same ode (579–669).[18] They petition the gods for mercy, asking that Jason, *mare qui subegit*, 'the one who subjugated the sea', be spared the terrible punishments that have caught up with the rest of the Argo's crew. Jason's tragedy, their catalogue suggests, is merely the latest in a grisly series perpetrated by the *dominus profundi* – Neptune, god of the sea – who continues to be infuriated (*furit*) by the 'conquest' of his territory. Here, *furor* is transferred away from Medea to a more primal source. The conflict is between the Argonauts and the gods, the *divi* (668) who are relentlessly avenging themselves, one by one, on the men who compromised the honour of the sea (*mare vindicastis*, 669). As the Chorus relate:

Every noble man who took up the oars
of that daring vessel (*audacis carinae*)

> and despoiled (*spoliavit*) Mt Pelion of the deep shade of its sacred grove
> [...]
> and returned as a robber of foreign gold,
> has paid with a fearful death for contravening
> the rights of the sea.
> The sea, provoked, has exacted punishment (*exigit poenas mare provocatum*).
>
> 607–9, 613–16

The Argonauts' trespass is figured in language both legal and religious, the sea attributed *iura* (rights) and designated as sacrosanct, only to have this sanctity violently disrupted (*rumpe nec sacro violente sancta / foedera mundi*, 605–6).[19] In this passage, not only the voyage itself but the very construction of the ship is predicated on sacrilege, the pine-trees from which it was built having been felled from sacred groves (*nemoris sacri*, 608). It is an intruder, a rapist, an abomination, and utilized for no nobler purpose than crude conquest and the illicit acquisition of wealth (*externi auri*, 613).

Quod fuit huius pretium cursus? The Chorus ask, rhetorically: 'What was the price/prize (*pretium*) of this voyage?' They answer themselves: as well as the Golden Fleece, their original objective, the Argonauts brought back Medea, *maiusque mari Medea malum, / merces prima digna carina*, a suitable cargo for the first ship (361–3). Again, the paradigm of trade and exchange renders Medea passive in this transaction. She is merchandise, *merces*, a bonus thrown in with the Colchian treasure; or rather, as it was impossible for the Argonauts to acquire the Fleece without her assistance, she is its necessary accompaniment, the time-bomb, the backlash waiting to happen. Seneca's formulation is elegant. Above and around Medea's personal motives for vengeance, he crafts a confluence of imagery that positions her as acting on behalf of the outraged gods and the violated sea.

Act 4 establishes further connections between Medea and the natural or elemental forces she embodies. More than a self-indulgent embellishment by Seneca or a surrender to sensationalism, the way in which Medea's witchcraft is represented embeds her deeply in a responsive, echolalic universe. Following on from the Chorus's insight that Jason is to suffer the inescapable wrath of the gods, what might otherwise seem gratuitous becomes instead a process of concentration, or again of personification, as Medea takes on the role of conduit for the global energies now ranged against the former Argonaut. Medea, unaware perhaps of anything but her own pain but nonetheless fully cognizant of her own capacity, dismisses as weak and common the 'weapons' (*tela*) born on earth and reaches instead to the heavens for more potent *venena* (poisons); that is, she will milk the venom of the constellation Draco and conjure back to life the great defeated serpents of mythology: Python, the Hydra, and her own Colchian dragon (700–4).

The ingredients of her *pharmakon* are all in some way emblematic or representative, either geographically or mythologically. The terrestrial serpents she summons approach from as far south as the Libyan desert and as far north as the Arctic tundra (682–3). These creatures emerge from her *penetrale funestum* (676), her deadly inner shrine, her spell collapsing logical space so that the places most distant are also to be found deep within. As well as venom, Medea uses poisonous plants which have been harvested from a dizzying itinerary, taking in the Caucasus, Arabia, northern Greece, Mesopotamia and more, zigzagging back and forth across the continents. None of the plants are identified by name, only by their origin, as though (like wine) they carry the distinctive qualities of the regions from which they were gathered. The inclusion of the geographical catalogue is not trivial, as it functions to make the whole world manifest in Medea's cauldron.

The spell also suggests that her claims in the previous scene to possess (or have access to) greater *vis* than volcanoes or hurricanes may not be exaggerated. Her magic can summon rain and turn the tides, bend constellations down to the sea and make seasons spontaneously change.[20] The reversals of natural processes which Medea has brought about seem to contradict, in one sense, her all-important alignment with *Natura*. On the other hand, given the ease with which she intervenes and the type of magic which she is able to perform, it could be suggested that in Seneca's dramatic universe the opposite is true, and it is *Natura* which must operate in concord with Medea. A paradox ensues, or rather a confusion over whether Medea should be regarded as the pawn of *Natura* or its mistress. For Littlewood, this relates to the question of whether Medea's magical *artes* are a form of artifice, a human craft as disruptive as the Argo, or a spontaneous current of power channelling natural resources.[21] Seneca appears to have it both ways. Medea possesses enormous power, but it is a power that has lost control. On the basis of previous successful magical acts, Medea believes herself (it seems, not incorrectly) to have the ability to charm snakes, rivers, stars, ghosts, and other natural phenomena into obedience. She is perhaps unaware, or will not become conscious until her simile of the clashing sea (940–3) of her surrender to the greater tides that are acting through her, placing her skills at the service of angry gods and driving her to break in a furious wave.

In the relationship of its protagonist to *Natura*, *Medea* takes up some of the fundamental questions addressed by Roman Stoicism (and of course by other philosophical systems): How is morality determined? Why does suffering exist? Do human beings possess free will? Insofar as an orthodox line can be traced through Seneca's philosophical writings and those of other Stoic practitioners,[22] the cosmos or universe is regarded as an organic, harmonious unity, and 'cosmic nature (*Natura*) … is rational, beneficent, and a model of morality'.[23] *Natura* is synonymous with Providence, Fate, and divinity (Seneca *NQ*. 2.45). By exercising reason (*ratio* or *logos*), humans thus bring themselves closer to perfected Nature rather than struggling in vain against circumstances which have been fated, such as the inevitability of death. Quoting another philosopher, Cleanthes, Seneca summarizes: *Ducunt volentem fata, nolentem trahunt*: Fate guides the willing, drags the reluctant (*Ep*. 107.10).

Three tensions arise from this position, however, and it is these tensions which Seneca explores in *Medea* and his other tragedies. First is the question of free will.[24] It is evidently necessary to use willpower in order to approach the perfection of rational behaviour and resist your spontaneous inclinations (towards laziness, for example, the pursuit of pleasure, or prestige). One cannot simply rely on predestination; the universe may have granted you the capacity for reason, but will not exercise it for you. Therefore, living rationally – that is, with a willing acceptance of fate – entails some form of independent decision-making. Secondly, Stoic morality rests on the a priori premise that *Natura* or the cosmos operates rationally and harmoniously. The tragedies tap into a vein of uncertainty already present in Stoic thought. Entropy is undeniable. Decay, disease, and decomposition also form part of the cosmic whole.[25] Eschatologically, Stoicism proposes that the universe periodically undergoes a purificatory cataclysm of fire (ekpyrosis; see *Ad Marciam* 26.6) or water (inundation; see *NQ*. 3.27), destructive episodes necessary for restoring equilibrium. The third tension subsumes the other two, and raises the most disquieting possibility. What if the basic condition of nature is in fact chaotic, irrational, and entropic, and human *logos* a futile attempt to hold back the tide? As a thought experiment, *Medea* explores the possibility that willpower may be applied to bring action into accordance with a fundamentally vicious cosmos.

Alternative readings of Medea's relationship with Stoic *Natura* have been proposed. For Norman Pratt, Medea is a negative *exemplum*, 'a dramatization of Neo-Stoic negative models', a 'chronically irrational figure' whose *ira* disrupts the operation of an otherwise orderly universe.[26] Pratt ignores Seneca's condemnation of the Argo's voyage as disruptive, however, and cannot account for *Medea*'s persistent depiction of natural energies as destructive (e.g. 408–14, 579–90, 680–736). Helen Fyfe and Thomas Rosenmeyer, on the other hand, both seek to uncover the affinity of Senecan tragedy with Stoic thought, Fyfe through a close reading of *Medea* and Rosenmeyer through a systematic examination of cosmological principles, in particular *sympatheia*. Fyfe argues that while Medea's wrath is 'an anti-civilization, anti-technology force', it is nevertheless a force of Nature. She points to the play's paradoxical insistence on the uncanny fecundity of death as a challenge to the assumption that growth and decay are opposites.[27] Rosenmeyer shows how Seneca's tragic universe functions according to the principles of Stoic physics, which envisage 'a coextension of the psychological and the cosmological'.[28] In a universe conceived as a fluid organic entity, movements in the psyche are reciprocated by movements in the dramatic environment, and vice versa. The natural forces which Medea embodies 'do not serve as icons' – in other words, they are not just metaphorical – but rather, 'they *are* the human energies, caught at a different angle'.[29]

These are persuasive interpretations. Neither, however, fully resolves the contradictions noted above. Medea is sometimes represented as (mis)directing natural forces, and sometimes as their puppet; she is fated to be criminal, yet has to force herself to fit the mould; and her so-called *scelus* satisfies a divine prohibition against human transgression and greed. She is not simply cautionary, but neither can she be fully recuperated for Stoicism. Rather, in *Medea* Seneca uses the medium of tragedy as a speculative vehicle for voicing doubts unspeakable elsewhere in his philosophy. The play invites us to consider the consequences of Stoic action in a universe inclined to rage, where death is the only reliable fact, and where, as Jason screams up from the wreckage of his ambition, there are no gods.

3.3 Now I'm Medea (*Medea nunc sum*)

As many scholars have observed, Seneca's Medea exhibits a high degree of self-consciousness about her role and identity, and the extent to which she is fulfilling it.[30] This has been linked to the Stoic practice of self-monitoring and striving for self-actualization, the use of inward dialogue, reflection, and discipline in order to bring oneself closer to a philosophical ideal.[31] It has also been read as an authorial comment on Seneca's own belatedness in the tragic tradition, an awareness of the prior literary models that necessarily inform the construction of his own text and its protagonist. As Stephen Hinds puts it, 'Medea is an intertextual heroine: every one of the limited number of moves in her story is multiply determined in literary history'.[32] In Chapter 2, we saw how previous iterations of Medea contributed factors which became inseparable from her composite mythological identity. After Euripides, she could no longer abstain from killing her children. Apollonius gave her relationship with Jason its full erotic value. A Hellenistic potter handed her the reins of flying serpents. Her spells took shape in Ovid's *Metamorphoses*.

Seneca exploits the prior knowledge of the myth possessed by his expected audience. This often creates dramatic irony, most notably when Medea appears to make oblique references to infanticide before she has settled on this course of action. *Parta iam, parta ultio est: / Peperi*, she declares ('It's born, my revenge is born: / I bore it', 25–6), ostensibly meaning that Jason is now cursed with children who will take after both their murderous mother and their treacherous father, but inadvertently also predicting their death at her hands. The dramatic interest is not that of suspense, but that of fulfilment. Seneca was working in a well-established tradition of Roman Medeas,[33] and his consciousness of this literary lineage surfaces in a number of Medea's own utterances. When Jason departs, advising her to moderate her feelings, she explodes: 'You're going? Have you forgotten who I am (*Vadis oblitus mei*) / and everything I've done? I've slipped your mind? / I will never be forgotten!' (560–2). If any member of the audience thinks it might be possible for Medea to be placated, they too have 'forgotten' what she is about to do.[34] For Seneca's audience, her previous actions include the infanticide she has performed in other poems, other plays.

This relates to the issue of characterization, and the much-debated question of what constitutes a dramatic character. Language on the page or in the mouth operates in conjunction with the performer's embodied self to create the impression of a coherent (albeit fictional) individual. For tragedy, one useful formulation has been developed by William Storm, who proposes the concept of the 'tragic field'.[35] Tragic characters, according to Storm, operate as 'symptoms of some larger condition . . . a ground that not only surrounds and includes the figures [onstage] but which also demonstrates its own particular identity, dynamism, and effect.'[36] A figure like Seneca's Medea, then, is the reflex of a field or condition which includes the passion of *ira*, the imperative for revenge, and the transgression of the Argo, all of which converge in the ongoing process of her characterization. The character's former incarnations also confer a depth and complexity beyond the surface of the script, for which the figure onstage functions as a kind of antenna. This resembles the concept of personification discussed above, relating also to the Stoic concept of *sympatheia* or the correspondence between Seneca's dramatic personae and their cosmos.

In relation to Seneca specifically, Erica Bexley points to the importance of recognition and consistency in the construction of the dramatic self.[37] It is Medea's Senecan utterance, in the same breath assertion and realization, 'I am Medea!' (910) that will come to define her in later receptions. About to take off in her dragon-drawn chariot, Medea taunts Jason, 'Do you recognize your wife? This is how I usually escape' (*Coniugem agnoscis tuam? / Sic fugere soleo*, 1021–2). Like *vadis oblitus mei* (560), this line is regularly understood as metatextual, referring not only to Jason's recognition but that of Seneca's audience. Medea is 'accustomed to flee' not only after acts of violence in her personal history, but also in her literary history, towed repeatedly away from a grisly murder scene by flying serpents. As Bexley observes, consistency is equally crucial for the Stoic self to be properly realized. 'Tailoring one's conduct to one's persona is the ethical equivalent of achieving a seamless performance: both activities require an outwardly directed display of self-coherence intended to guarantee recognisable identity.'[38] Seneca's Medea works towards behaviour which is consistent both with her previous actions – murder of family members – and with her pre-existing literary self. In a form of perverted *aemulatio* (artistic emulation), she also feels the need to improve on her crimes, in the same way that Seneca exaggerates aspects of his antecedent texts. In an impossible instance of bootstrapping, she is her own *exemplum*.

The progress of Medea's successful, if monstrous self-actualization may be tracked through the statements she makes regarding 'becoming Medea'. During their first exchange, the Nurse addresses her as 'Medea', and Medea replies, *Fiam* (171), 'I will be(come) [her]'. At this point, she feels incomplete, unrealized, her Colchian crimes a juvenile sketch of the finished portrait she imagines. After Jason has rejected her final offer, and revenge is the only option remaining, she urges herself to 'Go on, be daring now (*aude*), and begin / whatever Medea can do, and whatever she cannot' (566–7); in other words, be *audax*, and attempt the impossible, because it is only by outdoing or excelling whatever 'Medea' has done before that she can develop herself. Finally, once she has consigned Creon and Creusa to the grisly death we all knew was coming to them, she feels ready to take on the approaching *nescioquid*: *Medea nunc sum*, she realizes: now I am what is understood to be meant by the shorthand referent 'Medea', now I can lay claim to the title. 'Previously my *dolor* / was only practising (*prolusit*),' she exults. 'What could untrained hands / accomplish, and the rage of an immature girl? / [But] *Medea nunc sum*: my talent/ skill (*ingenium*) has grown along with my crimes' (907–10). The rehearsals are over, and Medea now steps onstage in her full capacity, prepared to commit the act that has defined her since Euripides made it hers. What the shrinking virgin of the *Argonautica* could never have contemplated, the towering tragic heroine will claim and own as her legitimate legacy.

As well as being metatextual, this reflexive technique can also function as metatheatrical, as the drama foregrounds its own performative artifice and Medea her identity as performer.[39] Traces of metatheatricality appear in many forms throughout the text. One is Medea's tendency towards self-address. This has been examined in detail by Christopher Star, who demonstrates that Seneca's dramatic avengers, just like the Stoic exemplars in his philosophical works,

> use the language of self-address to fashion themselves, battle against psychological fluctuation, and strive to achieve consistency of mind and action. [. . .] For Seneca, creation and maintenance of a consistent

> self are intensely rhetorical, based on the repetition of the figure of self-apostrophe and self-command.[40]

Like good Stoics, they pursue the virtue of *constantia*, i.e. integrity or steadfastness; but whereas the philosopher exhorts himself to moral improvement, these distorted individuals urge themselves aloud to commit the monstrous acts demanded by the role they have assumed.

Medea frequently addresses imperatives to herself without mediation. *Accingere ira*, she tells herself in Act 1: clothe yourself in anger (51). After Jason departs, her exhortations intensify as she talks herself into performing black magic: *Hoc age, omnes advoca / vires et artes* ('Go on, summon all / your strength and skill', 562–3). When her willpower begins to fail, she orders herself to 'seek out some form of punishment / beyond the pale' (898–99) and 'whip up your anger and stir yourself, lazy!' (902). She also addresses her *animus*, her spirit or courage: 'If you're alive, *anime*, if anything of the old / zeal remains' (41–2); and later, frustrated, 'Why, *anime*, are you stopping? [. . .] Why, *anime*, do you falter?' (895 and 937). The final form of self-address Medea employs is a little different. Instead of herself, her own mind or spirit, Medea singles out her pain (*dolor*) and her anger (*ira*) as separate states or entities apart from her speaking self.[41] Earlier in the play she begs her rising *dolor furiose* to be more lenient (139), but during her climactic deliberative soliloquy and after, instances of this emotional rupture become particularly concentrated. 'Find the material [for my/our/your revenge], *dolor*!' she incites her pain at 914, but by 944 has reconsidered, and pleads instead with her *dolor* to yield to maternal love. Finally, it is *ira* which she allows to take over: *Ira, qua ducis, sequor*, she pledges ('Anger, wherever you lead, I follow', 953). In the final scene, however, *dolor* resurfaces as the part of her which takes brutal pleasure in murder ('Enjoy this at your leisure, and don't hurry it, *dolor*', 1016) but also remains insatiable: once both children are dead, she regrets that 'I have nothing more, *dolor*, with which to appease you' (1020). This artificial split in Medea's being between the self which acts and the passion of *ira / dolor* which compels has been interpreted as pathological.[42] It is also dramaturgical. In vocalizing, almost personifying these *pathē* (passions),

Medea becomes an expressionist figure commentating on their operation at the same time as she suffers their effects.

Another means by which attention is repeatedly drawn to Medea's theatricality is the use of concurrent commentary on stage action. As discussed in Chapter 1, scholars have linked this unusual device to the performance conventions of tragic pantomime, in which medium a dancer mimed the movements of a scene while the libretto was sung alongside by a *cantor* or chorus.[43] Two passages in particular exhibit this feature. One is the Nurse's description of her mistress's frenzy at the start of Act 3:

> Like a maenad possessed, taking tottering steps
> as she raves with the onset of the god
> on the snowy heights of Pindus or the ridge of Nysa,
> she plunges here and there with wild movements
> and the signs of frenzied madness in her looks.
> Her face is flaming, she draws deep breaths,
> she cries out, bathes her eyes in flowing tears,
> and smiles again. All kinds of emotions grip her.
> She pauses, threatens, burns, laments, groans.
>
> 382–90

The other is the Chorus's description of her similarly frantic movements following the performance of the ritual, prior to the messenger's arrival:

> Where is the bloodthirsty maenad
> being forced headlong
> by her savage love? What crime
> is she planning in her unstoppable fury?
> Spurred by anger, her face
> grows rigid, and tossing her head
> arrogantly, with fierce motion (*feroci . . . motu*)
> she threatens even the king himself.
> Who would believe this exile?
>
> Her reddened cheeks burn;
> pallor chases the flush.

Constantly changing (*vagante forma*),
no colour remains for long.
She paces here and there
like a tiger bereaved of her young
roams on her furious path
through the groves of the Ganges.

849–65

It is to be assumed that Medea is physically present onstage during both of these concurrent descriptions, either duplicating (or anticipating) the actions mentioned in the verbal text, or providing some form of mimetic counterpoint.

Medea herself also comments verbally upon the bodily sensations she is supposedly experiencing or actions she is supposedly performing. 'My heart pounds in horror, my limbs freeze icy cold,' she says aloud upon realizing that it is her children who must pay the price for Jason's treachery, 'and my breast is trembling' (926–7). Whether derived from pantomime, from recitation, or both, this representational technique of having a character verbalize their physical distress instead of (or in addition to) displaying it is typical of Senecan dramaturgy.[44] It produces a similar effect to the split between physical enactment and verbal commentary identified above, albeit concentrated in a single performer. Insofar as pain is resistant to expression in language,[45] the suffering body described is a separate entity from the eloquent body of the speaking subject; in a sense, Medea is communicating herself as an object, a third-person self whose intense sensations do not impede their utterance.

A clearer illustration of this premise may be found towards the end of Act 4 in the self-harm performed by Medea as part of her ritual:

For you [Hecate], breasts bared like a maenad
I will put my arm to the sacred knife.
My blood will drip down on the altar.
Practise drawing the iron, my hand,
and enduring the loss of your own flesh and blood.
Now stabbed, I dedicate this sacred fluid.

806–11

Again, the stage directions are embedded in Medea's monologue. As in the pantomimic passages quoted above, the performer here has two basic options: s/he can either literally and mimetically duplicate the action described, supplying the audience with two simultaneous renditions, one visual and one verbal; or s/he can lend her body to the delivery of the text like a storyteller, and allow a more stylized physical attitude to support the rhetorical power of the discourse. In both cases, Medea's divided body is both the speaking, stabbing subject and the wounded object. Talking about this pain draws attention to the theatrical illusion, the means by which fictional suffering is evoked for the audience, whether this is achieved by convincing them through verisimilitude or persuading them through rhetoric.

The power of Medea's voice, her magical ability to effect change in the material world merely through speaking, is also a theatrical power. After all, words are the substance from which a (scripted) theatrical universe is formed, conferring imagined significance upon actions and objects, positing the existence of fictional space and fictional relationships; every onstage utterance is a speech act, in that it brings about a change in the configuration of dramatic reality. Once it is stated that we are in Corinth, we remain there until otherwise directed; we accept, unless disputed, that for the purposes of this narrative, the Argo's voyage was indeed resented by the gods. This capacity for effective fabrication is partly verbal, but also, in performance, partly vocal.[46] Roman tragedy could be sung (*tragoedia cantata*) as well as spoken (*recitatio*), poetry delivered in the mesmerizing medium of the *vox*.

Medea's vocal power is remarked upon throughout the play. The first scene opens with an invocation: *voce non fausta precor*, Medea comments reflexively ('I pray with an unholy voice', 12), summoning not only the goddesses of marriage and childbirth but also those of the underworld, including the Furies, snake-haired personifications of revenge. She commands their presence, repeating the keyword *adeste*, 'Come', or 'Be present' (13, 16), and in doing so brings it about, in theatrical terms. When Medea speaks of the Furies, in a wholly spoken medium, she evokes them for her listeners in an act of rhetorical *enargeia* as effective as that which evokes her immediate surroundings. 'Think when we talk of horses that you see them / printing their proud hoofs i' the receiving earth', instructs the Prologue of Shakespeare's *Henry V*, another dramatic form reliant on language to create multisensory impressions, printing the galloping of entirely imaginary horses in his auditors' minds as indelibly as the Furies' torches are now burned into those of Seneca. Diana Robin, in a psychoanalytic reading of female voices in Seneca, remarks that 'Medea binds and envelops the space of the theatre with the almost unrelieved continuum of her voice ... bathing the audience in the sounds of her hallucinations (as later she will inundate them with the screams of her children).'[47] The womblike theatre is filled with the mother's voice, immersing the auditors like unborn infants in its undulating flow. The presence of everything in Medea's world is contingent upon its presence in speech, meaning that the otherwise dominant distinction between the visible and the invisible, the tangible and the intangible, is erased.

It is perhaps for this reason that Creon is so concerned that Medea should not be allowed to speak to him, in case she should enchant him. Her touch might contaminate (188), but her words might likewise insinuate themselves like vipers into the cracks in his judgement. *Iubete sileat*, he orders his servants (who do not speak, and who only exist in Creon's words): 'Order her to be silent' (189). He will not even address Medea directly, speech being the conduit through which conviction passes, conceding acknowledgement of presence and the right of reply. Also fearing the consequences of her speech, the Nurse warns Medea to use silence for her own protection (150, 158) and to suppress her angry words (*Compesce verba*, 174). Jason attempts to cut off the flow of promises before seduction sets in (*longa colloquia amputa*, 530). Her threats, her arguments, and her persuasion are all represented as in some way dangerous.

The greatest concentration of references to Medea's voice occurs in the Act 4 spell-casting scene.[48] Her magic is predicated upon summoning vocally: invoking or evoking the powers of the underworld (*meis vocata sacris*, 750), calling on mythical serpents (*pestes vocat*, 681; *evocavit omne serpentum genus*, 705), drawing down the waters (*evocavi aquas*, 754), her vocatives irresistible, empowering the audience through her evocative song to sense the presence of the supernatural. Medea's magical chants physically 'pull' or 'drag' their subjects into her orbit, exerting a magnetic attraction, *tracta magicis cantibus* (684). At the very sound of its name, Python arrives (*adsit ad cantus meos . . . Python*, 699–700).

The other effect of Medea's enchantments is to bring about change in her environment. Like a stage set awaiting animation by the actor's voice, Medea's surroundings become an emanation of her speech. In midsummer, she causes the land to shiver as though with cold (*aestiva tellus horruit cantu meo*, 760), again drawing attention to the role of vocal intervention rather than – as elsewhere – using a more neutral verb such as *egi*, 'I forced' (755). Similarly, groves of ancient trees have been stripped of their shady leaves not simply at Medea's command (*imperio*), but explicitly at her vocalized command (*vocis imperio meae*, 768). The aquatic constellation known as the Hyades, associated with the onset of rain, likewise falters in its course *nostris cantibus*, as a result of Medea's songs.[49] It is no wonder that her voice is regarded as fearful, that the whole *mundus* – the 'world', but also in a wider sense, the cosmos – trembles as she approaches the altar. 'Listen', whispers the Nurse. 'It is the sound of her wild progress, / and she is singing (*canitque*). The *mundus* shakes as she opens her mouth' (*primis vocibus*, 738–9). Importantly, perhaps, it is not Medea's words (*verba*) which are so terrifying, but the sound of her *vox*, the moment of enactment where intent meets flesh as speech. The first word of her monologue, perhaps not coincidentally, is *comprecor*, 'I invoke'; meanwhile, the spirits she proceeds to solicit are spoken for in their silence (they are called the *vulgus silentum*, 740).

As well as performer, Medea is characterized as a poet. For Trinacty, Medea is 'quasi-author of the plot and active compiler of the texts she wishes to enact. Metapoetic language reveals her transcendence into a semidivine dramaturge, possibly standing in for Seneca himself'.[50] 'Metapoetic' language designates Medea as participating in the crafting and invention of her own scenario. For Creon, she is a deadly *malorum machinatrix facinorum*, a 'manufacturer' or 'architect' or 'designer' of evil deeds (216), her machinations having previously contrived the death of King Pelias and the implication of his daughters. She is a fabricator of murders. The Nurse describes her in similar terms, half admiring and half afraid of what she has raised, as a *scelerum artifex*, an artist, artisan, or inventor of crimes (734). Her witchcraft is the craft of the skilled creative practitioner. This conceit is not unique to *Medea*; Seneca uses a similar phrase of Theseus in *Phaedra*, who has caused the death of his son and refers to himself as a *leti artifex*, a master-craftsman of death (*Phaed.* 1220). The metaphors of *artifex* and *machinatrix* relate more to the atelier than to poetic composition, but Seneca evokes the literary domain via Medea's *carmina*, spells which are also songs (598). Medea refers moreover to her growing *ingenium malis*, her 'talent for malice', her evil genius (910). *Ingenium* can refer to any kind of creative, inventive gift, including poetic inspiration.[51] Jason seals the association by calling Medea a *sceleris auctorem*, an 'author of crime' (979). It is of course Seneca himself who is the ultimate *auctor* of the tragedy, but Medea who acts to bring about the plot's foregone conclusion.

*

Is Medea responsible for her actions? The sharp retort of Fitch and McElduff is that blaming external factors such as a family curse or runaway emotions is merely 'a way of shielding the self' from having to accept responsibility.[52] According to this reading, Seneca exhibits characters binding themselves to destructive personae in order to expose their blind adherence as a fallacy. Within Seneca's tragic cosmos, however, such adherence is presented as inescapable, and even overdetermined. It is inevitable that Medea will become Medea, however *invita* ('reluctant', 952) the hand that wields the knife. Agency does not necessarily entail autonomy. An agent also acts on someone else's behalf, just as Medea has killed for Jason and will kill again for Absyrtus, bereaving and polluting herself in the process. A poet is responsible for his utterances, but his utterances (and, to some extent, the poet himself) are also a reflex of language. Seneca's Medea is aware that she gives herself to *Ira*, and aware that she personifies the sea, but her perception is that these forces are in her service, not vice versa. This is reflected in criticism that represents her as a misguided individual, instead of revenge incarnate. The price of being able to say that where she stands, you can see the wrath of the gods is that the wrath of the gods will not spare her when it falls.

4

Language and Style

Seneca's hyperbolic, or more pejoratively, 'bombastic' style has often been denounced as untheatrical; that is, as too wordy and long-winded, melodramatic rather than properly 'dramatic', stilted in structure and over-the-top in its constant striving for maximum effect.[1] This impression, however, results partly (as we saw in Chapter 1) from a strain of twentieth-century criticism that valued theatrical naturalism, and partly (as I will demonstrate below) from the way in which early vernacular translators sought to render Seneca's Latin. His characters indeed speak in artificially elaborate monologues unlike the patterns of prose discourse, but they are not toneless tirades or devoid of dynamics. Rather, when examined closely, it becomes apparent that the density of their structure results from its tautness and leanness: there is not a single line that is not working hard, that does not contain some substance indispensable to the whole. Paradoxically, this lack of relief ratchets up an unremitting tension which can result in overload and start to blur into white noise. This is not due to any excess material, however, as implied by the accusations of 'bombast' or 'rant', but rather the opposite. Senecan poetics have been called 'baroque', meaning overly ornamented.[2] On the contrary, I would argue that they are fractal. Every moment is mined for its micro- and macroscopic resonances, unfolding into endless iterations like a hall of miniature mirrors.

4.1 Extreme passion

Seneca's poetics, or the way in which language is used to represent a given situation, are certainly hyperbolic; his dramaturgy, or the way in which these situations are arranged for the stage, is certainly melodramatic. These terms, however, need not be derogatory.[3] They can function as descriptors to distinguish this mode of writing from one which is minimalist or understated, and this mode of performance from one which is naturalistic.[4] *Medea*'s rhetorical artistry does not necessarily detract from the play's theatricality. Oratory in imperial Rome was an art form, and the ability of well-crafted speech to move and sway its listeners – in Greek, *psychagōgein*, to direct the mind or soul – was widely recognized and appreciated as an aesthetic quality.[5] Senecan tragic discourse participates in this performance culture. As scholars like Mastronarde and Herington have long argued in Seneca's defence, just because 'the drama is all in the word', as T.S. Eliot put it, does not in fact mean that the words are undramatic.[6]

Tragedy, for Roman authors, had its own unique register of expression, determining the type of vocabulary used and the emotional range to be covered. Horace outlines this principle in his 'Art of Poetry', written in 10 BCE:

> Comic matters don't need tragic poetry to express them.
> It would be outrageous, on the other hand, for Thyestes' cannibal feast to be
> recounted in verse appropriate (*dignis carminibus*) to the humorous and everyday.
> Each genre of writing has its own suitable place (*decentem locum*).
> Sure, sometimes comedy can raise its voice (*vocem tollit*)
> when angry (*iratus*) old Chremes bellows in exaggerated tones (*tumido ore*),
> and sometimes tragedy grieves (*dolet*) in common speech –
> when Telephus and Peleus, in poverty and exile,
> put aside their bombast (*ampullas*) and polysyllabic words
> in order to touch the spectator's heart with plaintiveness.
> It's not enough for poetry to be pretty; it also has to be moving (*dulcia*)
> to direct the listener's mind (*animum . . . agunto*) as desired.
>
> *A.P.* 89–100

Horace focuses on the attributes of genre, and the importance of applying appropriate language to the given situation, stressing that the choice of words should be suitable (*digna, decens*) except when the author intends to signal generic intrusion. The properties of tragedy as described here are applicable to Seneca: Thyestes' cannibalism is also the subject of a Senecan play, its scheming protagonist and gruesome climax comparable to those of *Medea*. Tragic characters, like Medea herself, are typically consumed by grief (*dolet*) or rage (*iratus*), and hence it is expected that they (should) speak in swollen or inflated discourse (*tumido*), attaining a more 'elevated' or 'heightened' mode of expression. Oratorical theory likewise distinguishes between 'plain' speech, suitable for mundane matters, and the more forceful representational mode required to encompass strong emotion,[7] which makes use of devices such as exclamations and direct address, rhetorical questions, phonemic repetition (alliteration, assonance),[8] repetition of single words (anaphora) or syntactic patterns, and an increased awareness of rhythm, in a sense becoming more musical and more highly wrought – paradoxically, more articulate – as the emotional pitch intensifies. In particular, Horace makes the suggestion that tragic language ought to be *ampulla*, which could be translated as 'bombastic'; synonyms include *tumida*, *grandia*, *inflata*.[9] There is a place, a *locus* for speech like Thyestes' or Medea's, and it is tragedy. The medium requires it, if it is going to be more than merely decorative (*pulchra*). To act upon the audience's soul, altering their perceptions, *agunto animum* – a Latin translation of the Greek concept *psychagōgia* – [10] the language of tragedy must also be *dulcia*, literally 'sweet', but with overtones of persuasiveness, seduction, and therefore rhetorical effectiveness. The auditor should feel themselves carried away ecstatically by the right combination of sounds.

Seneca, however, does not in fact exhibit those faults which typically turn tragic gravitas into pomposity ripe for satire. He uses neither archaic vocabulary nor experimental neologisms. His words are not what Horace terms sesquipedalian (long and obscure), unlike the playful onomatopoeic compounds of the earlier Roman Republican playwrights. The features of Senecan diction which have led it to be seen as bombastic are its syntactic formality and compactness; its intricate monologues; its fondness for catalogues and lists; its ellipsis, or omission of explication; and its verbal reiteration of particular concepts as keywords. *Medea* is also a study in uncontrollable passions, so these states are represented in sensorially vivid terms that could be regarded as overblown, were it not for their function within the play as superhuman forces.

To illustrate some of these features in action, consider this distinctively Senecan passage from Medea's opening tirade:

> Si vivis, anime, si quid antiqui tibi
> remanet vigoris, pelle femineos metus
> et inhospitalem Caucasum mente indue.
> Quodcumque vidit Phasis aut Pontus nefas,
> videbit Isthmos. Effera ignota horrida,
> tremenda caelo pariter ac terris mala
> mens intus agitat: vulnera et caedem et vagum
> funus per artus. Levia memoravi nimis:
> haec virgo feci. Gravior exsurgat dolor:
> maiora iam me scelera post partus decent.
>
> 41–50[11]

Evidently, this is not naturalism, but the self-addressed soliloquy is nevertheless an established dramatic convention.[12] Medea speaks to her *animus*, her mind or spirit, and also speaks about it in the third person, commentating on her own sensations. She does not require her mental agitation to be inferred from subtleties of tone or body language, but instead informs her audience directly that *mens intus agitat*. Ellipsis is apparent in the use of place-names to stand for the traumatic (*nefas*) events of her past: Phasis recalls her treachery, and Pontus her brother's murder. These acts are not named explicitly, but rather Seneca proceeds firstly to skirt around them adjectivally, enhancing their horror in a crescendo – *effera ignota horrida tremenda* – that culminates in the nonspecific keyword *mala*, which can usefully mean both suffering inflicted and misfortunes suffered. Again, however, she will not name the act of fratricide. Instead, another list comes out, this time an ascending tricolon (*vulnera* [1] *et caedem* [2] *et* [3] *vagum funus per artus*), fragmenting the same *malum* into disjointed, post-traumatic flashbacks. Seneca then draws an antithetical contrast between Medea's recollections and the grief to come using the sensory metaphor of weight (*levia ... gravior*). These words commence successive sentences and occupy the same metrical point in successive lines, the relevant noun – *scelera*, 'crimes', an important keyword – delayed until the groundwork has been laid for its gravity to be realized. Once spoken, it is then repeated almost immediately: *quae scelere parta est, scelere linquenda est domus* (53) in another finely balanced line, both metrically and syntactically, *scelere parta* mirroring *scelere linquenda*, and ending in the wistful pendant, *domus*, the home that Medea is perpetually denied. Seneca's poetry is mannered, but as a result of this intensely musical, and the myriad shifts of mood within each monologue are generated by the same rhetorical devices his critics find so inimical.

Seneca also uses patterns of repeated keywords, often clustered together to gather impetus by their association. *Scelus* (crime) is one of them, spoken aloud some twenty-five times over the course of the play.[13] Its importance is indicated not only by its frequency but also by its positioning. *Scelus* sounds in concert with Medea's other keywords – *ira*, *furor*, *odium*, *amor* – to create a tightly woven emotional texture in which strong feeling appears inseparable from doing harm, or alternatively in conjunction with Seneca's other term for crime, *crimen*, which has additional overtones of guilt (a further eight instances). *Nullum scelus irata feci*, Medea protests. *Suasit infelix amor* ('I committed no criminal act / in anger; ill-fated love made me do it', 135–6). Later, the Chorus join *ira* and *amor* together as dual motivators, both incapable of restraint: *Frenare nescit iras / Medea, non amores; / nunc ira amorque causam / iunxere* ('Medea knows no way to curb / her rages, nor her loves; / now rage and love have made / common cause', 866–9). Medea has been snatched away on a headlong descent by *amore saevo*, 'savage love' (850), which is glossed in the next line as *impotenti furore*, irresistible or ungovernable frenzy.

Amor is linked to *furor*, *furor* to *ira*, *ira* to *amor*, *amor* to *scelus*, *scelus* to *dolor* (pain): as in the passage discussed above (41–50), when the *dolor* becomes more severe, the crimes become correspondingly greater.

At the end of the play, the same association recurs as Medea gives her *dolor* permission to revel in criminal consummation: *Perfruere lento scelere, ne propera, dolor* ('Enjoy the crime at leisure, *dolor*, no need to rush', 1016). *Dolor*, however, is also elided with *ira*, Medea's dominant passion: Medea's heart becomes the battleground for waves of anger (*ira*) and maternal duty (*pietas*), and it is *dolor* which she pleads to give in to the promptings of tenderness (*cede pietati, dolor*, 944). Finally, all are connected to *odium*, or hatred. *Increscit dolor et fervit odium*, Medea reports, as the momentum of her passions hurls her towards infanticide ('Pain increases / and hatred seethes', 951–2). Jason sees her as a terrifying compound of grief and rage: *Furit, / fert odia prae se; totus in vultu est dolor* ('She is enraged, / she wears her hatred openly; pain is all over her face', 445–6). *Odium*, however, is also cognate to its apparent antithesis, *amor*. 'If you want to know, poor thing, what limit to put on your hatred', Medea tells herself, 'just imitate your love' (396–7). Both passions, for Medea, are unlimited, as the subsequent lines will make clear, aligning her *furor* (406) with the pulse of a well-regulated universe.

These reiterated keywords may seem excessive, but their repetition and proximity create a matrix where emotions have an explicit, verbally articulated presence, where they appear to operate independently of the character who suffers their attack. Their patterning may seem artificial and rhetorical, and quite unlike the erratic speech of someone genuinely caught in psychological turmoil, but it is precisely this careful musicality of language, the use of words as interbraided themes, which gives Senecan tragedy its suffocating sense of inevitability, Whichever way Medea turns, *ira* – even if masked as *amor* or *dolor* – is waiting.

For some things, there are no words. Two of Seneca's other core expressions are paradoxical in that they signify that the limits of language, and even of comprehension, have been exceeded. They are the word *nefas* ('unspeakable') and the word *nescioquid* ('something', or literally, 'I don't know what thing'). Unlike the liberal scattering of *ira*, *dolor*, and *furor*, they do not occur very often, but when they do, the effect is chilling; all the more so because Seneca otherwise has little compunction about making horrors explicit. For Seneca (or Medea) to draw back from identifying something, to confess a reluctance or inability to name it, makes whatever they cannot verbally confront appear truly monstrous. *Nefas* is used four times in *Medea*, each time in reference to the murders Medea has committed: her brother (44 and 122), King Pelias (261), and finally her children (931). This last, a *dirum nefas*, is glossed in apposition as an *incognitum facinus*, an unheard-of or unknown, unthinkable act, picking up some of the obscurity emanating from *nescioquid*. *Nescioquid* is used only once, but as in other Senecan uses of the term, it comes at a pivotal moment, foreshadowing what even Medea is unable at this juncture to conceive. Where, she asks her anger, are you directing me? She senses her soul has settled on *nescioquid ferox*, some ferocious thing, but as yet *nondum sibi audit fateri*, something which does not dare be spoken (917–19). To speak, on the Senecan stage, is to make manifest, and so long as this final atrocity remains unspeakable, unthinkable, there is a chance it may still be averted.

The gestural representation of emotion (*affectus*) on the Roman stage was correspondingly stylized. A common vocabulary of affect pertained across media, similar gestures occurring in oratory, dance, and the visual arts. In tragedy, as in oratory,[14] the words' emotional content and import were reinforced by nonverbal cues. The keys to their effectiveness were clarity and recognizability. Although some anecdotes show performers moved to genuine tears behind their masks,[15] consensus appears to be that too close an identification with the character's feelings risked inhibiting their effective communication and compromising the actor's primary aim of *psychagōgia*, or moving their audience. The actor playing Medea did not have to present a psychologically nuanced portrayal through his body language. Rather, his skill lay in the accurate application of an existing gestural repertoire to give each spoken phrase an appropriate affective colour.[16]

By analogy with other media, it is possible to recover a palette of the most significant gestures that would have accompanied verbal delivery of the text. *Ira*, for instance, may be indicated by a clenched fist held against the chest, although its stage performance may involve less subtle variations such as beating the sternum. Other percussive actions – stamping the feet, or thumping the thigh – were also thought to be effective (Quint. *Inst. Orat.* 11.3.123–4, 128). Beating the head and breast, or ripping and tearing at hair and clothing could also indicate violent grief, as in the choruses of Aeschylus's *Persians* or Seneca's *Trojan Women*. Grief could also be realized in some contexts as prostration (e.g. Eur. *Troades* 115–19; Ovid, *Met.* 2.342–7). Other actions or states of mind requiring embodiment when acting the role of Medea include arrogance or pride (*superba motu*, 855), which Quintilian attests is shown by raising the chin and throwing the shoulders back; and its converse, *supplicatio*, which Medea turns both on Creon (285–90) and on Jason (478–82). *Supplicatio* involves raising one or both arms imploringly and may also involve sinking onto the knees, which grants status and makes magnanimity possible. Should Medea wish to play the demure and subservient femme, she could do so by adopting the so-called *pudicitia* pose, one arm resting diagonally across her torso, chin propped on the hand; to transform this into a provocative invitation, she could slouch a little, incline her head coquettishly, thrust out a hip.[17] *Mania*, or delusional madness, is associated in tragedy with spinning or whirling.[18] While Medea does not explicitly perform this action in the text, she is *praeceps amore saevo / rapitur* (850–1) on a *cursu furente* (864), Nurse and Chorus both referring to her as a *maenas* (384, 849), doubling back on herself with *motu effero*, wild motion. Bacchantic ecstasy, according to Quintilian, presents in violently circling and tossing the head (Quint. *Inst. Orat.* 11.3.71; cf. Vir. *Aen.* 7.378–84).

This physical expressionism, at once impersonal and melodramatic, serves Seneca's convoluted script more readily than realism. The dominant performance media of Seneca's Rome, declamation and pantomime dance, both utilized variations on these gestures, and actors are frequently described as performing more exaggerated versions of oratorical gesture.[19] Dancers, moreover, are often compared with sculpture, and their plastic artistry to that of the sculptor himself.[20] Roman audiences brought to the theatre a literacy in body language that spanned different media, and the psychagogic effectiveness of such gestures was predicated on their repetition in different contexts. Like musical motifs, they enabled a performer to activate a cascade of associations with what might otherwise superficially appear a simple movement: covering the face, or kneeling, had the capacity to evoke intertextual resonances over and above its adoption in the fictional moment. Senecan bodies, if they had to bear with literal accuracy the pain heaped upon them by the text, would become inarticulate, just as speech would dissolve into inarticulate cries.[21] To retain its communicability, its performative effectiveness, Senecan *dolor* remains at one remove from the actor, who must commit to its signification while not allowing manufactured passion to consume her.[22]

4.2 Extreme rhetoric

One of the primary characteristics of Seneca's Medea is her self-identification as a performer, as an actress. Throughout the play she alternates blistering tirades that display her *furor* openly with scenes of role-play and dissimulation designed to persuade. As we have seen in Chapter 1, protective deception became a necessary survival strategy among the Julio-Claudian aristocracy, courtiers smoothing away rage and bitterness in order to appear submissive and thus diminish any sense of threat to those in power. Persuasive discourse was also a form of art and entertainment in its own right, as in the *suasoriae* or *controversiae*, mock orations on sensational topics such as the legal rights of a priestess captured by pirates, carefully quarantined from the praxis of political debate.[23] Three scenes in Seneca's *Medea* show off her deliberative skill to particular effect: her appeal to Creon (192–300), her address to Jason (447–559), and the climactic *tour-de-force* of her struggle against her own conscience (893–957). The witchcraft scene which comprises Act 4 is also intensely metatheatrical, an extended *mise-en-abîme* comparable to the equally unprecedented raising of Laius from the Underworld in Seneca's *Oedipus*; so much so, in fact, that it will be the independent subject of the following chapter. The three instances considered here share the common factor of persuasion, effected through both the temporary adoption of a persona (*ēthos*) and the artistry of sophistic reasoning.

The appeal to Creon can be divided into six movements, or six 'rounds' (see Table 4.1), if considered in terms of a sparring match.[24] Unlike Euripides, however, Seneca does not employ the form of the *agōn* or equal debate in which both speakers present their case in turn; the platform belongs disproportionately to Medea, showcasing her skill with her interlocutor as a foil. The first round, a stichomythic exchange initiated by Medea, establishes some of the main terms to which she will return. 'What crime (*crimen*) or what guilt (*culpa*) is punished by [my] exile?' she asks, ingenuously (192). As Creon attempts to deflect her, she keeps him talking, braiding together the concepts that will underpin her main defence: kingship and culpability. 'If you're acting as judge, you need to understand the case,' she tells him. 'Or you can play the tyrant, and issue [uninformed] commands' (194). Creon almost takes the bait and momentarily engages in an exchange about the nature of royal power. Realizing the danger, he tries to break away, ordering her once again to return to Colchis. Medea seizes the opportunity to insert her second theme: 'I will return,' she promises him eagerly, 'if the one who brought me here takes me away' (198). Again, Creon affects indifference, but when Medea insists that he can only be *aequus*, just, if he has heard her side, he caves in. *Sed fare*, he concedes, 'Speak.' Round one to Medea: she has the floor.

She embarks on the fifty-line monologue which forms the centrepiece of Act 2 with a certain amount of circumspection, approaching her

Table 4.1 Medea's appeal to Creon

Round	Lines	Argument
1	193–202	'Listen to my defence.'
2	203–25	'Kings should exercise *clementia*.'
3	225–36	'I have benefitted Greece.'
4	237–51	'I am owed a debt.'
5	272–80	'The beneficiary is also guilty.'
6	282–97	'Grant me one day.' (supplication)

subject obliquely and in such a way as to draw a parallel between herself and her addressee. It is Creon's royalty (*regale*, 204) which excuses his obduracy, something which she recognizes from her own upbringing in the royal house (*regia*, 206) of Colchis. This enables Medea to introduce a running antithesis, contrasting her former glory and status, the extent of her realm and her divine ancestry with her current abjection: *miseranda obruta, / expulsa supplex sola deserta*, she wails, piling on the pathos, 'overcome by disaster, / an exile, a suppliant, alone and deserted', 207–8, whereas formerly, in Colchis, *generosa, felix, decore regali potens, / fulsi*, 'blessed and noble, resplendent in royal power and finery, / I shone' (217–18). The rhetorical devices Seneca employs are asyndeton, or the omission of connectives in order to maximize intensity, and pleonasm, or the accumulation of synonyms. Medea draws from her antithesis the explicit moral of Fortune's reversal, a possibility which should haunt all kings: unpredictable (*praeceps*) and fickle (*levis*) Fortuna 'wrenched me from power, expelled me to exile' (*regno eripuit, exilio dedit*, 220). A ruler's greatest legacy, in sum, is the *clementia* he extends to pitiful suppliants like herself. This second bout, then, sets up an imagined relationship between two characters, a just and magnanimous king extending his mercy to fellow royalty now suffering wretchedly reduced circumstances.

Medea's next move is to demonstrate how her actions have benefitted Greece, and indeed Creon himself (round 3). She brought only one thing with her from her *Colchico regno*, but it was nothing less than the Argo and all its illustrious crew. This she glosses as a *munus*, a gift or dedication, dwelling on its impressive scale by cataloguing members of the expedition (228–33) and ending with the device called praeteritio: *nam ducum taceo ducem*, she demurs, 'I won't mention the captain of these captains,' drawing attention thereby precisely to the very man she is definitely not in any way referring to. In a syntactically balanced line, she sets Jason on one side of the scales and the rest of the Argonauts on the other: *vobis revexi ceteros, unum mihi*, 'For you I brought the others back, him alone for me' (235).

Moving into round 4, Medea now picks up the theme of her guilt, recalling her first attempt at gaining Creon's attention. The single (*solum*) *crimen* he can charge her with is the same as the single (*solum*) *munus* she brought from Colchis, the ship made to stand emblematically for the actions which retained it. She underlines her responsibility, and the inescapable reciprocity of crime and benefit, with a counterfactual proposal: supposing she had been alliteratively satisfied with virginal loyalty and paternal authority (*virgini placeat pudor / paterque placeat*, 238–9), the result would have been the loss of a whole generation of Greek aristocracy, and Jason – fulsomely referred to as Creon's son-in-law (*gener*) – the first to have perished. Medea uses the family relationship as a springboard to her main request, that Creon, if he persists in condemning her *culpa*, ought to give this *crimen* back to her in the shape of Jason himself, whom he now counts as part of his household. 'And I'm guilty, I confess it, Creon,' she concludes, 'You know I am' (246–7). If he cannot reverse the sentence, perhaps she can prevail upon him to grant a miserable *supplex* some rural, distant, meagre corner of his vast domains in which she can simply disappear. If he is not moved by pity, perhaps Creon will respond to obligation.

He does not. The strength of his revulsion towards Medea, and his need for a scapegoat (*purga regna*, 269), make him deaf to her entreaty. Medea tries again (round 5, 272–80), in an impassioned exhortation that starts with a rapid sequence of rhetorical questions and answers, peppered with repetitions that zigzag rhythmically across the verses (*redde fugienti ratem / vel redde comitem. Fugere cur solam iubes? / Non sola veni*, 272–4). A long crescendo follows, building up the litany of crimes with which Medea herself has been charged into a bombshell which she hurls at Jason, encompassing him, no, blaming him utterly as her beneficiary. The dust settles. Calmly, Creon asks in the terrible stillness why she is still delaying in idle talk. This bout, at least, is his.

Picking herself up, Medea reverts to what seems to have been her most effective tactic, playing the helpless victim and appealing to Creon's sovereign generosity.[25] As a retreating suppliant, *supplex recedens*, suggestive of the cringing posture adopted by servile characters,[26] she attempts one last, rather unexpected entreaty: that Creon spare her sons. Creon, now sure of victory, is delighted to oblige.

He will embrace them like their own father (284). Seeing a weakness, Medea presses her advantage, coming back for round six. She begs him (*precor*) in formal terms, by what she now calls Jason's 'auspicious' wedding-day, and by the royal power she knows Creon cannot resist exercising, that he grant her just a very short delay (*moram*, echoing Creon's own reference to *mora* a few lines before) to give her children a mother's last kiss, a mother who perhaps is dying (*fortasse moriens*). Tremulous, broken, finally beaten, Medea allows her voice to waver, risks introducing a sob. Creon's response is gruff, and Medea, perhaps in genuine desperation, bursts into tears (*lacrimis*, 293) accusing him of being the kind of bully who would deny a poor woman (*miserae*) even the time to weep. It is the turning point. He may have refused her everything else, but Creon reluctantly, crucially, offers her a single day. Even if all her eloquence was otherwise ineffectual, her half-feigned tears have prevailed. She may not have negotiated for Jason's return, nor a reprieve of exile, but she has gained the necessary time for carrying out revenge; and this, as we have seen, counts as an acceptable substitute.

Medea's attempt to placate Creon functions as a dress rehearsal for her address to Jason himself (447–559). Again, its movements are best analysed by beat or section, of which again there are six (see Table 4.2). Medea's opening tirade (447–89) contains three of them. In the first

Table 4.2 Medea confronts Jason

Beat	Lines	Movement
1	447–65	*Quo me remittis?* (Where are you sending me?)
2	466–77	*Revolvat animus . . .* (Turn your thoughts back. . .)
3	478–89	*Miserere!* (Pity me!)
4	490–514	*Meque teque in exitium.* (You and me, to the death.)
5	515–30	*Pro me vel scelus.* (Do a crime for me.)
6	531–59	*Bene est, tenetur.* (Good, I've got him.)

round, she batters Jason with rhetorical questions: where can she flee now? Where does he expect her to return, since everywhere they have previously lived, including her own homeland, has branded her a wanted criminal? The first two lines (447–8) make use of repetition, varying the parts of speech – a technique called 'polyptoton' – to emphasize that while the situation of exile is familiar, the circumstances this time are utterly transposed: *fugimus, Iason* (I've been on the run before), *fugimus* (I'm on the run again). *Non hoc est novum, / mutare sedes* (It's nothing new, changing homes): *causa fugiendi nova est* (but I have a new reason for running). Having listed the places that have been tainted by what she has done for Jason, she uses pithy antithesis – *quascumque aperui tibi vias, clausi mihi* ('Whatever routes I opened to you [on their way to Corinth], I closed for myself', 458 – and another instance of polyptoton, *exuli exilium imperas* ('You order the exile into exile', 459) to underscore the absurdity, the irony, and the cruelty of Jason's dissociation. With ferocious sarcasm, she suggests further punishments that the *regius gener*, the royal son-in-law, might like to inflict (462–5).

Her next approach is more conciliatory. The punchy staccato assault of her exordium (opening statement of grievances) is followed by a stream of longer, smoother phrases calling to mind the magical assistance she provided to Jason in Colchis. *Revolvat animus*, she invites him (466): turn your mind back, let your thoughts rewind. She then begins to place verbally before his eyes the challenges she helped him to overcome: the fire-breathing bull, from which her unguent protected him; the earth-born army which her advice defeated; and the dragon she charmed to sleep. Medea is drawing on her ability to enchant a listener with the vividness (*enargeia*) of her descriptions, a rhetorical technique known as ecphrasis.[27] Past events are described with the art of a storyteller, encouraging her auditor(s) to bring them to mind as though they were occurring in the present. This is of course a highly theatrical device, here itself embedded in the fictional scenario of Seneca's play in such a way that the enargetic skill of the character and that of the actor who delivers her words become indistinguishable.

The third section of Medea's speech (478–89) is a formal supplication, similar to that which she addressed to Creon at 285–90. At this point, it is not yet clear that Jason cannot be seduced back to Medea's side, so she grovels to him, begging him by their children, and by their adventures together – the monsters vanquished, the terrors they have faced – and by the sky and the waves that witnessed their union that he might pity her (*miserere*, 482). Using the same device as previously deployed to sway Creon, she contrasts the opulence of Colchis with her present destitution, adding this time that Jason was the recipient of this lavish 'dowry' (489) consisting of everything she sacrificed for him.

The fourth and fifth movements of the scene comprise mainly stichomythia (dialogue exchanged in single lines). Medea's stated objective is now to smear Jason with the guilt he is intent on repudiating, to implicate him in the shared past he has almost succeeded in escaping. Seneca gives us marital breakdown in the form of a tennis match. 'What crime can I actually be charged with?' Jason serves. 'Whatever I've done,' Medea smashes back (497–8). She has accused him of ingratitude (*ingratum*, 465), but Jason twists the word back on itself: *ingrata vita est cuius acceptae pudet*, 'No need to be grateful for getting a life you're ashamed of', 504; 'There's no shame in giving it up,' Medea points out, in parallel syntax (*Retienda non est cuius acceptae pudet*, 505). Were this purely a battle of wits, she would win; but glib retorts are not enough.

The mood shifts as Jason's resistance crumbles. Like Lady Macbeth, Medea begins to tempt him once again to trust her power and throw off his obligations to Creon. 'Tell me what I can do, then,' says Jason. Medea's eyes gleam. '[You can do] a crime for me [this time],' she replies (*Pro me vel scelus*, 516).[28] They plot in whispers, Jason hesitant, Medea tasting victory. She will take on kings and armies for him, and win. She paints an alternative future in which they escape together, dangles it before him, gives Jason every opportunity to seize it. If all the armies of Scythia were added to all the armies of Greece, they could not withstand the opposition of oceanic Medea: *demersos dabo*, she promises (528). I will submerge them, I will drown them all.

But Jason still hesitates. 'I'm frightened of mighty sceptres,' he whines. 'Stop talking, they'll suspect something' (530).

Persuasion has failed. Medea's rage breaks out. Invoking Jupiter, she calls down the lightning bolts which cannot help but strike the guilty, wherever they fall. *Omnenque ruptis nubibus mundum quate*, she thunders ('Split the clouds and shake the whole world'), recalling her own threats in the preceding scene (*sternam et evertam omnia*, 414; *cuncta quatiam*, 425). When she returns to their conversation, she has only one purpose: to identify Jason's weak spot (*vulneri . . . locus*, 550) where her revenge can cut deepest. Mentioning their children exposes him: *bene est, tenetur*, Medea gloats. It has been pointed out that this creates something of an inconsistency in Seneca's text, as Medea appears to have decided to use the children as a weapon well before her dramatic realization that they must die.[29] An alternative reading, however, is that she refers here only to their deployment as the messengers who deliver Creusa's poisoned garments. Closing the scene, Medea then cloaks herself in sweetness and asks that Jason forgive her *dolor*, and that all of her *ira* should be wiped from his memory (553–7). The immediate success of this *volte-face*, following so closely on her violent imprecations to Jupiter, makes it seem less a request than an exercise in mind-control, an act of magical speech anticipating the great spell to come. As if hypnotized, Jason is instantly soothed into complacency, and departs oblivious of Medea's cresting rage and of the danger he is in.

The last opponent Medea must face is herself (893–957). Her deliberative pendulum swings three times in this passage from vengeful *dolor*, to horrified repulsion, then back again (*rursus increscit dolor*, 951) to a renewed pursuit of revenge. Within these dominant movements are a multitude of smaller vacillations. Medea's habit of self-address is concentrated most intensively in this soliloquy. The first hint that she is not altogether united in jubilation at the news of Creusa's death comes almost immediately with the dissatisfied question, *Quid, anime, cessas?* – 'Why stop there, my spirit?' (895). She calls herself *furiose*, crazy, and accuses herself slyly of still having feelings for Jason, if this petty gesture is going to be enough. The aspect of Medea's self who is speaking here, the Gollum to her reluctant Sméagol, may perhaps be usefully designated as *Ira*, addressed as such in 916 ('Anger, where are you sending me?') and 953 ('Anger, where you lead, I follow'). *Ira* expresses herself in imperatives, ordering Medea's *animus* to reactivate her *veteres impetus*, her old destructive energies, and stir up the rage which is described as 'dormant' or 'sluggish', *languentem*; scarcely accurate, but an effective strategy for establishing a new scale of passion in which all former atrocities are dismissed as trivial (*levia*, 906) and recalled as pleasurable (*iuvat, iuvat rapuisse fraternum caput*, 911). This movement builds towards Medea's realization that the *nescioquid* which *ira* has implanted in her *animus* is that her children, now Creusa's children, must pay Jason's penalty (*pro paternis sceleribus poenas date*, 925).

This sophistry pushes her a step too far, and Medea recoils, reporting aloud how the thought has made her shudder and turn cold (926–7). Now she turns to address her *furor*, shocked that it could lead her even to contemplate such an *incognitum facinus*, an unthinkable act (931). But the Mephistophelean allure of syllogism, of concepts yoked together by a trick of the syntax, becomes irresistible: *Scelus est Iason genitor*, the children's only 'crime' is to have Jason as their father; *et maius scelus, Medea mater*, 'and the greater crime of Medea as mother' (933–4). They must die, therefore, on both counts: *occident, non sunt mei; pereant, mei sunt*, 'They shall be killed [because] they are not mine', that is, because Jason has denied her custody; and at the same time, 'they shall perish, because they are mine', and causing innocent deaths is Medea's trademark.

Love and anger struggle for her wavering soul (938–9). She feels them dragging at her like conflicting ocean currents and begs her pain to yield to *pietas*, familial affection and duty. In tears, she embraces her sons (945–7). For a moment, as when Jason was almost seduced, the tragedy's outcome rests on a knife-edge. It is the recollection of exile which tips the balance back again, and which sets in motion the final, fatal stroke of the pendulum by establishing another (il)logical equivalence: 'Let them be lost to their father's kisses / as they are to their mother's' (950–1). Medea hands herself over to *Ira* once more and the *antiqua Erinys*, the ancient spectre of Revenge personified. Hyperbole overflows, and Medea, now the mouthpiece once again of demented rage, regrets only that her womb was not as fecund as that of Niobe, whose fourteen children were killed by the gods to punish her for boastfulness (954–6). 'As a means of punishment, I am practically barren [by comparison]', she spits; but two are enough, she concedes, as compensation for her father and her brother. It is at this point that her brother's ghost appears, and the persuasion ceases to be verbal, effected instead by supernatural intimidation. Absyrtus's intervention, however, is by now rather superfluous. Medea has already beaten herself.

In all three scenes, Seneca proceeds through a compelling blend of argument and ornament, generating structural intricacy out of interlocking repetitions both phonological and syntactical. The scenes fall into units whose gear-shifts reflect the underlying movements of strategy, emotional impulse, and thought-process. In terms of performance, as the physical bearing and gestures of an orator were expected to support the phrasing and temper of his speech, so we might expect the outlines of Medea's movements to be found in the textures, dynamics, and pacing of her spoken discourse. The verbal twists and turns of these monologues, then, imply their embodiment. Medea's performance art consists not only in her adoption of deceptive attitudes, but also in the very substance of the rhetoric whose lineaments she fulfils.

4.3 Studley's *Medea*

Seneca's poetry is so compact, and so dependent on the compression which Latin uniquely affords – the absence of articles, for instance, and of auxiliary verbs ('would', 'ought', 'will', etc.), the almost unlimited options for arranging word order, and highly elliptical expressions that remain comprehensible (*'Medea –' '– Fiam,'*) – that its translation into English requires creative solutions. The first English translator of Seneca's *Medea*, John Studley, took an expansive approach which enabled him to encompass the content of Seneca's verse and convey what he felt to be its blasting effect, at the same time exploiting the conventions and possibilities of his native language. Studley's Seneca can elicit strong responses ranging from supercilious contempt to dumbfounded mirth,[30] but it repays examination in context, both as an experimental approach to dramatic translation and one which (for better or worse) laid the foundations for how Seneca came to be perceived by generations of English readers.

Studley, to be fair, was not single-handedly responsible for the construction of Seneca as wordy, ghoulish, and shamelessly fortissimo. Written in 1566 along with his translations of *Agamemnon*, *Hercules Oetaeus*, and *Hipploytus* [*Phaedra*] the following year, Studley's *Medea* was later incorporated by Thomas Newton into his anthology of Seneca's *Tenne Tragedies* (1581), which served as their canonical English translation even into the twentieth century.[31] Studley's style, however, is the dominant voice of the collection, and because of its pre-eminence has tended to drown out Seneca's own.[32] In this section, I will show how Studley magnifies particular features of Seneca's poetics in order to produce a text that, while retaining the overall structure, themes, and dramaturgy of *Medea*, is also magnificently other.

Like the other nine of the *Tenne Tragedies*, Studley's *Medea* was not written for performance and there is no record of it ever having been staged. This does not mean, however, that Studley regarded Seneca's play as unplayable. On the contrary, his translation followed immediately upon two performances of *Medea* in Latin at the University of Cambridge, where he was a scholar at the time (Trinity College in 1560–1, and Queens College in 1563).[33] It is not clear from the records whether these productions used Seneca's own text, or a neo-Latin version produced by a member of the college along the lines of George Buchanan's *Medea* of 1544. Based on contemporary practice, however, they are likely to have used Seneca as the core of an adaptation which grafted in new passages (perhaps a Euripidean messenger-speech?), perhaps new characters (such as Creusa or a Fury?), and moral sentiments more appropriate to a Christian community.[34] It is important to note that Studley's translations appeared at a time when Latin tragedy was in vogue among the English intelligentsia, and its vernacular equivalent would soon appear at the Inns of Court and on the public London stage (e.g. *The Misfortunes of Arthur* (1588), Christopher Marlowe's *Tamburlaine* (1587), and Thomas Kyd's *The Spanish Tragedy*, also in the 1580s).[35] Although not staged themselves, the publication in 1581 of the *Tenne Tragedies*, including *Medea*, provided a significant resource for the development of English tragedy as a genre.[36]

Compare, for example, the ten lines from Seneca's opening scene quoted above:

Si vivis, anime, si quid antiqui tibi
remanet vigoris, pelle femineos metus
et inhospitalem Caucasum mente indue.
Quodcumque vidit Phasis aut Pontus nefas,
videbit Isthmos. Effera ignota horrida,
tremenda caelo pariter ac terris mala
mens intus agitat: vulnera et caedem et vagum
funus per artus. Levia memoravi nimis:
haec virgo feci. Gravior exsurgat dolor:
maiora iam me scelera post partus decent.

41–50[37]

Studley retains the order and sense, but more than doubles the length of the passage, at the same time introducing a number of details unmentioned by Seneca:

If any lusty lyfe as yet within thy soule doe rest,
It ought of auncient corage still doe dwell within my brest,
Exite all foolysh Female feare, and pity from thy mynde,
And as th'untamed Tygers use to rage and rave unkynde,
That haunt the croking combrous Caues, and clumpred frosen clives,
And craggy Rockes of *Caucasus,* whose bitter colde depryves
The soyle of all Inhabitours, permit to lodge and rest,
Such salvage brutish tyranny within thy brasen brest.
What ever hurly burly wrought doth *Phasis* understand,
What mighty monstrous bloudy feate I wrought by Sea or Land:
The like in *Corynth* shal be seene in most outragious guise,

Most hyddious, hatefull, horrible, to heare, or see wyth eyes,
Most divelish, desperate, dreadfull deede, yet never knowne before,
Whose rage shall force heauen, earth, and hell to quake and tremble sore,
My burning breast that rowles in wrath, and doth in rancour boyle,
Sore thrysteth after bloud, and wounds with slaughter, death, & spoyle,
By renting rackéd lyms from lyms to drive them downe to grave:
Tush, these be but as Fleabytings, that mentionéd I have:
As weyghty things as these I did in greener girlishe age,
Now sorrowes smart doth rub the gall and fret with sharper rage.
But sith my wombe hath yeelded fruict, it doth mee well behove,
The strength and parlous puissaunce of weightier illes to prove.

One of Studley's self-imposed constraints is his use of the characteristically English verse form known as the 'fourteener', consisting of seven-foot iambic lines (iambic heptameter) arranged in rhyming couplets. This means that his basic sense-units are longer; where Seneca delivers an idea in one swift slash (*maiora iam me scelera post partus decet*), Studley spreads it lavishly over the full extent of the air-time his form affords: 'But sith [since] my womb hath yielded fruit, it doth me well behove / The strength and parlous puissance of weightier ills to prove'. Another, related result of this more capacious framework is that Studley frequently fills out his extra syllables with additional words that gloss or qualify those he retains from the Latin. Medea's soul is not only recalled to 'life' (*si vivis*), but 'lusty life'; her *femineos metus* are, in addition, 'foolish', and along with these Senecan fears, she is also to expel pity; the 'breast' (i.e. *mente*) which is to take on Caucasian rigour is 'brazen'; her crimes will cause hell to tremble, in addition to Seneca's *caelo ac terris*; her youth was 'greener' as well as 'girlish' (following *virgo*); and her forthcoming *scelera* will possess a 'parlous puissance' which Seneca's do not. The cumulative effect of these small enhancements, none of which have a lexical analogue in the source-text, is to make Senecan diction appear more ample, and Senecan speeches longer, louder, and more sonorous than their Latin allows. We also get a number of pleonastic redundancies: 'rage and rave', 'lodge and rest', 'quake and tremble', 'see with eyes', which likewise serve to fill out the meter, often with pleasing consonances, and at the same time enable Studley to pile on synonyms which would otherwise have to be relegated to the thesaurus.

The extra syllables in his sense-units also give Studley extra space which he devotes to the play of pure sound, realized most obviously in the form of rhyme and alliteration.[38] This delight in soundplay is reminiscent more of the Roman Republican tragic style which we saw in Chapter 2 than it is of Seneca. It is also a practice favoured by the Elizabethan poets who were Studley's stylistic models for creating a vernacular verse form suitable for tragedy. Recall Horace's advice that tragic subject matter requires a special type of language; recall also that Studley's translation precedes the canonisation of blank verse (Shakespearean iambic pentameter) as standard for English tragedy, and that of the alexandrine couplet, which in fact it closely resembles,[39] as standard for French. Studley's may not have been the conventions which stuck, but at the time they represented a sensible and not uninspired intervention into the development of Anglophone verse drama.

As well as embellishing Seneca's text on the level of individual words, Studley also adds entire lines. Where Seneca is content with *inhospitalem Caucasum*, Studley feels this is insufficient to convey to his early modern readers everything that the Caucasus entails. Medea's internal landscape is mapped in vivid detail:

> And as th'untamed Tygers use to rage and rave unkynde,
> That haunt the croking combrous Caues, and clumpred frosen clives,
> And craggy Rockes of *Caucasus*, whose bitter colde depryves
> The soyle of all Inhabitours . . .

Although Seneca does not mention tigers here, Medea does become a tigress at 863–5, so the simile is not inappropriate. Studley's idiosyncratic vocabulary, however, introduces the unprecedented impression of a glacial landscape where the ice creaks (or 'croaks') into great overhanging ('cumbrous') caverns, and clumps itself into 'cliffs', the ensuing soundscape issued in a frieze of alternating glottal consonants and low vowels, all of which echo the first sound of **co**ld, itself not uttered until the end of the third line, and that of **Cau**casus; also the croaking caw of the crows which simultaneously rises from the looming ice-caves. None of this is in Seneca.

Another characteristically Studleyan expansion of a Senecan concept occurs a couple of lines later. Medea's *nefas* ('mighty monstrous bloody feat', and, in apposition, 'hurly burly') will be seen by Corinth (*videbit Isthmos*) 'in most outrageous guise', Studley promises enthusiastically. Whereas Seneca's Medea regards her past actions as merely *effera* (savage) and *horrida*, for Studley they become at once 'most hideous, hateful, horrible to hear' and 'most devilish, desperate, dreadful deeds'. The patterned syntactic repetition and the hyperbole are Senecan tropes, albeit applied here with heavy-handed gusto, but the generous alliteration, the thunderous percussive build-up of repeated sound, is quintessential Studley. It reaches a crescendo in rendering the relatively restrained *mens intus agitat* as 'My burning breast that rolls in wrath, and does in rancour boil,' terms which again are borrowed from elsewhere in Medea's emotional vocabulary – notably 408–14 – but the images Seneca reserves for his moments of sharpest agony, Studley disperses and makes commonplace. Lines such as this were famously satirized by the next generation of English playwrights, and may sound most familiar from Shakespeare's parodic *Lamentable Comedy of Pyramus and Thisbe* ('Whereat with blade, with bloody blameful blade, / he bravely broached his boiling bloody breast', *MSND* 5.1.142–3). Moreover, whereas Seneca's Medea is at best ambivalent about the *dolor* that provokes her to murder, Studley's heroine 'sore thirsteth' to commit again the atrocities that she recalls, making her more immediately and straightforwardly complicit with the violent impulses of *ira*. She has already stated her intention to commit infanticide, declaring from the outset that 'at the Aulters of the Gods my chyldren shal be slayne, / With crimsen colourde bloud of Babes their Aulters will I stayne'.

Overall, Studley's language is more visceral than Seneca's own: his text contains more numerous explicit mentions of 'bloud', 'flesh', and other organs or body parts, especially the 'gut(s)' and 'stomack'. Studley uses the term 'stomack(e) stout' on several occasions as a synonym for courage, thus grounding the abstract firmly in the corporeal. Another example of this grounding impulse may be found in the passage above, where Medea describes her *levia mala* as 'Fleabytings'; just as her *animus* is now located in her stomach, so her juvenile crimes take on the bodily discomfort of a verminous itch. Studley's tendency towards increased corporeality is most immediately apparent in those passages relating the death of King Pelias, and those which describe the fire-breathing bulls faced by Jason in Colchis. At the start of Act 2, Studley interpolates these creatures, which are absent altogether from the corresponding passage in Seneca:

> The grunting firy foming Bulles, whose smoking guts were stuft,
> With smoltring fumes, that from theyr Jawes, & nosthrils out they puft.
> I stopt their gnashing mounching mouths, I quencht their burning breath,
> And vapors hot of stewing paunch, that else had wrought his death.

The monstrosity of Studley's bulls has a definite gastric aspect: they approach 'gnashing' and 'munching', ready to belch out (rather than more delicately breathing out) the 'fumes' or 'vapours' that have been 'stewing' in their 'guts', or their indecorous 'paunch'; elsewhere Studley has them issue from the monster's 'spewinge throat'. There is a physical grossness here which Seneca does not possess. Similarly, where Seneca has 'the limbs of old Pelias / boiled in bronze', Studley expands *membra* (limbs) into 'members all and mangled flesh', reminding us that they were 'with liquor scalding hot / ysodden [saturated]' before being 'perboyled ... in seething brazen pot'. The conceit that closes Seneca's third choral ode, which attempts to correlate Pelias's death with the transgressive Argonautic mission, has the old king 'burned up, wandering in his own miniature sea' (*arsit angustas vagus inter undas*, 667),[40] which in Studley's hands becomes a kind of grotesque stew:

> Perboylde in glowing cauldron hoate with fervent heate hee fryes,
> And fleering peece meale up and downe in water thin he lyes.

Each such instance is not remarkable in isolation, but when no opportunity for extra viscerality is let slip, the cumulative effect is to flesh out the bare bones of Senecan discourse with the very bloodthirstiness of which the Roman playwright later stands accused.

Studley performs a similar exaggeration of corporeality, in conjunction with some characteristically undignified vocabulary, in his translation of the serpents which Medea summons at the start of Act 4:

> She mumbling conjures up by names of ills the rable rout,
> In hugger mugger cowchéd long, kept close, unserchéd out:
> All pest'lent plagues she calles upon, what ever *Libie* lande,
> In frothy boyling stream doth worke, or muddy belching sande:
> What tearing torments *Taurus* breedes, with snowes unthawéd still
> Where winter flawes [rivers], and hory frost knit hard the craggy hill,
> She layes her crossing hands upon each monstrous conjurde thing,
> And over it her magicke verse with chanting doth she sing:
> A mowsye, rowsye, rusty route with cancred Scales Iclad
> From musty, fusty, dusty dens where lurkéd long they had,
> Doe craull: a wallowing serpent huge, his combrous Corps out drags,
> In fiery foming blaring mouth his forkéd tongue hee wags.
> He stares about with sparkling eyes, if some he might espy,
> Whom snapping at with stinging spit he might constrayne to dy:
> But hearing once the magycke verse he husht as all a gast,
> His body boalne [bloated] big, wrapt in lumps on twining knots hee cast.
> And wambling to and fro his tayle in linkes he rowles it round.

> Omne explicat
> turbam malorum, arcana secreta abdita,
> et triste laeva comprecans sacrum manu
> pestes vocat quascumque ferventis creat
> harena Libyae quasque perpetua nive
> Taurus coercet frigore Arctoo rigens,
> et omne monstrum. Tracta magicis cantibus
> squamifera latebris turba desertis adest.
> Hic saeva serpens corpus immensum trahit
> trifidamque linguam exertat et quaerit quibus
> mortifera veniat; carmine audito stupet,

tumidumque nodis corpus aggestis plicat
cogitque in orbes.

678–90[41]

Although Medea's 'magicke verse' is later elevated to 'chanting', it is initially represented as indistinct 'mumbling'; the very opposite, in fact, of Seneca's *explicat*, which means to unravel, lay out, or clarify. Medea's *turbam malorum* are not simply a crowd or a host, but a 'rabble rout', an unruly mob, which has moreover been kept colloquially 'hugger mugger'. Libya and Taurus are both given familiar Studleyan touches. In addition to the tautological and alliterative 'pestilent plagues', Libya's desert acquires 'boiling' streams and sand which is not only rustically muddy but also, recalling the bulls' steaming gullets, 'belching'; while Taurus, in imitation of Colchis, adds 'craggy hills' and knitted frost to its smoother Senecan surface of ice and snow. The 'rout' (crowd) of serpents are inactive and 'rusty', their scales 'cankered', and the dens which they have left, in which Studley attains an absurd ecstasy of internal nonsense-rhyme, 'musty, fusty, dusty'.

Note the re-use of the term 'cumbrous' to describe the serpent subsequently singled out. In Seneca, his mouth is neither fiery, foaming, nor blaring, although all of these resonate with the play's scheme of imagery, so do not seem necessarily out of place. The 'snapping' and 'stinging spit' are likewise interpolations, supplying some enjoyable and not inappropriate sound effects. 'Wagging tongue', however, despite accurately picking up *linguam exertat*, brings with it unfortunate overtones of gossip. Studley's serpent becomes comical rather than menacing: encumbered by his lumbering body, he fancies himself sharp-eyed and deadly but moves in fact in a 'wallowing' wobble of blubber, tongue hanging out in puppyish excitement, even before Medea's song reduces him to a purposeless, wambling (wandering, wavering, ambling, bumbling, utterly humbled) jelly.

Further expansion is produced by the insertion of digressive material to explain mythological references. Meleager, for example, one of the Argonauts whose death is mentioned in passing by Seneca in his choral catalogue of divine revenge (644–6), becomes for Studley a more important figure. The potential parallels in Meleager's story are not pursued by Seneca, but Studley allows them space to flourish. One of the magical ingredients added by Medea to her potion is the firebrand used by 'Althaea the avenger', *piae sororis, impiae matris* (dutiful sister, unnatural mother) to punish her son:

Loe heere the fatall brand, which late the fatall sisters three
Conspyred at *Meleagers* byrth, such should his dest'ny bee,
To save alyve his brethyng corpes, while that might whole remayne,
Which safe his mother *Althe* kept, till he his uncles twane,
(That from *Atlanta* would have had the head of conquered Bore,)
Had reft of lyfe whose spightfull death *Althea* tooke so sore,
That both she shewed her ferventnesse in systers godly love,
When to revenge her brothers death meere nature did her move,
But yet as mother most unkynde, of nature most unmylde,
To hasten the untymely grave of her belovéd chylde,
Whyle *Meleagers* fatall brande she wasted in the flame,
Whose swelting guts and bowels moult consuméd as the same.

None of this background is given in Seneca, who passes over the firebrand in two short lines (789–90). A prophecy at Meleager's birth had predicted that he would live as long as a branch of wood, then beginning to char in the hearth, remained intact; Althaea removed it and kept it safe, until Meleager killed her two brothers during a dispute over hunting spoils. In revenge for her brothers' death, Althaea retrieved the branch and thrust it into the fire. Meleager died in agony, as if consumed from within by invisible flames.[42] The structural echoes in the tragedy of a mother 'most unkind, of nature most un-mild' moved to revenge her brother's death by killing her own son ('to hasten the untimely grave of her beloved child') are clear. In showing *pietas* ('sister's godly love') towards her murdered brother, Medea must become her children's killer. Dwelling on the death of Meleager also gives Studley another opportunity for dishing out the guts and gore as the sometime Argonaut's 'swelting [sweltering, sweating] guts and bowels moult [molten, melting]' are burned alive. The image is not altogether gratuitous, however, as a similarly hideous death will overtake the unfortunate Creusa as a result of Medea's poisoned robes. As John Henderson has shown,[43] the deaths of the Argonauts in Seneca's catalogue (607–69) all in some way anticipate Medea's own revenge, but it is not until Studley opens up the *penetrale funestum* (*Med.* 676) of this glancing reference that the typological significance of Meleager becomes properly apparent.

*

Studley's writing is truly baroque: voluptuous where Seneca's is lean, unravelled where Seneca's is taut, explicit where the Roman playwright is elliptical. The difference between the two modes illustrates what is distinctive about Senecan style, showing how another poet in another language makes use of the traditions, devices, and resources at his disposal to fashion a very different *Medea*. This chapter has shown how Senecan rhetoric functions as a theatrical medium, and has identified those features of its poetics which taken together characterize the playwright's style. In particular, the set-piece arguments crafted for delivery by Medea are rich in rhetorical devices which should be regarded less as ornamental than as psychagogic mechanisms intended to persuade. This persuasion takes the form of syllogism (the assertion that X is Y, that *ira* is *amor*, for instance, or that benefit is culpability), ecphrasis (as in the vivid verbal depiction of Colchis), and *ēthos* (adoption of an attitude, such as the suppliant or the seductress). While Medea particularly excels at the latter, she is by no means unpractised in other aspects of oratorical performance. Her metatheatricality emerges in these skilful, albeit not always successful manipulations of the play's internal auditors as much as it does in her role-plays, self-conscious autopoiesis, and assumption of control over the plot.

5

Witchcraft and Stagecraft

Seneca's fourth act, in which Medea prepares the poisoned robes and crown that will destroy Creusa, has no equivalent in Euripides. As we have seen, Medea's identity as a witch is integral to her representation in Ovid's *Metamorphoses*, but Ovid directs her magic towards the rejuvenation of Jason's father, the elderly Aeson. Moreover, the great spell performed by Seneca's Medea is not merely reported in the past tense, as an event which occurred long ago, but rather staged in the dramatic present. Even if its likeliest forms of staging consisted of stylized pantomime dance, concert opera, or poetic recital, as opposed to a full-cast production crammed with realistic props,[1] the delivery of this elaborate ritual in real time – weighing in at a challenging 180 lines – creates a chilling assimilation of character and performer. An invocation of Hecate, for instance, is spoken aloud in both the fictional world and the performance venue. The speech-act performed by 'Medea', composed of enchantment, deception, and exertion of will, is identical to that which is performed by the singer: the singer entrances their audience into accepting the illusion cast by stage-magic, or what Amy Wygant calls 'glamour'.[2] While on one level we have been admitted as audience into the preparation behind the scenes of a show(down) that will happen offstage, entitled The Beguilement And Death Of Creusa, on another we have ourselves been willingly beguiled into attending, appreciating, and perhaps applauding the ingenuity – the virtuosity – of the *artifex malorum*.

This chapter analyses Seneca's witchcraft scene in two contexts: firstly that of Julio-Claudian Rome, and secondly in translation as a component of Pierre Corneille's 1635 *Médée*. Corneille's translation shows how Medea's sorcery, her command of the *merveilleux*, came into its own in the early Parisian theatre. In the decades before the so-called *Règles* or 'Rules' of neoclassical tragedy had squeezed theatrical action down to what was strictly *vraisemblable* (believable), theatre-makers experimented wildly with generic fusion, composite sets, and special effects. French baroque theatre was magical, in love with both illusions and the consciousness of illusion. As such, as reimagined by Corneille, Seneca's *Medea* was its embodiment.

5.1 The Roman witch

Evidence for the perception of witchcraft in the Roman era comes from two main sets of data, the representation of literary witches like Medea and material sources pertaining to the practice of magic. Attempting to separate 'magic' in the ancient world from religion, medicine, philosophy, dream-interpretation, poison, or divination is difficult, as magical practices overlap with all these fields. One working definition, however, is that magic involved 'the socially unsanctioned use of supernatural powers and tools to control nature and compel both humans and superhuman beings to do one's will'.[3] Magic, then, was illegitimae, or illicit; and rather than petitioning the gods or observing the occurrence of natural phenomena, it sought to impose the practitioner's will forcibly upon the cosmos. It was carried out either through plant-based philtres, incantations, or a combination of both, accompanied by the performance of ritual acts.

The most common type of evidence for magical practice in the early empire consists of *defixiones* or 'curse tablets', of which approximately two thousand examples have been found,[4] spanning the whole Mediterranean region. *Defixiones* are thin sheets of lead a few inches wide on which a curse or a binding-spell has been inscribed using a sharp stylus. The lead slip was then folded, twisted, and sometimes pierced through with a nail before being deposited in some ritually significant location. Many have been found in springs or cemeteries. Although predominantly erotic, seeking to 'bind' a lover's affection, take revenge for infidelity, or constrain a rival, *defixiones* could also be used to influence business dealings, court proceedings, or the outcome of a sporting event. The extent to which professional practitioners were employed in the manufacture of *defixiones* is unclear, and probably variable. Daniel Ogden suggests that experts may have been consulted on the content of spells or engaged as scribes, but as other *defixiones* exhibit scripts that are highly idiosyncratic or even illiterate, it seems that one did not need to be a *magus* or a *straga* in order to deposit a curse.[5]

The *Papyri Graecae Magicae* (*PGM*) are a collection of papyrus documents from Egypt dating from the first few centuries CE. Many of them are templates for producing *defixiones*, of the 'insert name here' variety. Their language is graphic and disturbing: 'Let desire settle in [the victim's] heart and burn her guts, her breast, her liver, her breath, her bones, her marrow, until she comes to me, loving me, and until she fulfils all my wishes … Turn her guts inside out, suck out her blood drop by drop' (*PGM* 4.1529–45). Repetitions lend the curse an incantatory quality, enhanced by the frequent inclusion of strings of nonsense letters, supposedly the names of esoteric gods or daimones – Ipsentanchoucheouch (*PGM* 4.5), Araracharara (*PGM* 4.1796) – who will assure the spell's success. More conventional deities, such as Hecate and Hermes, are also invoked.

Clandestine but widespread, then, the practice of magic complemented activities such as the deposition of votive offerings or consultation of oracles. Literary witches, however, such as Horace's Canidia and Lucan's Erichtho, developed their own identity and a set of tropes or iconic characteristics which by the time of *Medea*'s composition were well entrenched.[6] Canidia appears as a character in Horace's invective poetry, his *Satires* and *Epodes*. Decrepit and grotesque, she is an essentially comic figure, subverting the genres of epic and bucolic poetry as she and her crony Sagana attempt to summon a ghost at night in the gardens of Maecenas, an endeavour which is rudely interrupted by a farting statue.[7] Her practice already exhibits aspects that will become canonical: she uses *carminibus … atque venenis* (incantations and poisons, *Sat.*1.8.19), having gathered 'bones and harmful plants' (22); during the ritual, 'barefoot and hair spread loose' (*pedibus nudis passoque capillo*, 24), she shrieks and howls (*ululantem*, 25) as she calls on Hecate and the Fury Tisiphone. In a more violent passage (*Epode* 5), the witches prepare to murder a child in order to produce an erotic charm. This time, Canidia's hair is *implicata viperis*, braided with snakes (*Ep.* 5.15–16). She makes burnt offerings that include the feathers of a screech-owl and 'plants from Iolcos and Hiberia / full of poisons'. The flames which leap up are called 'Colchian' (*Ep.* 5.25). Canidia justifies her escalation to murder because the *dira barbarae . . . venena Medeae*, the 'dread poisons of barbarian Medea' are proving ineffectual (*Ep.* 5.61–2). Horace makes another reference to Medea in *Epode* 17, where the narrator himself is suffering the effects of Canidia's binding-spell:

> Hercules smeared with Nessus' black blood
> didn't [burn] like this, nor the boiling flames
> that live in Sicilian Etna. Until I am borne away
> as dry ash on the baleful wind, will you
> keep scorching me with your Colchian poisons?
>
> 17.31–5

As it has been noted more than once, Canidia is the 'anti-Muse' of the Epodes, 'the embodiment of the collection as a whole'.[8] Just as the *puella*, the unattainable beloved, inspires elegiac verse, so the vile Canidia is the substance of invective, the inescapable hate-object without whom the poem would not exist.

Witches are metapoetic figures.[9] In Book 6 of the *Bellum Civile* (*Civil War*), an epic composed by Seneca's nephew Lucan in the early 60s CE, the Thessalian witch Erichtho is consulted about whether Caesar or Pompey will win the decisive battle to come. An accomplished necromancer, Erichtho drags a fresh corpse off the battlefield and recalls its ghost from the Underworld to deliver the required prophecy – which, as prophecies tend to be, is riddling and inconclusive: both leaders will ultimately lose, and the only question is which one of them will be buried by the Nile, and which the Tiber.[10] Erichtho has much in common with Seneca's Medea. Thessaly is introduced as the land where 'the Colchian' gathered her herbs (*BC*. 6.441–2). The powers of Thessalian witches, reversing natural processes and constraining the gods, also resemble Medea's (*BC*. 461–84), and at their spells the moon-goddess Phoebe 'turns pale (*palluit*) and burns with a dark and fearful glow' (*BC*. 502; cf. Sen. *Med.* 793). Erichtho herself is discovered composing *incognita verba*, 'unknown words', and 'fashioning a song for unheard-of purposes' (*carmenque novos fingebat in usus*, *BC*. 576). Both her craftsmanship and the novelty or originality of her production recall Medea, who is similarly determined to commit unheard-of crimes and similarly associated with poetic creativity. Erichtho scorns the regular *crimina* of witches as *nimiae pietatis* ('too much like piety', *BC*. 508; cf. Sen. *Med.* 904–5). She likewise reaches beyond the natural world into the realms of the supernatural. Medea's words are 'no less to be feared than her poisons' (*Med.* 737–8); Erichtho's voice (*vox*) is similarly 'more powerful than her drugs (*herbis*) at enchanting the infernal gods' (*BC*. 6.685–6). Erichtho's metapoetic function has been discussed in depth by W.R. Johnson and Jamie Masters.[11] She has been identified as the vatic mouthpiece of the poet, her chaotic, nihilistic prophecy borne out by the unavoidable events of history. Both she and Lucan, as Masters points out, speak what is *nefas*, unspeakable.[12] A cosmos in which Rome is torn apart by civil war and oppressed by Caesarian autocracy cannot be overseen by the Olympian pantheon of Virgil's empire-building *Aeneid*. Its presiding forces are those of Erichtho and Medea.

Seneca's ritual (see Table 5.1) is structured in six sections, followed by a brief coda. The first two function as a prologue, preparing the way for Medea's entrance. As the Nutrix catalogues the venomous serpents (670–704) and poisonous plants (705–39) that will supply the ingredients of her mistress's concoction, she lays essential groundwork of mood and atmosphere. Suspense is created, and Medea's power enhanced by this warm-up act. The Nutrix begins by declaring her own fear (*pavet animus, horret*, 670), and warning that Medea is preparing some monstrous evil greater than anything previously committed

Table 5.1 Seneca's ritual

Movement	Lines	Action
1	670–704	Ingredients: venomous serpents
2	705–39	Ingredients: poisonous plants
3	740–70	Medea's invocation
4	771–86	Offerings made at the altar
5	787–816	The sacrifice
6	817–42	Infusing the robes
7	843–8	Coda: Medea dismisses her sons

(674–5). Then, taking on Medea's voice, she relays the ominous intimation that terrestrial *mala* are too meagre (*parva*) and common (*vile*), and this spell must source its ingredients from constellations such as Draco (the Dragon), Ophiochus (the Snake-catcher), and the many-headed Hydra. From the perspective of the plot, the Nutrix's long catalogue is digressive and dilatory. Dismissing it as purely decorative, however, ignores its thematic function and dramaturgical mode. Senecan theatre often slips into a mode of representation that might be termed epic, or rhapsodic. As opposed to events being enacted mimetically, they are related verbally, in the manner of the messenger-speech in Greek tragedy or the way in which a professional bard would deliver Homer (and Roman poets their own works of epic poetry).[13] Reporting Medea's direct speech in lines 690–704 requires the performer singing the role of the Nutrix to engage in the rhetorical technique called prosopopoeia, or occupation of a secondary character. In the performance context of *orchēsis* (pantomime dance), we might imagine a dancer wearing the mask of the Nutrix adopting the choreography and gestures characteristic of Medea.[14]

The second movement of the scene (705–39) has Medea gathering the sap, flowers and leaves of *frugis infestae*, poisonous plants, from locations scattered across the known world. The expansive geographical coverage of this catalogue takes in not only Greece and the Caucasus, regions associated with Medea's personal backstory, but also Arabia and Parthia (Persia), Mesopotamia, the cold forests of northern Europe, the Danube frontier, the banks of the river Hydaspes in India, and the Iberian province of Baetica, where Seneca himself was born. This itinerary conflates Medea's spatial range anachronistically with the extent of Roman geographical knowledge and the expansion of the empire. At the end of *Medea*'s second choral ode, men from India arrive in the Caucasus, signalling a reversal of north-south cultural polarity, and Persians in Germania, signalling a disruption to the Roman world's conventional east-west axis. There is no apparent logic, however, to Medea's meanderings as she assembles her pharmacopoeia, and no indication of how she travels. In Ovid, she flies smoothly above the landscapes of northern Greece (*Met.* 7.218–36). Seneca's abrupt, erratic leaps from the Balkans to the Tigris and Suebia to Spain are more akin to teleportation.

Medea enters with an invocation (section 3, 740–70), summoning the supporting cast whose assistance is required for this performance. Among others, she calls on prominent figures from the Underworld: Ixion, punished on a wheel for attempted rape; Tantalus, tormented by food and drink forever out of reach; and the daughters of Danaus, 'taunted' by their impossible task of collecting water in sieves.[15] She also summons the moon-goddess, addressed in this instance as Phoebe (770), although the moon is also identified with the chthonic goddess of witchcraft, Hecate.[16] *Vocata sacris*, 'called by my ritual', the moon appears *minax*, threatening, and possessing Hecate's triple face (751). Like the catalogue of poisons, the catalogue of supernatural supernumeraries also serves both dramaturgical and thematic functions. In addition to the divine (or infernal) favour conferred by Hecate-Phoebe, the shades who are summoned appear to fulfil a silent choral role, or that of an internal audience. The play's spectators are made conscious of their invisible presence as they are invoked, or literally called into being by Medea's utterance of their names within the fictional space.

Comparable invocations occur elsewhere in Senecan drama, notably in *Hercules Furens* and *Agamemnon*, with similar connotations of spectatorship. In the prologue to *Hercules Furens*, the goddess Juno summons an army of chthonic personifications – Conflict (*Discordia*), Crime (*Scelus*), and Rage (*Furor*), among others – to drive Hercules into a state of murderous delusion. *Tibi et ostendam inferos*, she hisses: 'I will show you hell, right here' (*HF.* 91). Although not visible as *dramatis personae*, Juno's Hades will erupt onto the stage in the form of Hercules' own destructive *insania*. In another variant of the trope, the prophetess Cassandra describes the visions she alone can 'see', populated by the ghosts of the Trojan War and the fall of Troy. 'Open up, for a while, the lid of the Underworld,' she addresses the death-gods, 'so that the Trojan crowd (*turba*) can see (*prospiciat*) Mycenae' (*Ag.* 756–7) – and take pleasure in watching their persecutor's murder. Spectatorship is emphasized in Cassandra's language, as she repeats references to her own sight (*ecce, cerno, video*), while bringing her visions before the mind's eye of her auditors. Then, with a rhetorical twist, she presents them with a mirror image of their own spectatorship in the ranks of the dead Trojans rising to her call.[17] *Hercules Furens* makes the comparison even more explicit. The great *turba* of the deceased who flock down to Hades move like a crowd through city streets *ad novi ludos avidus theatri*, 'eager to attend the show in a new theatre' (*HF.* 838–9). Ghosts, in other words, behave like theatrical spectators; and theatrical spectators, by implication, watch in turn like ghosts.

Recalling the magic that Hecate has previously enabled her to perform, including disrupting the seasons and controlling the seas (752–69), Medea demonstrates what her vocal power can accomplish. The scene is replete with references to calling and summoning: she calls the serpents (*pestes vocat*, 681 and *evocavit omne serpentum genus*, 705); she appeals aloud to the occupants of Hades (*comprecor*, 740) and to Hecate-Phoebe (*meis vocata sacris*, 750; cf. 802, 813,815). A particularly high concentration of such references occurs as Medea recounts her prior proficiency in spell-casting: 'I have called (*evocavi*) rain from dry clouds' (754), she boasts, and 'ancient groves have shed their leaves at the command of my voice' (*vocis imperio meae*, 767). Another way in which her vocal power is manifested is explicitly as singing. In the same passage, 'the summer earth turns wintry at my song' (*cantu meo*, 760), and 'my songs (*nostris cantibus*, 769) make stars drop from their courses'. Astral bodies such as the snake caught by Ophiochus similarly arrive *ad cantus meos* (699), and the giant python is hypnotized when she croons to it (*carmine audito stupet*, 688). Her words, the Nutrix informs us just prior to Medea's entrance, are to be feared no less than her drugs (*verba non illis minus / metuenda*, 737–8). The sound of her crazed footsteps is heard, and she is singing to herself as she approaches (*canitque*, 739). 'When she first gives voice, the cosmos trembles' (*mundus vocibus primis tremit*, 739). This irresistible vocal power which mesmerizes and commands, strips and shakes, summons and curses, coaxes and enthrals is an idealized oratorical or theatrical voice, which exercises a quasi-magical authority over auditors.[18] In particular, it persuades them to 'see', to bring before their eyes (*ante oculos*) the content of the speech.[19] Techniques of ecphrasis or vivid description were integral to Roman rhetorical training, and informed the craft of actors, poets, and playwrights no less than that of orators.

In a different meter, Medea enumerates the offerings she is bringing to Hecate's altar (section 4 of the scene, 771–86), all of which are relics of intersecting myths. Typhon's limbs, *Typhoeus membra* (773), recall Medea's identification with Mt Etna, the volcano where defeated giant Typhon supposedly lies imprisoned. Nessus's blood was the poison which infused Hercules' robe and caused his fiery death on Mt Oetaeus (775–8), a death horribly similar to Creusa's. Althaea's burning branch, as we have seen, consumed her son Meleager. The feathers of the Harpies and the Stymphalian birds serve to bind Medea's vengeance to the afterlife of the Argonauts and Hercules' labours respectively. Resistant to conquest, the monsters supposedly defeated return here in Medea's hellish brew; later, Medusa and the Chimaera make an appearance (828, 831). In this way, Medea's revenge is augmented by physical cross-references to other myths, indicative not only of how far her influence extends, but also in some cases disclosing an alliance with demigods such as Prometheus and even Olympian deities such as Vulcan, making them accessories to her crime (822–5).

The next section (787–816) forms the core of Medea's ritual: the sacrifice (*sacrum sollemne*, 799). Everything up to this point has been preparatory – the ingredients, the summoning, the offerings – but now Medea plunges into the ritual itself. The meter speeds up again, galloping in furious anapaests towards its bloody climax. The moon is visible in her incarnation as the triple goddess Hecate or Trivia, whipping her chariot across the sky, her face weirdly shadowed as if by imminent eclipse. 'Pour your bitter light down on us!' Medea shrieks (792–3). She vocalizes her props (torch, wand, blade), her movements (tossing head, arching neck), and, reflexively, the sound of her own voice (*voces dedi*, 803). She even describes in words the moment of her sacrificial self-harm, initially approached in the future tense (*sacro feriam bracchia cultro*, 807), then uttered as an imperative (*assuesce*, 809), and finally as a *fait accompli* (*laticem dedi*, 811).

Blooded, she commences the last full movement of the scene, the infusion of the robes with the potion (817–42). The snakes' function becomes apparent: as well as supplying venom, they supplied secrecy, burning Creusa with *serpens flamma*, a 'serpentine flame' (819) that will slither unseen into her entrails. As a finishing touch, several more relics are added with associations of burning, particularly of flame concealed. Prometheus, who stole fire from the gods, has taught Medea how to 'bury' it (*condere*, 823) in gold, while Vulcan, god of craft and metalwork, has likewise given her fire hidden in sulphur. She has similar 'gifts' (*dona*) from the fire-breathing Chimaera, from Phaethon who fell like a meteor from the Sun's chariot, and flames that she herself extracted from the throat of her father's fire-breathing bulls. Hecate is enjoined to ensure that the poison remains invisible and inert until activated by Creusa. *Fallant visus*, Medea prays. 'Let [these objects] deceive the eyes' (835). In this, she sums up the props' theatrical duplicity. To Creusa, they will appear harmless, but in fact are deadly; to the play's spectators, they now appear deadly, whereas in fact they are harmless. Such duplicity (or complicity) also manufactures the theatricality of the whole scene, and indeed that of the play in which it occurs.

5.2 The French witch

In 1635, young Parisian playwright Pierre Corneille composed his first tragedy, *Médée*, for performance by the troupe du Marais. Corneille's previous plays had been comedies or tragicomedies, a blended genre especially popular at the time, and his translation of *Medea* follows this generic inclination. Corneille would go on to become one of the foremost tragedians of the seventeenth century, the so-called *grand siècle* of French drama, his later works including Roman history plays *Horace* (1640), *Cinna* (1641), *The Death of Pompey* (1643), and a version of Seneca's *Oedipus* (1659). In 1660, he composed the libretto for a fantastical opera on the theme of the quest for the Golden Fleece (*La Toison d'Or*).[20] Corneille's career as a playwright spans the three decades during which the neoclassical *Règles* ('Rules') of dramatic composition were first introduced into French theatre.[21] His *Trois discours sur la poème dramatique* (*Three Essays on Dramatic Poetry*, 1660) were an attempt to reconcile the theory behind regulation with what he perceived as the demands of professional practice, and to defend the dramaturgical choices made earlier in his career, including in *Médée*. As Corneille maintains in *Médée*'s dedicatory preface, 'The point of dramatic poetry is to give pleasure, and the Rules which are prescribed to us are nothing more than guidelines (*addresses*) to make the poet's job easier'. It is on the same pragmatic grounds that he defends the 'crime' against verisimilitude of representing Médée's flying chariot onstage.[22] It was only retrospectively, however, that such flights of fantasy had become inconceivable in a proper, well-regulated tragedy. *Médée* slipped in just prior to the 1635 foundation of the regulatory Académie Française, and the history of Senecan reception is the richer for it.

Seneca, and *Medea* in particular, already had a presence in French tragedy prior to Corneille. In fact, the earliest translation of a classical tragedy into French was the *Médée* of Jean de la Péruse, written in an academic setting, the Collège du Boncourt, in 1553. Corneille, indeed, may have been familiar with La Péruse's translation,[23] although apart from their common source-text the two versions are quite dissimilar. Aside from interpolating Euripides' messenger-speech, La Péruse sticks closely to Seneca, whereas Corneille diverges considerably in response to the preferences of his popular marketplace. Despite its academic treatment, there is evidence that La Péruse's *Médée* made it into the repertoire of one of the touring companies of players who staged vernacular tragedy. An outdoor production in 1572 is recorded which included fireworks (*feux artificiels*) and other *singularités*, or special effects, one of which was presumably a chariot drawn by dragons.[24]

In 1629, a watershed in French theatrical history occurred when the Comédiens du Roi (the 'King's Men') took out a permanent lease on a performance space in the Hôtel du Bourgogne. The Théâtre du Marais soon followed in 1634. The Marais was not purpose-built, but rather adapted from a games room, a *salle des jeux-de-paume*, which was converted into a long, narrow auditorium with the stage at one end. It was not at all suitable for productions of serious drama. The sightlines were restricted and the acoustics poor, and the audience did not expect to sit in silence, but 'brawled, tippled, diced and wenched' throughout the performance.[25] The stage itself was occupied on both sides by boisterous spectators who punctuated the performance by heckling and harassing the cast.[26] When Corneille protests that the point of theatre is to be entertaining, it is the raucous *parterre* (stalls) of the Marais that he has in mind.

Permanent indoor performance venues, on the other hand, also afforded new possibilities for staging. Backdrops, scenery, trapdoors, and in particular mechanized special effects such as flight became available. Contemporary stage convention made use of a practice which became known as *décor simultané*, in which different parts of the stage represented different locations, indicated by an item of set such as a ship, an arbour, or a prison cell. Unused items were simply covered by a curtain until the setting was required, at which point it was revealed, casting its identity temporarily over the stage-space as a whole. This playful acknowledgement that stage-space is fluid and its referentiality transient contrasts with the central principle of neoclassical and other naturalistic forms of theatre, *unité de lieu* or 'unity of place', according to which all action must occur in a single setting so as not to break its hold on the imagination with disruptive set-changes. For earlier French dramatists, however, these disruptions could be an opportunity for creating spectacular effects and periodically re-engaging an audience who were not otherwise obliged to remain attentive. The extant set-designs of Laurent Mahelot, resident scenographer at the Bourgogne and later the Comédie Française, show both how elaborate some of these early sets could be, and how they developed over a thirty-year period to accommodate a more minimalist and concentrated aesthetic. Unfortunately, we do not possess the designs for Corneille's *Médée*, but Corneille's explicit Act 5 stage direction that Médée appears *en l'air, dans un char tiré par deux dragons* ('aloft, in a chariot pulled by two dragons') may be illustrated with reference to Mahelot's comparable record of a contemporary tragicomedy, Jean Rotrou's *Hercule Mourant* (1634):

> In the fifth act, a thunderclap, then the heavens open, and Hercules descends from on high in a cloud: the globe should be surrounded by the twelve signs [of the zodiac] and the twelve winds, burning stars, the sun in a transparent sphere, and other fantastical ornaments, according to the artist's fancy.[27]

Corneille, then, was adapting Seneca's *Medea* to be staged in a theatrical context governed by its own constraints, expectations, and technical possibilities. Unlike La Péruse seventy years earlier, he had the advantage of a permanent public theatre and theatre-going public; unlike later playwrights for whom unity of place was *de rigeur*, he could exploit less restrictive scenographic conventions. The resulting play is evidently an incarnation of Seneca's *Medea*, but filtered through the French Baroque enthusiasm for charm, illusion, the unpredictable and the incredible.[28] *Médée* captures Senecan tragedy at a particularly unruly moment in its performance history.

What makes Corneille's adaptation such a clear-cut and entertaining case study in reception is its juxtaposition of passages closely translated from Seneca with episodes that have no ancient antecedent. The play's denouement, meanwhile, draws on other Senecan tragedies to produce a climax even more gruesome than envisaged for *Medea* by either Seneca or Euripides. Although mentioned in the play's prefatory

Examen, Euripides actually furnishes little apart from the (almost unrecognizable) character of Aegeus / Aegée. Corneille's *Médée* is a Senecan creation. At the same time, however, it also displays considerable divergences. Structurally, the absence of a chorus strips the tragedy of the thematic and philosophical resonances which their odes bring to Seneca. The introduction of new characters onstage (Aegée, the princess Créuse, and interlocutors Pollux and Cléone) disperses perspectives and transforms Médée's single-minded pursuit of revenge into one facet of a political refraction. Her ability to overcome any opposition simply by exerting her magical powers comes to seem, in this new world of statecraft and strategy, rather unfair, like a fist through a chessboard.[29]

Corneille opens with a dialogue between Jason and his old pal Pollux, conveniently just arrived in Corinth and therefore requiring an exposition of Jason's recent adventures. Jason relates how Médée used her magic to restore his father's youth, then tricked the daughters of usurping tyrant Pélie by promising them marvels (*merveilles*) and 'filling their ears with the power of her art' (1.1, 62), which could refer equally to her magical art and the art of her persuasive oratory. Like a mountebank, she contrived Pélie's death by setting up a scene of faked magic, preparing a cauldron containing only water and *herbes sans force*. Pollux describes the carnage resulting from her theatrical proficiency as a *tragique spectacle*, (1.1.89), highlighting both its generic affiliation and its macabre showmanship and foreshadowing Médée's forthcoming spectacular revenge. It is in her capacity as sorceress, not in her role as abandoned wife, that Médée is introduced. Indeed, hearing of Jason's plan to remarry, Pollux warns him that however politically expedient, he runs the greater risk of incurring Médée's resentment, and 'You know better than me what her spells (*charmes*) can do' (1.1, 145).

Médée's first appearance takes Senecan form. Instead of lamenting indoors or soliciting sympathetic collusion, she blasts onstage calling on the gods of marriage to witness her betrayal, and alongside them the 'troupe vicious in your dark savagery, / daughters of Acheron, ghosts, Furies / fierce sisters . . . / and your serpents' (1.4, 206–8); this picks up Seneca's *nunc, nunc adeste, sceleris ultrices deae, / crinem solutis squalidae serpentibus* (*Med.* 13–14) from Act 1, possibly merged with *vulgus silentum vosque ferales deos* (*Med.* 740) from Act 4.[30] She is incredulous that Jason, even having seen first-hand every atrocity that she has committed – her father betrayed, the elements brought under her command (*forcés*), and a brother's limbs scattered on the water – still dares to oppose her:

Tu t'abuses, Jason, je suis encore moi-même.
Tout ce qu'en ta faveur fit mon amour extrême,
Je le ferai par haine; et je veux pour le moins
Qu'un forfeit nous sépare, ainsi qu'il nous a joints;
Que mon sanglant divorce, en meurtres, en carnage,
S' égale aux premiers jours de notre marriage,
Et que notre union, que rompt ton changement,
Trouve un fin pareille à son commencement.

1.4, 237–44

You are mistaken, Jason, I am still myself.
Everything I did to oblige you from excessive love
I will now do from hate; at least, I want
that we should separate in crime, just as we were joined:
that my bloodstained divorce, in murder, in slaughter,
should equal the first days of our marriage,
and that our union, which your infidelity has torn apart,
should find an end that corresponds to its beginning.

Seneca's verses are rearranged, but the sentiment of reciprocity and structure of payback remain. Her former crimes were mere *coups d'essai*, practice shots, and now 'I must accomplish my masterpiece (*chef d'oeuvre*), and my final work (*ouvrage*) / must surpass by a long way my feeble apprenticeship' (1.4, 247–50.) Corneille has retained Seneca's language of self-development and craftsmanship, Médée depicting herself as an artisan honing her skills or an author preparing the crowning achievement of her career. His purpose is not to produce a line-by-line translation of his source-text, but rather to pick out those passages that still make compelling theatrical sense when spoken by a seventeenth-century Medea.

Another Senecan retention is the keyword *fureur* (*furor*), which is applied to Médée's state of mind by various characters, including Médée herself, on numerous occasions throughout the play.[31] As Médée announces her intention to swoop down on Corinth in the chariot of the Sun, smash the Isthmus, and allow the seas to converge – cf. lines 32–6 in Seneca – her companion Nérine (Seneca's Nutrix) advises silence and dissembling. 'What is left to you?' asks Nérine, and Médée gives her quintessentially Senecan answer, *Moi: moi, dis-je, et c'est assez* ('Me: me, I say, and that is enough', 1.4, 317). She elaborates: 'Yes, you see in me alone (*seule*) iron and flame, / the earth and the sea, Hell and the heavens, / the sceptre of kings and the thunderbolt of the gods' (cf. Seneca, *Med.* 166–7). This isolation, of Médée *seule* (alone), is a Senecan hallmark. Alone she makes her entrance, cursing; alone she will cast her master-spell; alone, she will escape in the finale. Whereas the concentration of Seneca's text into the mouth of this overwhelmingly dominant figure makes his whole play almost a monologue, however, Corneille counterposes other relationships and interactions, notably between Jason and his new wife Créuse, thereby placing her solitude in relief. This allows Corneille to weave an alternative plot in which Créuse intercedes with Créon on Jason's behalf to request that his children be allowed to remain in Corinth; she then demands that he fetch her a jewelled robe belonging to Médée as recompense for her pains. Médée's poisoned gift therefore exploits Créuse's own greed and insensitivity.

Créon's exchange with Médée is shorter than in either of the ancient playwrights, its main import being that Créuse has successfully persuaded him to reprieve the children from exile. Nevertheless, Corneille does take from Seneca Créon's almost superstitious fear of Médée; he instructs his guards to prevent her from approaching him, and orders her, 'Go, purge my land of a monster such as you' (*Va, purge mes États d'un monstre tel que toi* (2.2, 376); cf. Sen. *Med.* 190–1, <u>*vade*</u> *veloci via / <u>monstrum</u>que saevum horribile iamdudum avehe*, and also 269: *Egredere, <u>purge regna</u>*). With Médée consigned to exile and Jason's allegiance secured, the only remaining impediment to Créon's plans is the comic sub-plot, Aegée. Créuse's former suitor, Aegée is less than impressed to have been thrown over for 'a fugitive, a traitor, a murderer of kings' (2.5, 615). Créuse rationalizes her decision to Aegée in person. Not only love, but sound political reasoning motivated her: instead of moving to Athens as Aegée's wife, leaving Corinth without an heir, she can remain as queen in her own homeland with Jason installed as Créon's successor. Fuming impotently, Aegée resolves to punish this insult to his rank and dignity with an armed assault on the Corinthian citadel, a threat which he follows through unsuccessfully in Act 3.

Aegée is a stock comic character, the *viellard amoureux* or besotted old man. That his age makes him risibly incongruous as a romantic match for Créuse is emphasized on several occasions. Even Créon remarks that un *viellard amoureux mérite qu'on rie* ('An amorous old man deserves to be laughed at', 2.3, 534), even though he swiftly clarifies that Aegée's royal status exempts him from mockery. Aegée is not so self-assured. 'Go on,' he growls, 'laugh at my passion, laugh at your shame: / favour those among your courtiers / who best deride my declining years . . . / Youth may have left me, but courage has not; / Kings do not in any way lose their strength with age' (2.5, 690–8). Nevertheless, his attack is an ignominious failure, and Aegée is thrown into prison. Structurally, Aegée and Médée complement one another, their interests coinciding in their opposition to Créon and Créuse's dynastic plans, each of them having been rejected by one of the royal newlyweds. In other respects, they are diametrically contrasted, not least in Médée's embodiment of high tragedy while Aegée, not altogether unwittingly (however reluctantly) plays the buffoon.

As in Euripides, it is Aegée who offers Médée asylum in Athens. Corneille, however, motivates this offer by having Médée rescue him from prison. The rescue is staged as a magical *coup de théâtre*: Médée strikes the prison gate with her wand, and it opens of its own accord; she then gives another blow to the iron chains that hold the Athenian king, and they fall away. 'Recognise Médée by this sign', she tells Aegée, spectacular feats of magic being her trademark. Recognition is also part of her arc of development in Seneca, as in her mocking question to Jason, *coniugem <u>agnoscis</u> tuam* ('Do you recognize your wife?', *Med.*

1021). Whereas Euripides' Aegeus is reluctant to jeopardize relations with Corinth and limits his assistance strictly to asylum, Aegée in gratitude offers Médée anything she wants, including the backing of his army. She refuses, however, on the grounds that it would demean her to scrounge for help from any human source (4.5, 1255). 'Is there, after all, any who can withstand me?' she asks. 'Does one who has Nature at her command have need of assistance?' (4.5, 1258). Like a fairy-tale princess, Aegée has been magically rescued from his tower, his release coinciding precisely with Créuse's receipt of the poisoned robe. If Médée's dramatic trademark is spectacle, Corneille's is symmetry.

Corneille retains from Seneca the extent of Médée's magical powers and the way in which they are exercised, through control over the natural world. Nérine gives a glimpse of the type of vengeance we might expect:

> One word, and the heavens send thunderbolts from on high;
> The oceans await only her order to submerge everything;
> The earth offers to open up beneath the palace of the king;
> The air holds the winds ready to follow her anger.
> Thus has fear made Nature the servant of her displeasure.
> And if all these elemental forces are not enough,
> Hell itself will issue forth at her command.
>
> 3.1, 714–20

Corneille's formulation is more condensed and formulaic than Seneca's, and rather more generic, essentially elaborating on Médée's claim to embody 'seas, and lands, and gods, and thunderbolts' (Sen. *Med.* 166–7) with a tour through ocean, earth, and air, bracketed by deities celestial and infernal. Corneille has dropped the geographical specificities of Seneca's comparanda, such as the Sicilian whirlpool Charybdis and Mt Etna (408–10) or the rivers Rhone and Hister in spate (583–90) which align Seneca's Medea and her rage with iconic features of the Roman world. Similarly, the effects of Médée's spells, such as the seasons reversed or the river Phasis flowing backwards (Sen. *Med.* 760–4) are no longer in evidence. It is merely her general authority over the elements that is asserted, along with a Senecan emphasis on the power of her voice to issue *commandements* and lay down *lois*. A single word (*mot*) could cause a lightning strike. Médée's is still a very vocal magic.

Although Corneille retains the scene of spell-casting, positioned similarly at the start of Act 4, it is considerably shorter, and curtailed by Nérine's report of Aegée's failed attack on the palace. Nevertheless, it is a recognizably Senecan passage. The ingredients of the *liqueur* in which Médée steeps her robe follow a basically Senecan recipe: 'You see how many serpents, at my command, / have not lost a moment in coming here from Africa,' she croons, compressing the Nutrix's twenty-five-line exposition into a couple of couplets. She moves onto Seneca's plants, again dispensing with the geographical catalogue, but presenting a haunting image of herself 'making the moon turn pale, / when, hair floating loose, arms and feet bare, / I plucked them long ago in an undiscovered country' (*climat inconnu*), 4.1, 995–6. The loosened hair and bare feet are borrowed from elsewhere in Seneca's Act 4 (752–3, *Tibi more gentis vinculo solvens comam / secreta nudo nemora lustravi pede)*, and the moon's pallor from another stage of the ritual where the lunar goddess appears *facie livida* and *pallida* (790, 793). What Corneille does include at length are Médée's mythological ingredients, such as the blood of the Hydra and Nessus, the Harpies' black plumage, Althaea's branch and fire that fell from the sky along with Phaethon (4.1, 997–1008). Médée conducts the scene *seule, dans sa grotte magique*, emphasizing both her isolation (*seule*) and her relationship with stage-space.[32] *Décor simultané* permitted this special *penetrale funestum* to be realized scenographically. Unlike much of Corneille's dialogue, which takes place in unspecified locations, Médée requires sets to shift and coalesce around her even as she stretches and transforms their capacities. She permits the *grotte magique* to open up; she visits Aegée's prison, only to render its pretend bars and chains ineffectual as restraints; and she will break all theatrical rules at the end of the play by turning a mechanical platform from a balcony into a *char tiré par deux dragons* (while all along we know it is still being played by a mechanical platform).

The spatial confusion engendered by Médée reaches its climax in an unprecedented scene, inserted by Corneille, in which Créon and Créuse die horribly in full view. Owing nothing to Seneca's *Medea*, although perhaps something more to Euripides, the passage it most closely resembles is Hercules' fiery death in the pseudo-Senecan *Hercules on Mt Oeta*. Hercules has likewise been poisoned by a robe soaked in the blood of the centaur Nessus, and he relates how it is eating away his flesh and consuming him from within. This surreal coupling of an eloquent verbal commentary with the inner agony it purports to display is likewise performed by Créuse, who – instead of simply screaming – describes both her own movements ('I stagger, I fall', 5.3, 1439) and her own sensations ("This fire which consumes me, inside and out . . . / This burning which devours me, which I deserve, / surpasses in its cruelty the Promethean eagle', 5.3, 1404–6). In what may be a further reference to *Hercules Oetaeus*, Jason compares his wife's suffering to a scorpion's sting, recalling Hercules' perception of the poison as 'a scorpion in my entrails' (*HO.* 1218). It is possible that Corneille's exposure to *Hercules Oetaeus* came via Jean Rotrou's translation, *Hercule Mourant*, which had premiered the previous year. Classical mythology, self-referential commentary, and poetic hyperbole spill from Créuse's tongue even as she expires: 'I burn, I die, I am nothing but a flame,' she exclaims (5.3, 1437), a typically Senecan representational technique in which the rhetorical density of the language intensifies according to the extremity of the pain it is supposed to express.[33]

In another, somewhat shocking departure from both ancient precursors, Corneille's Jason proposes to kill the children himself, to sacrifice the *petits ingrats* at Créuse's tomb 'so the witch (*sorcière*) will start to suffer through you, / so that her first torment will be to see your death' (5.4, 1567–8). It then transpires that Médée has beaten him to it: she appears aloft to gloat, first *sur un balcon*, and then, abruptly, 'in the air, in a chariot drawn by two dragons', which Jason watches helplessly as it disappears in a puff of smoke (*ce char volant, disparu dans un nue*, 5.7, 1613). After a rambling monologue of self-reproach, Corneille's Jason then commits suicide, the final stage direction: *il se tue*.

Médée is referred to four times as *sorcière* in this closing scene,[34] and indeed magic has been her defining feature throughout. Corneille's adaptation has extracted and magnified the Senecan (Ovidian) witch, and placed her on a stage where her showmanship could be exploited to the full. Ironically, this experiment was to be almost the last of its kind in the French Baroque reception of classical tragedy. Spectacular flourishes and an embrace of the *merveilleux* moved sideways into opera and masque, as 'straight' theatre came to define its representational mode by an adherence to spatial unity, credible action, and appropriate behaviour or *bienséances*. Seneca's transcendent rhetoric and Medea's utter disregard for human boundaries created a potent brew, however, and even as the parameters of Western theatricality shifted, she continued to find places to resurface.

6

Becoming Medea

Seneca's *Medea* exists – and has existed – in a multiplicity of states. The play is not only a text, and a textual history; it is also a composite history of translations, performances, and reader or audience experience, a polyvalent entity comprising both written instantiations (the script, the edition) and renditions that are material or performative.[1] The meaning and potential meanings of an ancient play are not exhausted by their manifestation as text. As scholarship on performance and performance reception has shown, the manifold contingent factors which impinge on staging are equally determinant of how a work of dramatic poetry may be (and has been) understood. In the absence of an ur-performance in antiquity, Senecan tragedies are in fact less tethered to ideas of 'original' staging than their Greek counterparts, which can be a liberating condition.

There is often some difficulty in disentangling the strands of Euripides in any given reception of *Medea* from those of Seneca, and it may depend on whether we consider the presence of Senecan traits in themselves to constitute a form of reception, or only the declared affiliation of a production; whether direct contact needs to be established between the modern playwright and (an edition of) the Latin text; whether a Medea can ever take place which is not in some way shadowed by Seneca, as consciously or unconsciously each Euripidean attribution participates in a philhellenic discourse with a stake in constructing Medea (the archetypal outsider, the stateless cosmopolitan, the Black Sea princess, Seneca's global backlash) as Greek.[2] It is true that the reception history of Euripides, particularly in the nineteenth and twentieth centuries, offers more to choose from. This chapter surveys some instances of Seneca's Medea in performance,[3] some stating their relationship aloud while others more covertly embed identifiable motifs, sometimes as brief as a single line, a single word (*Je reste!*). Such glancing references may be recognized as receptions of a sort insofar as they represent a point where something Senecan survives, where some part of the Roman concept of 'Medea' or *Medea*, formal or verbal, structural or thematic, has been retained.

6.1 Reconciliations

Whereas Euripides entertains no possibility of a reconciliation, Seneca's Medea gives her ex-husband one last opportunity to reconsider. 'Do a crime for me', she dares him, proposing that they skip town again together leaving Corinth in flames behind them, Bonnie reunited with Clyde, the genre suddenly flipped to picaresque. Two playwrights who pursue a similar course are Richard Glover, writing in 1761, and Jean Anouilh in 1946. Glover's version of *Medea* contains some Senecan elements, but at the same time is typical of trends in eighteenth-century theatre. A shift in theatrical aesthetics had drained the blood out of English classical tragedy, although by the 1790s it began to bubble up elsewhere into Gothic melodrama.[4] A turn towards domestication meant that audiences preferred to see characters whose troubles they could more easily relate to: 'sorrows like your own', as one prologue promised.[5] This was accompanied by a distaste for the extravagant rhetoric and stylized 'heroic' monologue that had persisted on the English stage until well after the Restoration, and a preference for characters who expressed their dilemmas in dialogue, and even, on occasion, in prose. As attending the theatre became a social marker of gentility, more delicacy was required in the stage representation of violence and gore. In a production of Seneca's *Thyestes* from 1707, for example, the king's cannibal gorging was transmuted into a single goblet of blood from which he symbolically sipped.[6] Female violence was particularly problematic. Who could possibly relate to a woman who committed murder, and worse still, who became the murderer of her own children? Glover's solution, as Edith Hall argues, was to compromise Medea's agency.[7] In order that she should appear less responsible for the act, he has her stricken by insanity and unaware of what she is doing. In this way, he satisfied the double purpose of making Medea both a suffering heroine – a bereaved mother – and a sympathetic character whose circumstances could generate pathos: an appropriately tragic victim. An engraving of actress Mary Ann Yates in the role (Figure 6.1)

Figure 6.1 Mary Ann Yates in the character of Medea, by William Dickinson after Robert Edge Pine (1771). NPG D36243 © National Portrait Gallery, London.

shows her silhouetted against a thunderous sky. A weeping child tugs at her skirt and a dagger's hilt protrudes from her robes. Her fists are clenched, arms outflung on a taut diagonal, like lightning caught mid-strike. Her eyes, wide and frantic, are fixed on invisible visions.

Despite this departure from Senecan ferocity, however, some aspects of Glover's *Medea* are recognizably derived from her Roman antecedent.[8] Crucial among these is a climactic spell-casting scene in which Medea summons Hecate from the Underworld. Her signature prop is a magic wand, as in Corneille, a 'potent rod / which grew a branch of ebony o'ershadowing / the throne of Pluto' and has been ritually dipped in the river Lethe. The wand (*tristis Stygia ramus ab unda*, 805) is only one of Medea's many Senecan accoutrements, but in Glover's adaptation it acquires its own focal identity. Medea calls on the goddess whose power stops the moon in its course, 'controlls [sic] the rapid planet's speed / and dims the constellation's fires' (3.6, p33). Compelled by Medea's 'strong constraining spell', Hecate ascends in the aspect of a Fury, 'wreath'd in snakes' and bearing a flaring firebrand. Unable to secure relief from the pangs of desperate love, Medea settles for vengeance, but follows up with a querulous query from her 'yearning heart': 'Will Jason ever more be kind?' (3.7, p. 35).

The contradiction haunting Glover's Medea throughout is that despite her hyperbolic boasting, her magical abilities are utterly powerless where it counts. She might be able to 'range with Nature to her utmost bounds' and 'rock the iron throne of Pluto' (3.4, p. 32), but none of this will bring Jason back to her. This produces an uneasy discrepancy between what Medea asserts she can accomplish and the helplessness she actually exhibits, fainting and weeping and sighing like a textbook sentimental heroine. Glover partially resolves this by having Medea 'scorn the arts / which may command his person, not his love' (3.8, p. 36). Another option, of course, would have been to suppress Medea's supernatural abilities altogether, as many later playwrights have done, following Euripides.[9] It seems, then, that the Senecan Medea still exerted an irresistible pull on Glover, who was prepared to dispense neither with the irony of an all-powerful creature brought to abjection, nor the dramatic effect of the spell-casting scene.

Medea's hallucinatory madness also takes Senecan form, as she relates a terrible vision:

> Ha! What art thou, grim shape embru'd with gore?
> Why dost thou wave that Stygian torch around?
> Art thou Revenge from Tartarus enlarg'd?
> To aid Medea? Come then, shake thy brand
> Before my steps.
>
> 4.3, p. 42

The apparition is not her brother, however, but a personification of Revenge. Absyrtus is not among the victims of Glover's protagonist. Neither, in fact, are Creon and Creusa. Instead, Jason stands up to Creon and renounces the princess of his own accord. He imagines a future in which he and Medea, reconciled, stroll by the moonlit river while 'her tongue / Unfolds the pow'rs of heav'n's resplendent train, / Of magic numbers, and mysterious spells, / And feasts with knowledge my enraptur'd soul' (4.13, p. 49). Ironically, Jason's change of heart comes too late, and Medea, raving, has already stabbed both children. Her declaration of victory is as Senecan as her vision of revenge, and similarly framed as delusional:

> Now to complete my vengeance I shall mount
> The burning chariot of my bright forefather;
> The rapid steeds o'er Corinth will I drive,
> And with the scatter'd lightnings from their manes
> Consume its walls, its battlements and tow'rs,
> Its princes, people, palaces and temples:
> Then, as the flames embrace the purple clouds,
> And the proud city crumbles from its base,
> The demon of my rage and indignation
> All grim and wrapt in terror shall bestride
> The mountainous embers, and denounce abroad
> To gods and men my wrongs and my revenge.
>
> 5.2, p. 52

As Robert Miola has argued in relation to Shakespeare's use of Senecan leitmotifs,[10] this type of excessive discourse can only find a place in domesticated tragedy if it is offset in some way from the main action; the character speaking is insane, for example, or playing a role. Only insanity could now license the type of speech which made perfect sense when spoken, for instance, by Christopher Marlowe's godlike Tamburlaine in the 1580s.[11]

During the nineteenth century, Medea lost her Senecan aspect in favour of the pathos of the abandoned wife and mother.[12] It is not until Jean Anouilh's post-war *Médée* in 1946 that the Senecan tigress comes snarling back, variously characterized as a hyena, an eagle, a vulture, and a wolf, a 'cornered beast' who identifies shamanistically with the 'beasts of the night' as she senses them hunting and killing 'under water and grass, in the trees, under the earth'. She addresses them as 'My sisters! Medea is a beast like you! Medea is going to glow and kill like you! [...] I utter with you your obscure scream ... Beasts, I am you! All that is hunting and killing tonight is Medea' (pp. 356–7).[13] This invocation occupies the position of Seneca's spell, replacing the chthonic with the carnivorous but still reiterating Medea's unbreakable connection with wild Nature.

Although diverging considerably from his ancient source-text, Anouilh also keeps points of contact in some of the key lines spoken by Médée. As editor E. Freeman observes, Anouilh made liberal use of the 1924 translation of Seneca's collected tragedies by Léon Herrmann, several of these lines being identical word for word with Herrmann's.[14] The trope of 'becoming Medea' is pursued so vigorously that it verges on parody. When Jason's betrayal is reported to her, Médée exclaims, 'Oh, lost strength (*O force perdue*)! I have found myself again. Have I been dreaming? Now I am Medea (*C'est moi. C'est Médée*, p. 333)!' She continues: 'Tonight it is over, Nurse, I am become Medea again. How good it is [...] Jason, you put her to sleep, but now Medea is awakening again' (p. 335). The Nourrice asks her what she intends to do, and she replies, 'What I did for him when I betrayed my father, when I had to kill my brother so we could escape. What I did to old Pelias ... But this time, at long last, I do it for myself [. . .] What can I not do? . . . I am Medea, all alone (*toute seule*), in front of this wagon . . . but nothing is too much for me!' (p. 335) – in other words, *incipe / quidquid potest Medea, quidquid non potest* (Sen. *Med.* 566–7). 'What have you left?' the Nourrice prompts, and Médée gives the expected response: *Moi!* (p336).

Her defence to Creon is also taken straight from Seneca: 'Do not let me go alone. Give the ship back to the exile. Give her companion back to her. I was not alone when I came. Why discriminate between us now?' (pp. 340–1, cf. *Profuge cogis? Redde fugienti ratem / vel redde comitem. Fugere cur solam iubes? / Non sola veni . . . Cur sontes duos distinguis?*, 272–6). Her crimes, she argues, are also Jason's. Addressing Jason himself, she uses Senecan language:

> I am running away, Jason! Running away! There is nothing new for me in changing my abode. Only the cause of my flight is new, for until now it was for you that I fled. [. . .] Where do you want me to go? Where are you sending me? Shall I get to the Phasis, or Colchis, my father's kingdom, the fields soaked with my brother's blood? You are driving me away. To what country do you order me without you? What unexplored seas . . . All the paths I opened for you I have closed for myself. I am Medea, loaded with horror and crimes.
>
> p. 343

Finally, as she immolates herself and her children in their burning caravan, she cries ecstatically, in Herrmann's words, and beneath them Seneca's:

> Now I have found my scepter again. My brother, my father and the fleece of the golden ram are given back to Colchis. I have found my country again and the virginity which you tore from me. I am Medea at last and forever!
>
> p. 360

Despite these Senecan assertions, Anouilh's central scene, the confrontation between Médée and her estranged husband, is unique. In place of violent histrionics and flimsy self-justification, Anouilh charts the irreparable breakdown of a mature relationship with blame, infidelity, and regret on both sides. The sometime adventurers have grown incompatible. Jason feels for Médée, but no longer loves her, and can no longer live in her chaotic world. Intractable, intransigent, she is steeped in the guilt and bitterness he is determined to put behind him and forget. Whereas Seneca flirts with the possibility of a marital reconciliation, and Glover experiments with the irony of changing Jason's mind too late, Anouilh depicts a couple inextricable in their mutual loathing and the length of their history together. 'If I told you I was going to try with you now, would you believe me?' Médée asks. 'No,' Jason replies, and Médée responds, after a pause, 'You would be right' (p. 354). And yet, as Jason walks away, she calls out after him, pleading that if he turned back, he could 'save us all' (p. 355). For a moment, it is possible; but Jason keeps walking. The tragedy returns to its accustomed course.

6.2 Rituals

In the same year, 1946, the tragedy of *Medea* was reworked as dance in *Cave of the Heart*, choreographed and first performed by trailblazer of modern ballet, Martha Graham. Nurit Yaari contends that 'Martha Graham's dances are anchored in the Classical Greek tradition',[15] and Graham certainly belongs among the century's great interpreters of ancient myth, but ignoring the Senecan elements in a piece such as *Cave* risks attributing to Euripides some vital aspects of Graham's Medea which do not actually derive from the Greek playwright's version.[16] *Cave of the Heart* belongs to a mid-century move to recover what were perceived as the ritual elements of ancient theatre, a perception that also informed Jorge Lavelli's 1967 *Médée* and Pasolini's film of 1970.

Cave, originally entitled *The Serpent Heart*, condenses the action and relationships of *Medea* into the tragedy's essential love-triangle – Medea, Jason, and the Princess – to explore Medea's catastrophic, corrosive jealousy. The children are not included. Like Corneille,

Graham chooses to focus on Medea's murder of the Princess, who here assumes the role of innocent victim. The climax of the ballet is a visceral solo which Graham describes in an interview as referencing an allegorical woodcut of Envy / *Invidia*, in which a woman is eating her own heart.[17] Agnes de Mille captures the solo's abject fury:

> It was a dance of such animal anger and frustration as to defy sense and sensibilities. It almost evoked disgust. And it was done on the knees, a long *pas de bourrée* on the knees, including a passage of quivering, carnivorous rage in which Medea would half squat, half kneel, and vibrate her knees in and out like a hungry insect in spasms of evisceration and digestion – an effect which makes the blood run cold.[18]

Medea's 'heart', or what could equally be called in Senecan terms her *cor* or her *animus*, is represented in the solo passage by a glistening, rust-red ribbon, about a metre long, which Medea (played in the filmed version by Takako Asakawa) withdraws from her breast and addresses interactively. She pulls it taut around her waist like corset strings, she swims towards it, kneels before it, adores it like a fetish, whips it with her hair; she chews it up and spits it out, her face a mask-like rictus of possession. Having devoured this more than cannibal meal, this displaced organ, she is consumed by it in turn as it coils itself around her and she bends repeatedly from the waist, scooping it up in a final, pulsating, clawing handful. At the end of the movement, she steps inside a slender wire frame that shivers as she turns her face skywards, enclosing her like a spider's web, a halo, a cage. This dialogue between Medea and her externalized *animus*, or the jealous rage which she was initially responsible for generating but which has come to take her over, is central to Seneca's version and its Stoic treatment of human passions. Graham's choreography shows Medea animating an independent object which then appears to be animating her body in turn as she wrestles with it, as it spins her around and bends her double. *Quo te, igitur, mittis?* gasps Seneca's Medea. 'Anger, where are you sending me?' (*Med.* 916). There is no vacillation or resistance in Graham's dance, but the separation of corporeal self from the driving force of a murderous wrath is certainly made manifest.

Snakes, as Oliver Taplin has demonstrated,[19] do not feature in Euripides, but they are everywhere in Seneca. The Furies bring them from the Underworld (*crinem solutis squalidae serpentibus*, 14; *ingens anguis excusso sonat / tortus flagello*, 961–2); Medea summons *omne serpentum genus* (705) in order to decant their poison (684–704), and departs in a chariot drawn emphatically by *gemini serpentes* with scaly backs (1023).[20] Graham's original title, *The Serpent Heart*, indicates that snakes were very much part of the ballet's initial conception. The ribbon which Medea dances with resembles a snake as it twists and writhes around her, and her costume is likewise covered in serpentine designs. In her rehearsal notes, Graham refers to the passage as her 'snake solo' and to the prop as a 'snake', e.g. 'fall forward to pick up snake – eating snake... Spasm-like contraction toward snake'.[21] *Cave*'s designer, Isamu Noguchi, explains how he understood the snake as a ritualistic symbol:

> We start with the snake. The snake is water. It is the passage from which the gods evolve ... One finds the worship of the snake from the American Indian all the way to the Greeks. So I used the snake. In *Cave of the Heart*, Medea dances with a red cloth in her mouth. She is dancing with the snake in her mouth. Then she spews it out of her mouth like blood.[22]

Ritual, and snake-based ritual in particular, occurs centrally in Seneca, but has no part in Euripides' play. Similarly, although Yaari feels that Medea's magical identity is understated,[23] Graham herself described the dance as derived from 'the legend of a sorceress' (rather than, for example, that of a mother who kills her children).[24] It is an elemental, visceral, Senecan Medea in thrall to her own venomous *furor* that Martha Graham chooses to portray.

Narrative dance (*tragoedia saltata*) and excerpted aria (*tragoedia cantata*) were two of the most common performance media for tragedy in Seneca's Rome, and, as discussed in Chapter 1, both art-forms left traces in the dramaturgy of *Medea*. Medea, as McDonald and Reynolds have shown, has been a perennially popular subject for opera, not least because the role shows off star performers to great advantage.[25] As always, however, there is a tendency to overlook the Senecan attributes of *Medea*'s operatic adaptations in favour of Euripides. The twentieth century's most famous incarnation of Medea, the diva who also came to define what is commonly meant by 'prima donna', Maria Callas, appeared first in the Cherubini opera and later in a film version of *Medea* directed by Pier Paolo Pasolini. Both the opera and the film have Senecan affinities, meaning that Callas's embodiment of Medea is also in part an indirect reception of *tragoedia cantata*.

Cherubini's opera, composed in 1797, was revived in Florence in 1953. Callas went on to perform it internationally, including productions in the USA (1958), Covent Garden (1959), and Epidaurus (1961). Medea became a role which defined her, personally and professionally.[26] In 1970, her operatic career behind her, Callas was then cast by Pasolini in his modernist art-house film. Cherubini's libretto, originally in French, was translated into Italian by Carlo Zangarini, and this is the text sung by Callas. It contains a number of Senecan motifs, accessed most plausibly by way of Corneille. Foremost among these is Medea's reflexive reiteration of her identity and her name. Arriving ominously and anonymously at Jason's wedding feast, she is recognized first by her voice: *Quale voce!* Jason exclaims. Creon demands to know who the stranger is: *Io? Medea!* she replies, and the Chorus set up a terrified echo of *Medea, Medea*. Her voice at first low and cajoling – the coloratura fireworks will come later – she delivers her threat. Neris (Corneille's Nérine, or Seneca's Nutrix) warns Medea that she should fly from Corinth, as all is lost. *Io resto*, Medea insists, or in French, *Je reste*, I remain, Corneille's translation of Seneca's *Medea superest*. The Latin implication – and Corneille's – is that she herself is what remains when everything else is gone, a remainder, a survival. Cherubini's libretto shifts the action of remaining to one of persistence or endurance: I remain, I do not leave.

Deciding on a suitable revenge for Jason, Cherubini's Medea seeks a punishment *più grave, più orrido* (worse and more horrific) than

Creusa's death: *All' onta crudel la vendetta sia par. / Ah, s'egli un padre, se fratelli avesse! / Che? Non ha dei figli? / Ah, dove mi parti, / sdegnato mio cor?* ('My revenge will equal my shame in cruelty. / Ah, if he only had a father, brothers! / What? Does he not have sons? / Ah, where am I going, / my outraged heart?'). Seneca's Medea similarly desires that her vengeance should be equal to the pain she has suffered (49–55), wishes that Jason had a brother (*utinam esset illi frater*, 125), and asks her rage where it is taking her (*Quo te igitur, ira, mittis?*, 916) upon realizing that Jason's sons would represent an adequate alternative. She also treats her heart as a separate entity (*cor pepulit horror*, 926). Contemplating the death of her children, Medea almost relents, but is brought back to herself with a sudden recollection: *E che? Io son Medea! E li lascio in vita?* ('What's this? I am Medea. And I'm letting them live?')

The death of the children, moreover, is figured as a sacrifice. Opening Act 3, Medea summons the 'infernal gods' (*Numi, venite a me, inferni Dei*) to assist her in accomplishing her 'work' (*opra / oeuvre*). Her children in this case are dedicated as an 'offering' to the 'dark Furies', *votati son dell' atre Erinni al nume*: 'I here sacrifice you (*io sacro*) to the dark Goddesses of hatred', Medea pledges. It is a different form of compact from that which Seneca establishes, children's blood for that of a brother, but the motif of reciprocity is nonetheless dominant here in a way that it is not in Euripides, and the children's function as sacrificial victims is emphasized.

Sacrifice is even more prominent in Pasolini's film, which includes a long sequence depicting a young man being dismembered in a Colchian fertility rite, his blood smeared on the crops. Medea presides as priestess over this grisly ritual. The film overall falls into two halves, Colchian backstory and familiar tragedy, both treated from Medea's point of view.[27] In Colchis, very little dialogue is spoken, the soundtrack consisting of chanting, discordant pipes, and insistent cicadas. Wide shots of an arid landscape alternate with choral ritual action and facial close-ups, particularly of Medea and a moody adolescent it will later become apparent is her brother Absyrtus. Upon Jason's arrival, Medea co-opts Absyrtus into assisting with the theft of the Fleece, and they abscond together with Jason's retinue. Pursuit is imminent and without hesitation, Medea seizes an axe and cuts Absyrtus down. The discordant music that accompanied the sacrifice returns as she lifts it and strikes, again and again, watched silently by the Argonauts, who can see what we cannot, the carnage taking place in Medea's chariot. Finally, Medea tosses Absyrtus's head unemotionally into the dust, and the Argonauts gallop away. The efforts of Aeetes' attendants to collect Absyrtus's corpse with sufficient dignity resemble the macabre reassembly of the dismembered youth Hippolytus in Seneca's *Phaedra* (1247–70). Pasolini's corn-king ceremony may owe more to Mircea Eliade and James Frazer than it does to Seneca,[28] but his inclusion of the Absyrtus episode as a precursor to the children's deaths is part of a Senecan, and not a Euripidean tradition.

Medea's identity in Pasolini's film is that of priestess rather than witch, but her power is still embedded in the earth and dispensed by the sun. It is Helios who recalls to her the abilities she thought had been wiped out by her deracination from Colchis. 'Speak to me, Earth,' she begs, running in desperate circles on a parched Greek plateau. 'Speak to me, Sun. Where must I go to hear your voice... You are disappearing, never to return again. I can no longer hear what you are saying.' Her Colchian self is recovered in the murder of Jason's sons. The language of ritual pervades Seneca's *Medea* from her opening invocation onwards, concentrated in Act 4 but never far from the surface: the curses she calls down upon Jason, for example (531–7), or the charm that erases her anger from his memory (553–7), and of course her sacrificial infanticide. Seneca's Medea offers up one child in explicitly sacrificial recompense, as a *victima* (965–71), and she also applies the language of Roman religious practice when she urges herself *Hoc age*, 'Perform this thing' (562 and 976).[29] The second child's death is marked as sacrificial with the verb *litare* (1020), which denotes a sacrifice successfully carried out.[30] Seneca's undeserved reputation for a pompous and stilted style has tended to obscure the extent to which his tragedies tap into a ritual vein, often more readily in fact than their Greek counterparts.

The 1967 *Médée* directed at the Odéon-Théâtre-de-France by Jorge Lavelli took a similarly ritualistic approach. The production's climactic scene is preserved on film.[31] Medea appears on a raised platform above the heads of the clustered Chorus. Jason faces us. His eyes are hollow. He speaks in a stricken monotone, repeating the ominous words, '*Medea. Mon fils. Medea. Mon fils tué*?' He sinks to his knees in a slow, deliberate glide. Medea raises her arm like a claw or a salute, and begins to invoke her appointed destiny, implicitly calling on her ancestor, the sun: '*Jour . . . jour éclatant . . .*' in an ascending scale, as inevitable as the sunrise, and as unstoppable. '*Tu es là*,' she says, with regret. The Chorus begin a low hum as Jason bends backwards like a bow, offering his own breast to the knife. '*Tue-moi*,' he intones, '*tue-moi . . .*'

'*Me demandes-tu la pitié*?' Medea replies, in the same emotionless drawl; and then her hand falls. Jason howls. The clip ends.[32]

Lavelli's translation (by Jean Vauthier) lends itself to theatrical ritual. One of its singular devices is the punctuation employed to indicate the continuity of thought or action between the spoken words: ellipsis, slash, dash, exclamation mark, indices of non-verbal intensity. The scene above contains a high proportion of these markers:

MEDEA
Ce jour, jour éclatant / !___
Jour tu es là . . . ! . . . ! . . .
Instant.
O vengeance justicière.
Un certain temps m'est accordé.

JASON
___ Tue-moi. Tue-moi! ______________
Veuille bien me tuer. . . . . Hâte-toi. Hâte-toi.

MEDEA
Me demandes-tu la pitié?
– Jason!. . . . . .
C'en est fait . . . .

. . . .
O mon ressentiment /
Je ne pouvais t'offrir d'avantage.
. . . .
– Jason.
Jason l'ingrat / regarde.
Reconnais-tu ton épouse?
. . . .

pp.108–9. Ellipses in original.[33]

Despite its lower verbal density, Vauthier's *Medea* is unmistakably Seneca's. It follows the Senecan structure and scene-content, including characteristic lines and distinctive passages. Lavelli, who later went on to direct opera sought to create a ritualistic, 'ceremonial' atmosphere by applying musical principles to a verbal text, treating the script like a score.[34] Spoken text, he believed, demanded the same scrupulous attention to rhythm, dynamics and tone, not to create the impression of lifelike discourse but to exploit the musical possibilities of the human voice. Treating Senecan speech as incantation reactivated its psychagogic potential. This potential was likewise realized by Peter Brook, who directed Seneca's *Oedipus* in 1968, two years before the release of Pasolini's *Medea*. Like *Medea, Oedipus* includes two scenes of enacted ritual, an extispicy and a necromancy.[35] Whereas for Corneille and Glover, 'theatre' and Medea's theatrical practice could be synonymous with 'magic', the 1960s saw a move towards conceiving of theatre as ritualistic,[36] and it is from this zeitgeist that Pasolini's film and Lavelli's staging emerged.

6.3 Landscapes

The moral ecology implied by Stoic *sympatheia* has found a new resonance in the late twentieth and early twenty-first centuries. In a period marked by environmental degradation and the increasing pressure of climate change, Seneca's *Medea* exhibits a haunting prescience. From an ecocritical perspective, the play becomes an indictment of human exploitation on a planetary scale. Medea's identification with the natural environment is a theme which recent productions have realized in diverse ways. Although Stoic physics is a factor quite remote from these interpretations, they nevertheless make manifest above all the reciprocity between the protagonist and her world.

Heiner Müller's *Medeamateriel* trilogy, first staged in 1983, frames a monologue delivered by Medea ('Medeamaterial') with two pieces of more abstract poetic text, the speakers of which are unassigned (entitled 'Despoiled Shore' and 'Landscape with Argonauts'). The ostensible setting of 'Despoiled Shore' is 'a lake near Straussberg', a muddy wasteland strewn with garbage and banal slogans, but the presence of Medea 'on the ground ... cradling / The brother hacked up to pieces' (*DS*, p130) brings a mythological undercurrent to Müller's montage of contemporary East German degradation. The surreal cacophony of 'Landscape' draws both layers into a post-apocalyptic nightmare. Müller envisaged all three acts as being performed simultaneously rather than sequentially,[37] the branches of the dead tree on the fouled lakeshore also those of the dead tree 'in the paradise of the bacteria ... masked with clouds' (*LA*, p134), standing as well for the transgressive Argo that once grew as pine on Pelion ('the slaughtered tree', *LA*, p133). Compressed into Müller's central monologue, Medea's Corinthian murders are set as in Seneca against the Argo's voyage and its consequences. For Müller, these consequences are nuclear. 'The theatre of my death had opened / As I stood between the mountains', cries the anonymous, prophetic voice that closes the triptych (*LA*, p135). The 'expected airplane' and its bomb-blast take the place of Medea's airborne chariot, scouring the plateau and sweeping the speaker/s before it on a 'reeling flight' into oblivion, as 'I felt MY blood come out of MY veins / And turn MY body into the landscape of MY death'. It is a form of radical *deus ex machina*, 'what my grandmothers used to call God', but in Müller's case a manmade engine of destruction erases the distinction between human bodies and their environment, reducing all to toxic ash.

'Medeamaterial' also contains other Senecan affiliations. Medea makes explicit references to her brother's murder, including the assertion which she repeats on three occasions that 'You still owe me a brother, Jason'. Juxtaposed with the tableau of Medea cradling her brother's limbs, this reiteration of debt recalls her Senecan motive for revenge. 'Today is payday, Jason,' she snarls. 'Your Medea will collect her debts today' (*MM*, p132). Prior to Jason's arrival, Müller's Medea looks into a mirror, and in an ironic negation of the Senecan tradition, disowns her own identity. 'This is not Medea', she tells her reflection. Fouled, dismembered and denied, Müller's classical source-text is scarcely recognizable. Nevertheless, the ecological relationship which Müller establishes between this text, its eponymous speaker, and their devastated setting also replicates the way in which Seneca's Medea speaks for a Roman world corrupted by exploitation and *luxuria*.

Reminiscent of Vauthier's elliptical typography, and also of the poetic form developed for Peter Brook's 1968 *Oedipus*,[38] Henry Stead's 2011 translation of *Medea* likewise informs the delivery of the text by means of its arrangement on the page. With minimal punctuation, Stead's free verse instead uses line breaks to indicate phrasing and spaces of varying size to suggest the length and timing of pauses. It is a lean, punchy translation by a poet who understands how actors speak, how dramatic poetry is realized through oral as well as aural sensations. Collaborating with Stead, I directed a production of *Medea* in March 2011 at the Burton Taylor Studio in Oxford.[39] Without explicitly updating the script, we wanted to escape the suffocating prolixity of versions like Studley's, and the stifling inheritance of Seneca's reputation as 'unstageable'. To this end, much of the mythological material was excised, and at the same time Stead retained a number of exclamations and invocations verbatim in Latin – *toto in vultu est dolor* (446), *cor pepulit horror!* (926), *parve sunt mala et vile telum est ima quod tellus creat* (690–1), for example – which speakers break into when English will not suffice. The only verbal anachronism reflects the similar temporal collapse performed by Seneca at the end of the second chorus. Stead replaces Seneca's global movement of people with the global movement of electronic data, and the prospect of lands beyond Thule with the prospect of worlds beyond worlds:

Every edge has moved cities
build walls in new lands individuals
build walls online in bedrooms
The world is full of noise
The world never sleeps
it chokes on endless information
The world is open
Nothing is left in its original place
A time will come when the world will be a city
building walls in different lands
Space will be ocean chains ruptured by noise
Universe will stretch open its vast blackness
twist into colour The Moon
will be a stone's throw away

Medea herself was performed by an ensemble of five women, who also worked together as their own Chorus. Three of them stepped out of this composite character to act temporarily as Jason, Creon, and the Nurse, whose voice could alternatively be interpreted as a cautionary note in Medea's own psyche. The effect was twofold, embodying Medea's fragmentation while at the same time ensuring her total dominance of a stage on which quite literally no-one else appears. Apart from some of the main dialogue sections, lines were not distributed beforehand. The actors discovered their own paths through the text in rehearsal, synchronizing their breath, moving together like water. Their costumes were identical loose blue garments, their faces tattooed with identical blue knotwork patterns.

There was to be something alien about Medea, something not quite human, which designer Hannah Cornwell realized in the representation of her children. In place of human infants, Cornwell constructed two cylindrical chrysalids, just over a foot in height, which we suspended over the stage. Medea 'killed' them by ripping open their velcro fronts, releasing a generous shower of 'blood': thousands of red adzuki beans, which I painstakingly swept up every night and Hannah stuffed back inside the chrysalids. Creon, Jason, and the Argo were other key design elements, conceived as objects rather than people. 'You get fatter with self-love every day', Stead's Medea jeers at Creon (*tumidus imperio Creo*, Sen. *Med.* 178). Creon's head (Medea Naomi Setchell) bobbed atop a billowing expanse of fabric like a floral parachute under which three other Medeas crouched to form his king-sized body. This grotesque puppet was paralleled by Jason, who was a small, excitable, jointed marionette (manipulated by Medea Bess Roche). During the Argonautic ode (301–63), the Argo was performed by a miniature model ship with its sails unfurled, navigating the treacherous (*perfida*) shoals and reefs and inlets presented by the archipelago of female bodies who permitted its passage. Curious and disinterested as Catullus' Nereids (*Carm.* 64.12–18), oceanic Medea conducted the voyage of the fragile craft (*rate fragili*), wafting it onwards, bearing it maternally towards certain death.

*

If you start with a volcano onstage in Act 1, it has to erupt in Act 5. The production of Seneca's *Medea* staged as part of the Greek theatre festival at Syracuse in 2015, adapted and directed by Paolo Magelli with a set design by Ezio Toffolutti, made Medea's wrath a volcanic event. *Quaeve anhelentem premens / Titana tantis Aetna fervebit minis?* fumes Seneca's Medea. 'Crushing the panting Titan, / could Etna seethe as threateningly as I?' (409–10). This comparison was put to the test in May 2015, as Magelli's production coincided with one of active Etna's regular, albeit infrequent eruptions. Some fifty miles up the coast of Sicily from the teatro Greco di Siracusa, lava was welling down the gullies, and ashen smoke billowing vast and cloudlike from the mountainside. The Sicilian landscape played an inescapable, indispensable role, partly through the stage design and partly as a result of the theatre's location, a factor typically exploited by directors participating in Siracusa's annual festival of ancient drama. As at Epidaurus, the semi-circular Hellenistic seating banks have been refurbished and the orchestra restored to accommodate outdoor productions of ancient tragedy and comedy in translation. The season is traditionally a trio of Greek plays, but in recent years Seneca has also made it onto the programme. Translation extends to the set and costumes, the style of acting, and the use of modern sound and lighting technology. These are not museum pieces, but contemporary classics. Nevertheless, the continuity of the location itself provides a deep-rooted fourth (temporal) dimension, implicit beneath every gesture as a subterranean sounding, the echo of the rattle of pebbles flung into an abyss.

There was nothing archaic about Magelli's *Medea*, whose title role was played by an incandescent Valentina Banci. The stage was covered in white sand, sloping up to an abstract, geometric concrete-and-sheet-metal structure entered through a square tunnel that retracted telescopically, like an airport boarding bridge. In contrast, the forestage presented a microcosmic natural landscape, consisting of two knee-high cinder cones of sand, like volcanoes in miniature, and half a dozen rectangular ponds like rockpools left by the receding tide, or if regarded on a different scale, caldera lakes. A number of bright red Argonautic oars were propped against a third, somewhat larger cone further upstage. As written by Seneca, Medea has a Sicilian persona: she is more rabid than Scylla, hungrier than Charybdis, more molten than Etna (408–10). As if these lines became a geographical key, Magelli placed her in a setting that reproduced the surrounding landscape.[40] At the same time, the cones created a distorted sense of scale, the interpretation of which became intrinsic to how Medea's power is to be perceived. If, as she stamps on them, writhes in them, kicks them and tosses sand around in furious handfuls and mashes Creusa's gold dress into the summit, these mountains are simply piles of sand, then her rage is a childish tantrum in a sandpit; if, on the other hand, they are the seas and mountains they appear to represent, then Medea bestrides them like a colossus, the earth beneath her quaking as she tramples human ruin underfoot.

Watching, we slide in and out of each perspective. Giusto Picone's modern Italian translation was delivered with the hysterical intonation of soap opera, a reminder that when stripped of its antique gravitas and mythological trappings, the core of Medea's drama is simply infidelity.

Her battered coat and boots, the pile of travelling trunks, were a reminder of her impending statelessness. Ignoring the mountains, we could receive these interactions as purely interpersonal, albeit heightened, and contemporary. The cones' continuous presence, however, and their relationship to the environment in which the theatre itself is sited, brought to the performance the geological, even cosmological dimension of Stoic *sympatheia* or resonance with *Natura*, an important Senecan theme that could not otherwise be embodied by the human stature of actors alone.

The most profound, and profoundly moving episode in Magelli's production was its ending. While utterly contradicting Seneca's, it nevertheless made manifest two of the Roman playwright's most central, most disturbing intimations. There is the possibility that the cosmos is malignantly disposed towards humanity; and the alternative, no less chilling possibility that Medea has successfully convinced both herself and her audience of this fallacy, leading her to perform a tragically unwarranted sacrifice. At the end of Magelli's play, she cannot leave. She staggers back and forth as if drunk, kicks at the sand, tries to draw her magic circle and call her customary dragons, but this time it does not work. This time, the palace roof is occupied by grim-faced, fire-fighting guards. Blocked from escape, she kneels and lowers her head to the sand. Her dress, golden now, is the same colour, blending in the twilight into the earth. The Chorus emerge from the tunnel, one by one, carrying red metal bins. We stir, suddenly conscious that the end we anticipated will not come to pass, and it is perhaps this time the Chorus who will be avenged on Medea for centuries of burnt temples and smothered infants. We feel a dreadful misgiving: what if Medea's power was all a lie, and her claims all false? If she never summoned the moon at all, and if, as in Glover, her natural alignment and supernatural authority were nothing but so much glamour, *herbes sans force*? What if all this is only madness, an hysterical delusion in which we have all become complicit? Surely now she will turn, and prove us part of something greater, something necessary, something fated.

There are no gods!

The Chorus empty their red buckets, one by one, over the crouching Medea. I thought it would be water. I thought, if she cannot be victorious, at least let her be cleansed. Return her to the sea. What came out of the buckets was a shattering inversion. What came pouring out of the buckets were long, cascading streamers of sand, over and over again, until Medea was buried in sand, until it choked her, until it drifted across the stage like smoke. And now, at the last, another mountain is growing, a fourth cone rising over the fiery core that was once Medea, just as Etna presses down upon the restless limbs of Typhon. She has taken root here, another mountain in the chain, a mountain of grief, an Ovidian metamorphosis, fundamental. Her limbs, her contours are still visible, but covered in a fine veil of sand so she no longer appears human. She has become a statue, a grieving Niobe: but Niobe, all tears, was permitted to weep down her rockface, while Medea's grief is become a drought, a waterless desert, a wasteland where *there is no water*. This ending is the most terrible punishment that could have been contrived for *maiusque mari Medea malum*, Medea the goddess of the ocean, the river in spate, the summoner of summer storms: buried alive in sand, the voyager and eternal exile fixed in place, immobile and immovable. Be careful what you wish for.

Then the scale resolves itself one final time, and in the most unexpectedly breathtaking reversal of all, Medea is redeemed. Assimilated by the land, her body in mountainous captivity assumes godlike proportions. She is the myth beneath the skin of the range, the fire that fuels tectonic movements. And I remember that earth, too, is liquid, if you drill it deep enough; if you reach the pitch where elemental distinctions collapse, where boiling rocks give birth to springs of fire, Medea remains.

Notes

Chapter 1

1 *Medea superest. Hic mare et terras vides, / ferrumque et ignes et deos et fulmina* (Sen, *Med.* 166–7).

2 This builds on methodology developed in Slaney 2015.

3 Fischer-Lichte 1999, 17 likens postmodern adaptations of Greek tragedy to Dionysiac *sparagmos.*

4 Sophocles is known to have written at least one. Radt 1977, 239–46.

5 Kragelund 2016, 369 notes dissent regarding *Octavia*'s authorship as early as 1371, but also (p. 145, n. 4) that some scholars persist in the attribution. Boyle 2008, lxxix–lxxxiv discusses how Renaissance tragedy made use of 'the only surviving *fabula praetexta* . . . which came with the authority of "Seneca".'

6 Fitch 1981. Boyle 2014, xix suggests 'late Claudian or early Neronian', which would place its composition either during the period of Seneca's exile or shortly after his recall. Arcellaschi 1990, 329–45 argues for a date between the autumn of 63 CE and the summer of 64, which is certainly plausible, although the evidence remains inconclusive.

7 Ahl in his introductory essay to *Two Faces of Oedipus* (2008), 14–15.

8 Kohn 2003. See also Rosenmeyer 1989, 8 for a brief survey of 'the separatist hypothesis' from late antiquity onwards, and Ker and Winston 2012, 7–11 on Seneca's medieval and early modern identity.

9 Wilson 2014, 78; Griffin 1976, 59–60.

10 Griffin 1976, 77–9.

11 Griffin 1976, 148.

12 *Octavia*'s date is uncertain; Kragelund 2016, 297–343, surveys the evidence and proposes 68 CE, shortly after Nero's fall; other options are Flavian or late antique. Boyle 2008, xv.

13 On Roman suicide: Edwards 2007, 113–60; Hill 2004, esp. 145–212; McGuire 1997.

14 When slitting his wrists proves ineffectual, Seneca drinks hemlock, which also fails; finally he suffocates in a steam-bath. Tac. *Ann.* 15.63–4. See Ker 2009a.

15 Ker 2009a, 72. As Hill 2004, 146 remarks, 'Seneca is obsessed with suicide'.

16 Phaedra and Jocasta; an argument could also be made for Astyanax in *Troades* jumping before he is pushed.

17 *Non quam diu, sed quam bene acta sit, refert. Nihil ad rem pertinent quo loco desinas. Quocumque voles desine: tantum bonam clausulam inpone* (*Epistle* 77).

18 E.g. *Epistles* 4.6–7, 5.5–6.

19 See e.g. Bartsch and Wray 2009, 3; Wray 2009, 239.

20 See *De Ira* 3.36 on the daily review, with comment by Ker 2009b; see also Seneca's *Epistle* 83.

21 On perverted appetite, see Seneca *NQ* 4B.13.5–11; cf. *NQ* 3.17.2–18.7.

22 For a contextualization of *De Ira* see Harris 2004, esp. 112–16, 220–3, 251–3.

23 Argued, for example, by Pratt 1983, 73–131, esp. 81–91; more sophisticated formulations of the position may be found in Bartsch 2006 and Nussbaum 1993.

24 Rosenmeyer 1989, 22.

25 Schiesaro 2003, *passim* on *Thyestes.*

26 So Schiesaro 1997, 110: 'To mobilise the psychagogic qualities of poetry to represent negative passions meant an inevitable degree of ambiguity.'

27 *De Ira* 3.14–15 gives several examples of historical occasions when it was expedient to flatter tyranny, concluding, 'this is how you must behave, if you eat with kings'. Suicide is one way out, but 'it is easier to bear any yoke quietly than struggle against it; anger will only make your subjugation more painful.' (3.16.1)

28 Gill 2009 and 1997; Harris 2004, 362–90.

29 The similarity in symptoms is also noted by Costa 1973, 108; Hine 2000, 154.

30 Pratt 1983, 90 briefly cites this passage, among others in *De Ira*, as possessing a 'stylistic link' to imagery in *Medea*.

31 E.g. Bexley 2016, 36–43; Star 2012, 76–80; Schiesaro 2009, 228; Bartsch 2006, 255–81; Johnson 1988, 93–100.

32 Bartsch 2006, 255–81, esp. 259–65, 272: 'Medea does go through a process very like the Stoic's own self-training to actualize an ideal and "recognizable" self.'

33 Ker 2009b analyses this passage of *De Ira* in detail.

34 Bartsch 2006, 194.

35 Bartsch 2006, 259.

36 Bexley 2016, esp. 36–43 discusses the operation of 'the theatrical metaphor of Stoic *persona*-theory' in *Medea*; more generally, see also Rosenmeyer 1989, 47–56. Seneca's *Epistles* 74, 80, 88, and 120 all mention the theatre or acting. *Epistle* 11 suggests imagining an ideal spectator for one's actions.

37 Rosenmeyer 1989, 140.

38 Star 2012, 4.

39 Wray 2009, 238. See also Johnson 1988, 96–7.

40 Henderson 1983, 99.

41 Fyfe 1983, 86–7.

42 Catullus, *Carmen* 64; Horace, *Odes* 1.3; Valerius Flaccus, *Argonautica*. See discussion in Chapter 2 below, and in Davis 1990.

43 Mentioned by Suetonius, *Life of Vitellius* 13. On trade, see Young 2001. On *luxuria*, Edwards 1993, 19–24, 137–206.

44 Wilson 2014, 199.

45 For Seneca's views on *luxuria* see *Epistle* 13.8; cf. *Ep.* 42, 89, 95, 119.

46 Kragelund 2016, 214–16 notes that *Octavia*'s author creates a 'vivid impersonation of the real Seneca' by using vocabulary taken from his philosophical essays.

47 The relationship between decline and technology is a literary commonplace, as found for example in Virgil's *Georgics* and *Eclogue* 4, and satirized by Petronius (*Satyricon* 119–20). For comment on the Argo's place in the tradition, see Davis 1990, esp. 57–61.

48 Sallust, *Cat.* 37.5; cf. Lucan, *Bellum Civile* 7.404–5; Juvenal, *Satire* 3.

49 McGuire 1997, 147–84.

50 Creon does not state this explicitly, but Jason suggests at line 526 that if he were to defect to Medea, Creon might join forces with the Thessalian usurper Acastus; with Creon's support, on the other hand, Jason has a chance to reclaim his birthright.

51 Bartsch 1994, 1–35.

52 As does Littlewood 2004 and Schiesaro 2003.

53 *Pace* Kohn 2013, esp. 81–92 who argues that Senecan dramaturgy is consistent with full staging.

54 Fantham 1982, 48; cf. Fantham 2000 for a reiteration of her arguments against performance.

55 Notable exceptions: Herington 1966; Calder 1976; Kelly 1979; Sutton 1986; Dupont 1995; Boyle 1997 and 2014; Davis 2003; Kohn 2013; and Harrison (ed.) 2000, especially Marshall's chapter in this volume.

56 Eliot 1951 [1927], 76 and 67.

57 Mendell 1941, 72 and 90. The phrase is also used by Duff 1960, 210.

58 Zwierlein 1966, 92.

59 The chorus in *Troades*, for example, state their disbelief in the afterlife when they have just witnessed a ghost; and the chorus in *Thyestes* rejoice in the reconciliation of the brothers just after Atreus plots his revenge. One scene which seems to cause particular consternation (Zwierlein 1966, 13–18; Mayer 2002, 30–1) is *Phaedra* 1144–200, but having directed a production of this play (Melbourne, 2007) I can attest that none of the issues raised are insoluble.

60 In 67 BCE, the Lex Roscia reserved fourteen rows for equites. The Lex Iulia Theatralis, part of Augustus's reforms of 22 BCE or 19 BCE, further segregated social ranks, women and slaves. Beacham 1999, 122–6; Rawson 1987; see documents collected in Csapo and Slater 1994, 309–12.

61 Sear 2005; Vitruvius, *De Arch*. 5.6.

62 Pliny, *Natural History* 36.113–15.

63 Pliny, *Natural History* 36.113–15. Beacham 1991, 167 notes 'extensive informal benefaction from prominent and wealthy citizens who in effect bought status by building or refurbishing provincial buildings and monuments, often including theatres'. Rome's first permanent theatre, the Theatre of Pompey, was dedicated in 55 BCE, shortly followed by the Theatre of Balbus (13 BCE) and Theatre of Marcellus (11 BCE), after which euergetism in the capital was restricted to the imperial family. Beacham 1991, 157–62; cf. Beacham 1999, 61–72.

64 For visual evidence, see Taplin 2007, *passim*; Beacham 1991, 7–9, 123, 186–8 and 1999, 6–7, 141; Bieber 1971, 129–66, 227–50.

65 Horace, *Epistle to Augustus*, 207: an actor wears *lana Tarentino violas imitata veneno*; Pliny 36.115 mentions *Attalica veste*, or cloth woven with gold thread.

66 Tarrant 1985, 31: 'There is no trace in Seneca of the strophic responsion on which most Greek choral song is based . . . For the most part Senecan lyrics

are stichic – that is, a single basic meter is used in every line of a section or even an entire ode.' Boyle 2014, cxliv adds that anapaestic dimeter is Seneca's most commonly used meter.

67 Calder 1976.

68 Petronius, *Satyricon* 53 and 59; Pliny the Younger, *Epistle* 7.24. Beacham 1991, 244 n.115.

69 See comment by Sherwin-White 1966, 115.

70 Plutarch, *Quaest. Conv.* 7.8: 711–12 endorses group recitations of Platonic dialogues and New Comedy; tragedy is also considered, but rejected as unsuitable for light entertainment. Bexley 2015, 781 makes the point that *recitat* is always a singular verb.

71 Fantham 2002; Gunderson 2000.

72 Edwards 1997, 66–95 shows how actors, along with prostitutes and gladiators, were subject to the legal disqualification known as *infamia*. 'Those who sold their bodies for the pleasure of others forfeited the protection Roman law accorded to the bodies of other citizens', p. 76.

73 Especially Alessandra Zanobi, who argues persuasively for 'the influence of the aesthetics of pantomime on Seneca's tragedies' (Zanobi 2014, xi). See also Zanobi 2008; Zimmerman 2008; Slaney 2013b; Dodson-Robinson 2011.

74 See Lucian's dialogue *On the Dance* and Webb 2008, 61–94, 160–1.

75 Zanobi 2014 identifies several others: the tragedies' episodic structure, themes of madness and obsession, absence of the chorus from the action, self-reflexive monologue, *ecphraseis topou*, and development of set-piece narrations at the expense of plot. The unstable settings and other continuity errors noted by Zwierlein may also result from a pantomimic idea of tragedy and pantomimic performance conventions.

76 Zanobi 2014, 93; cf. 95–7.

77 The conventional view is that of Robin 1993, 107: 'In keeping with the tastes of his era, Seneca's tragedies contain a number of explicitly bloody scenes.' Glenn Most 1992, 400–2 regards this connection as rather diffuse, however, preferring a stylistic explanation for the Neronian period's 'rhetoric of dismemberment'.

78 Boyle 2014, 266; Costa 1973, 119.

79 Costa 1973, 159 cross-references these lines.

80 Coleman 1990.

81 Barton 1993, 15–36.

Chapter 2

1 Bartsch 2006, 231–2, 263; Gill 2009 and 1997; Star 2012, esp. 78–9.

2 Trinacty 2014, 99–100. On other aspects of metatheatricality in *Medea*, see Boyle 2014, cvii–cxviii; Schiesaro 1997, 91–7; Littlewood 2004, 148–71. Littlewood identifies internal spectatorship in Senecan tragedy generally as a species of metatheatre.

3 Other examples of literary epithalamia include Catullus, *Carmen* 61 and 62 and Statius, *Silvae* 1.2. Hersch 2010, 232–6. Trinacty 2014, 102–3 shows how Seneca references Jason's wedding procession in Ovid's *Heroides* 12.

4 On Fescennine verses, see Treggiari 1991, 166; Hersch 2010, 151–6.

5 The river Phasis is in Colchis, often used in Roman literature as a way of referring to the whole region.

6 It was Pelias who dispatched Jason and the Argo on what he thought was an impossible quest. On the heroes' return, Medea persuaded Pelias's daughters that if they plunged the old king into a cauldron of boiling water, he would be restored to youth.

7 Trinacty 2014, 158–64 shows how the ode reworks themes found in Augustan poets Horace and Virgil.

8 *ultima Thule*. The identity of Thule is insecure; it may refer to Shetland, Norway, or (most likely) Iceland, but in Roman poetry generally signifies the furthest point of geographical knowledge. Roller 2006, 78–81; Romm 1992, 157–62, 204–11.

9 On which see Lawall 1979, esp. 420, 424–5.

10 Manuwald 2013 surveys the literary heritage. A more extensive treatment may also be found in Corrigan 2013.

11 Two fragments are quoted by Quintilian (*Inst. Orat.* 3.8.5, with additional comment at 10.1.98) and Seneca the Elder (*Suasoriae* 3.7) Nikolaidis 1985 summarises the evidence. See also Arcellaschi 1990, 247–66. Hinds 1993, 34–43 reads *Heroides* 12 as a 'prologue' to Ovid's tragedy.

12 Trinacty 2014, 95–126; Corrigan 2013, 41–66; Manuwald 2013, 127–30; Arcellaschi 1990, 267–312. Hinds 1993 defends the authenticity of *Heroides* 12 and discusses its relationship to *Heroides* 6 (to Jason from Hypsipyle). Trinacty 2014, 97 remarks that 'Seneca defines his tragic Medea as the culmination of Ovid's elegiac and epic Medeas'.

13 Literally, 'having caught fire, she will outdo my passion'.

14 Trinacty 2014, 99–100 points out that this also has a metapoetic resonance, namely that Ovid's forthcoming tragedy *Medea* will be a greater 'act' than this mock-epistle, and Seneca's tragedy claims to be 'greater' (*gravior*, *maiora*) than both.

15 Trinacty 2014, 95–126.

16 For further reading on Apollonius, see e.g. Byre 2002, Clare 2002, Hunter 1993, and Beye 1982.

17 Tsetskhladze 2006, lxvi; Boardman 1980, 238–55.

18 Williams 1991, 185–203.

19 On foundation-myths and Greek colonies overseas, see Dougherty 1993.

20 For a discussion of Medea's role in Apollonius, see e.g. Clauss 1997; Beye 1982, 120–66.

21 This is not Apollonius's innovation; Medea's fratricide is attested as far back as the fifth century BCE. Bremmer 1997, 85–6.

22 Trinacty 2014, 158–62; Davis 1990, 51–3.

23 Edwards 1993, 22–4, 147–8, 173–206 and see Chapter 1 above.

24 Slaney 2013a, 418–19.

25 Ohlander 1989, 26–191, esp. 26–8, 49, and 118–24.

26 Medea promises to provide Aegeus with drugs that will cure his childlessness.

27 Ohlander 1989, 63 argues that 'Euripides, no doubt, had a good sense of how far he could go in portraying a vindictive Medea at this point in the play without losing their support for his main character.'

28 See Pucci 1980 on Euripides' 'economy of pathos' in *Medea*.

29 Ohlander 1989, 118–24.

30 Erasmo 2004, 22 does not believe this can be the case; nor does Boyle 2006, 59. On Ennius's *Medea* generally: Arcellaschi 1990, 37–98; Manuwald 2013, 117–20.

31 Jocelyn 1967, 113.

32 See Boyle 2006, 72.

33 Jocelyn 1967, 118 does not regard this line as part of the quotation, but cf. Boyle 2006, 74.

34 Jocelyn 1967, 120. Erasmo 2004, 25–6 follows Jocelyn in keeping these as separate fragments; I follow Boyle in combining them.

35 Erasmo 2004, 45. On Accius's *Medea*, cf. Arcellaschi 1990, 163–96.

36 Taplin 2007, 119. This pot is discussed on pp. 122–3.

37 Sourvinou-Inwood 1997, 269–74. See also Taplin 2007, 117–21 and 124–8.
38 Creusa's death was also popular, as on Taplin 2007, 115–16 and 255–7.
39 Museo Archaeologico di Napoli Inv. 8976, 8977, 8978, and 114321.
40 Varner 2000. See also Boyle 1997, 18–20 on Seneca's 'iconosphere'.
41 Pliny, *NH*. 35.136.
42 Lada-Richards 2003.

Chapter 3

1 Terminology borrowed from Winkler 1985.
2 Kerrigan 1996, 6–12, 20–6; also 88–110 on some permutations of Medea.
3 The literal translation of *nescioquid* is 'I don't know what [thing]'. The term is used in Senecan tragedy to designate particularly ominous phenomena. See n. 9 below.
4 Karamanou 2014 relates 'Medea's multifaceted otherness' to the tetralogy in which Euripides' play was first staged in 431 BCE; in the same volume, Van Zyl Smit 2014 discusses her postcolonial reception.
5 Some of the Argonauts, of course (notably Heracles) do not return, but none of their deaths or departures occur while Medea is on board.
6 Under Roman law, Medea could expect the dowry to revert to her upon divorce; she could sue her ex-husband if he failed to comply voluntarily. Treggiari 1991, 323–40, 350–3. Guastella 2001, 206–8 also remarks on Medea's desire for repayment of her marital debt or adequate compensation.
7 As remarked by Schiesaro 2003, 209–13. Return as a structuring principle is also discussed in Schiesaro 2009, 229–33: 'Seneca's Medea upgrades *reddere* from a circumscribed, technical use to an embracing, metaphysical dimension: she wants nothing less than the undoing of her life so far [. . .] a compulsion [which is] satisfied against the requirements of logic and reality'.
8 On repetition as a trope with similar prominence in Seneca's *Agamemnon* and *Oedipus*, see Gunderson 2017.
9 The tragic logic of revenge, and its flaws, is discussed by Kerrigan 1996; Burnett 1998.

10 Other examples of *nescioquid*: *Phaedra* 858 and 1019; *Hercules Furens* 1146–7; *Oedipus* 334 and 925; *Thyestes* 267.

11 In the *Eumenides*, Clytemnestra's ghost incites the Furies to pursue her son, but does not haunt him herself. *Hecuba* contains two ghosts: Polydorus appears to Hecuba in a dream and relates the circumstances of his death through Polymestor's treachery, but what he wants is burial (Eur. *Hec.* 49–50); it is Hecuba who takes it upon herself to be revenged on his killer. Achilles' ghost is also reported as having demanded the sacrifice of Polyxena as his *geras*, his war-prize, but his motive is honour, not revenge. See Burnett 1998, 157–76.

12 Segal 1984 and 1986 makes a similar argument regarding landscape in Seneca' *Phaedra*.

13 Turcan 1998; Beard, North and Price 1998, 158–60 on *Dea Roma*. The phenomenon is not unique to Rome; see e.g. the essays collected in Stafford and Herrin 2005, especially Huskinson in this volume.

14 Jones 1990, 169 (*Libertas*) and 319–20 (*Victoria*).

15 Cf. *NQ*. 6.3.1 on the causes of earthquakes and other disturbances: *quibusdam vitiis, ut corpora nostra turbantur, et tunc, cum facere videntur, iniuriam accipiunt* ('they [the earth and the heavens], are disrupted like our own bodies by their imperfections, and when they seem to be doing damage, they are really receiving it').

16 'A greater evil than the sea' would be a more literal translation, but as *malum* can refer to misfortune as well as malignancy, 'accursed' captures both senses.

17 Ovid makes Scylla the traitor and Scylla the monster two different *virgines* (*Met.* 8.1–851 and 13.730–14.74), but there is also a tradition which conflates them.

18 For further commentary see Henderson 1983.

19 As noted by Henderson 1983, 101.

20 These abilities are not unique to Medea. Boyle 2014, 319 ad loc. comments that 'Power over nature . . . is a common property of the literary witch' in Roman poetry and beyond. See e.g. Apuleius, *Metamorphoses* 1.8 and Lucan, *Bellum Civile* 6.461–84. Further discussion in Chapter 5 below.

21 Littlewood 2004, 168.

22 Inwood 2005 provides an excellent analysis of Seneca's philosophy and its contexts.

23 Pratt 1983, 52.

24 Rosenmeyer 1989, 63–90 discusses the Stoic paradox of (multiple) causality versus free will, showing how 'the Stoics from the very beginning wrestled with the problem of how the moral requirement of free choice is to be integrated within their larger vision of the causal network' (p. 76).

25 Rosenmeyer 1989, 126–8.

26 Pratt 1983, 89 and 84.

27 Fyfe 1983, 88 and 83.

28 Rosenmeyer 1989, 132.

29 Rosenmeyer 1989, 133, emphasis original.

30 Bexley 2016, *passim*; Bartsch 2006, 255–81; Fitch and McElduff 2002, 19 and 26–31; Henry and Walker 1967, 175–7.

31 Bexley 2016, 36–43; Star 2012, 76–80; Bartsch 2006, 255–81; Johnson 1988, 93–100.

32 Hinds 1993, 46.

33 Manuwald 2013, 130: Medea's self-awareness refers in part to 'the literary heritage of the character'.

34 Noted by Hinds 2011, 28.

35 Storm 1998, 92–121.

36 Storm 1998, 108.

37 Bexley 2016, esp. 33–5. Cf Boyle 2014, cxvi.

38 Bexley 2016, 38.

39 Boyle 1997, 128–33 and 2014, cvii–cxviii; Littlewood 2004, 148–71 and 172–93; Schiesaro 1997, 91–8.

40 Star 2012, 62–3.

41 On the function of *ira*, *furor*, and *dolor* as motivating forces in Seneca's tragedies, see Dupont 1995.

42 Gill 1997.

43 Zimmermann 2008; Zanobi 2008 and 2014; Slaney 2013b.

44 Slaney 2015, esp. 18–21, 50–4.

45 Scarry 1985, esp. 60–1, and 35: 'Intense pain is also language-destroying: as the content of one's world disintegrates, so the content of one's language disintegrates; as the self disintegrates, so that which would express and project the self is robbed of its source and its subject.'

46 On the difference between *vox* and *verba*, see Butler 2015.

47 Robin 1993, 109. Robin's overall generalization, however, that the female voice in Senecan tragedy 'must ultimately be circumscribed and repressed', does not apply in *Medea*.
48 Schiesaro 2003, 87 and 90–1 discusses the comparable metatheatricality of Atreus's sacrificial ritual in *Thyestes*.
49 Fitch 2002 deletes these lines but they are retained by Boyle 2014, Costa 1973, and Hine 2000. Boyle ad loc. takes them as referring to current events rather than past achievements.
50 Trinacty 2014, 94. See also Schiesaro 1997, 97–8.
51 As in Propertius, *Elegies* 1.7. Ovid refers to his *ingenium* as the cause of his exile (e.g. *Tristia* 2.1,1–2).
52 Fitch and McElduff 2002, 32.

Chapter 4

1 The *locus classicus* is A.W. Schlegel, in his *Lectures on Dramatic Art and Literature* (1808): 'beyond description bombastic (*schwülstig*) and frigid, unnatural both in character and action, revolting from their violation of propriety'.
2 Segal 1984, 311; Johnson 1988, 85.
3 France 1991 recuperates hyperbole; Brooks 1984 does the same for melodrama.
4 Dupont 2007; Slaney 2015.
5 Plutarch, *How young people should listen to poetry* (*Moralia* 14–37) warns of its dangers; Schiesaro 1997, 110 comments that 'to mobilise the psychagogic properties of poetry to represent negative passions meant an inevitable degree of ambiguity', as the auditors might be swayed despite themselves. See also Webb 2009 on *enargeia*, and Gellrich 1994 on *psychagōgia* in Platonic dialogues.
6 Although concluding (p. 314) that Senecan tragedy is 'not stage art', Mastronarde 1970 is sensible of its qualities as poetry. For Herington 1966, 460, however, 'Senecan tragedy . . . proves to possess many of the qualities that we still associate with the greatest drama.'
7 Cicero's opinion (*Orat.* 100) is that eloquence consists of treating 'trivial matters in a plain style, matters of moderate significance in the tempered

style, and weighty affairs in the grand style' (trans. Hubbell). Cf. Quintilian, *Inst. Orat.* 12.10.58–72; Dionysius, *On the Style of Demosthenes*, 1–8; Demetrius, *On Style*.

8 Segal 1982, 241 remarks that the alliterations *Medea malum*, *Medea mater*, and *Medea monstrum* 'reflect in the microcosmic structure of phonemic patterns the tension between monstrosity and maternity that constitutes the dynamic force of Medea's tragedy.'

9 Brink 1971 ad loc.

10 Brink 1971 ad loc.

11 'If you're still alive, my spirit, if anything remains / of your former vigour, cast off feminine self-doubt / and clothe your mind in the harshness of the Caucasus. / Whatever unspeakable things Phasis and Pontus saw, / Corinth will see. Savage, unknown, horrific, / evils for heaven to tremble at as well as earth, / are stirring in my mind: wounds and murder and limbs / stiffening in death [lit. 'death wandering through limbs']. These things I recall are too trivial: / I did them as a girl. Worse pain now surges up: / greater crimes become me, now I have given birth.'

12 See Tarrant 1978 on Seneca and comedy, and Miola 1992 on Seneca and Shakespeare. Self-addressed soliloquies occasionally feature in Greek tragedy too, e.g. Euripides, *Troades* 98–152; Sophocles, *Ajax* 815–65; and of course Euripides, *Medea* 1021–80, and cf. 386–407, esp. 401–2.

13 By comparison, *ira* occurs 24 times, *dolor* (or *dolo*) 17, *furor* (or *furo*) 12, amor 10, *crimen* 8, and *odium* 4.

14 On which see Graf 1991, 41.

15 Quintilian, *Inst. Orat.* 6.2.35; compare Aulus Gellius, *Noctes Atticae* 6.5.7–8. See Lada-Richards 2002.

16 Koortbojian 1995; Lada-Richards 2004, 28 discusses 'the reciprocal interconnection of the stage and the plastic arts.'

17 Smith 1991, 84–9.

18 Llewellyn Jones 2005, 92, with reference to Aesch. *Ag.* 1216.

19 Cicero, *de Orat.* 3.220 and Quint. *Inst. Orat.* 11.3.88–91, 103

20 Lada-Richards 2003 and 2004.

21 Scarry 1985, 4: 'Physical pain does not simply resist language but actively destroys it, bringing about . . . a state anterior to language, to the sounds a cries a human being makes before language is learned.'

22 See Kemp 2012, 145–54 on the alternative techniques of method preparation.

23 Seneca the Elder, *Cont.* 2. On the entertainment value of declamation, see e.g. Lada-Richards 2007.
24 The eighteenth-century playwright and critic Gotthold Lessing called Seneca's characters 'prizefighters in cothurnoi'. (Lessing 1984, 30). These could just as easily be called 'beats' or 'action units', to use the term preferred by Kohn 2013.
25 Seidensticker 1969, 141–2 uncovers the irony in the terms of her appeal.
26 Quintilian, *Oratory* 11.3.83. See also the illustrations of comic slave characters in Terence compiled in Jones and Morey 1930–1.
27 Webb 2009, *passim*. Ecphrasis in poetry most commonly refers to the verbal description of visual art or a landscape, but the same techniques are used in rhetorical discourse to reanimate past events, e.g. in forensic (courtroom) oratory.
28 An alternative translation would be 'For me, [you could] even [commit] a crime', but the sense of reciprocity is important. See Costa 1973 ad loc.
29 Costa 1973, 119 ad loc. Boyle 2014, 265–6 ad loc. is keen to emphasize the dramatic irony generated by the aside. Bexley 2016, 39 reads Medea's hints as contributing to the persona she is progressively assuming.
30 'Tedious' and 'ludicrous', according to Studley's DNB entry.
31 Eliot's edition was produced in 1927.
32 Ker and Winston 2012, 51–6 discuss further examples of Studley's style, as does Norland 2009, 55–8 on *Medea* specifically.
33 Norland 2009, 46–7.
34 This is suggested on the basis of William Gager's 1592 adaptation of *Phaedra*, on which see Sandis 2015.
35 Slaney 2015, 77–88; Norland 2009, *passim*.
36 For more on the *Tenne Tragedies* and their immediate reception, see Heavey 2015, 52–60; Ker and Winston 2012; Norland 2009.
37 'If you're still alive, my spirit, if anything remains / of your former vigour, cast off feminine self-doubt / and clothe your mind in the harshness of the Caucasus. / Whatever unspeakable things Phasis and Pontus saw, / Corinth will see. Savage, unknown, horrific, / evils for heaven to tremble at as well as earth, / are stirring in my mind: wounds and murder and limbs / stiffening in death. These things I recall are too trivial: / I did them as a girl. Worse pain now surges up: / greater crimes become me, now I have given birth.'
38 On which see Butler 2015, 59–88.

39 Alexandrines are rhymed iambic hexameters, or six- as opposed to seven-syllable lines. Stapleton and Austin 1994, 230, observe that fourteeners were 'considered an appropriate medium for tragedy.'

40 The preceding line, *ustus accenso Pelias aeno* ('Pelias, burnt up in heated bronze', 666) appears to have been an interpolation, but Studley doesn't care. See Boyle 2014 ad loc. Costa 1973 retains it.

41 'She discloses her whole / host of evils: occult, secret, hidden. / Appealing with her left hand to the awful shrine / she summons all the poisonous creatures born in the burning / Libyan sand, and those that in perpetual snow / frozen Taurus holds fast in Arctic cold – / every monstrosity. Drawn by her magical songs, / deserting their lairs, the scaly swarm approaches. / A vicious serpent comes dragging its massive body, / extending its three-forked tongue and seeking those to whom / it might bring death. Hearing her song, it is stupefied. / It twists its swollen body into a multiplication of knots / and forces it into coils.'

42 The episode is treated in Ovid's *Metamorphoses* (8.515–25) and later became the subject of tragedies by William Gager (1582) and Alexandre Hardy (1624).

43 Henderson 1983.

Chapter 5

1 Kohn 2013, 17 and 87 believes that even in a full production, this scene would be 'mimed' without the use of any physical objects, which seems like an odd concession to economy; especially the knife, which is so crucial symbolically (compare Hippolytus's sword in *Phaedra*).

2 Wygant 2007, 9–10, 19. Marin 1992 reads Médée as the 'épiphanie' of absolute (monarchic) power.

3 Stanley Spaeth 2014, 42. I am using 'magic' as synonymous with 'witchcraft'.

4 The figure is from Ogden 1999, but as remarked by Gordon and Simón 2010, several new caches have been discovered since.

5 Ogden 1999, 15–25 (on deposits), 31 (types of curse), 55–60 (literacy).

6 Witches also feature in the prose fiction *Metamorphoses, or the Golden Ass* by Apuleius, but I have not examined this text here as it was written a century later. Apuleius, a self-professed natural philosopher and mystery-

cult initiate, was himself indicted for witchcraft and published a learned and playful *Apologia* in his defence.

7 Paule 2017, 39–45.

8 Paule 2017, 134–7, with bibliography.

9 Littlewood 2004, 148 argues that Seneca's Medea activates 'the meta-literary potential of . . . that most familiar poet-surrogate, the witch.'

10 Neither died on the battlefield at Pharsalus. As Lucan's readers would have been aware, Pompey was assassinated in Egypt in 48 BCE, Caesar in Rome in 44 BCE.

11 Masters 1992, 205–15; Johnson 1987, 20–9.

12 Masters 1992, 215.

13 Suet. *Vita* 27–33; Juvenal, Satire 1. Bexley 2015 argues for the performativity of *recitatio*.

14 Libanius's reference to dancing one role 'through' another (*Orat.* 64) may be the pantomime equivalent of prosopopoeia.

15 Sisyphus, on the other hand, condemned to push a boulder perpetually uphill, is cursed to be run over by his own rock, as punishment for being an ancestor of Jason's (745–6).

16 For a comprehensive study of Hecate generally, see Serafini 2015.

17 Compare the Greeks assembling to watch Astyanax's execution in Seneca's *Troades*, 1075–87, and Polyxena's sacrifice in a valley which *crescit theatri more* (1125).

18 On the dangers of persuasion, see Gorgias, *Encomium for Helen*; on poetry, see Plutarch, *How young people should listen to poetry* (*Moralia* 14–37). Speech could be figured as enchantment (*thelxis*) or a drug (*pharmakon*). See further De Romilly 1975.

19 Quint. *Inst. Orat.* 6.2.29–32 with comment by Webb 2009, 87–106.

20 Technically a *pièce à machines mêlée de chant*, a 'machine play with songs'. Its focus was the special effects, including monsters and storms at sea, but it did include music. *Pièces à machines* were a phase in the development of French opera. Akiyama 2010.

21 On the Règles, see Bray 1951; Dupont 2007. On Richelieu and the creation of the Académie, see Couton 1986.

22 *Trois Discours*, p180. Médée is a powerful *magicienne*; coming after all the wonders she has already performed, 'ce char volant n'est point hors de la vraisemblance, et ce poème n'a point besoin d'autre préparation, pour cet

effet extraordinaire'. Aristotle may be justified in accusing Euripides of inadequate preparation, 'but the same cannot be said of Seneca, nor of myself'.

23 Wygant 2007, 92.

24 Coleman 1985, xvi–xvii. For more on theatre in this period, see Meere 2015; Biet 2013; Mazouer 2002; Jondorf 1990.

25 Lawrenson 1986, 231. On conditions in the Bourgogne and Marais, see also e.g. Viala 1997.

26 Mittman 1984.

27 Mahelot 1920, 103.

28 Hobson 1982 calls this *papillotage*.

29 Marin 1992, 240: 'Elle est sur scène l'incarnation de la puissance dans sa verité infra-politique'.

30 'Now, now be present, goddess-avengers of crime, / hair foul with rippling snakes'; 'the silent throng [of ghosts] and you, death-gods'.

31 Lines: 146 (Jason), 276 (Médée), 344 (Nérine), 353 (Médée), 762 (Nérine), 926 (Médée), 1117 (Créon), 1350 (Médée), 1363 (Médée), 1561 (Jason), 1630 (Jason).

32 Marin 1992, 241 and 249–50 discusses Médée's transgression 'des règles de la répresentation théâtrale'.

33 Slaney 2015, 52: 'Senecan characters tend to be cast by *dolor* not into linguistic breakdown but into linguistic overdrive.'

34 Lines 1541, 1567, 1634, 1658.

6 Becoming Medea

1 Perris 2010 articulates the operation of these parallel reception strands. Other chapters in the same volume (Hall and Harrop 2010) offer varying perspectives.

2 Despite equal coverage of Seneca and Euripides in the introduction (Macintosh 2000a), the essays in Hall, Macintosh and Taplin 2000 almost exclusively assume the Euripidean *Medea* as their primary source-text.

3 A complete list of *Medea* receptions may be found in Boyle 2014, cxix–cxli, and on the APGRD database.

4 Slaney 2016.

5 Rowe, *The Fair Penitent* (1703).
6 Crébillon, *Atrée et Thyeste* (1707).
7 Hall 2000, 53–5.
8 Slaney 2015, 196–8. *Hercules Furens* is another Senecan source.
9 Macintosh 2000b.
10 Miola 1992.
11 Compare e.g. *Tamburlaine* Part II, 4.1.181–205.
12 Macintosh 2000a, 12–19; 2000b, *passim*.
13 Translations of Anouilh are by Luce and Arthur Klein. Page references refer to the translation. Ellipses in brackets are added to indicate omitted text; those without brackets are in the original.
14 Freeman 1984, xxxix.
15 Yaari 2003, 242; see also Corey 1990.
16 They do not necessarily come directly from Seneca, either, but most likely via a more diffuse route. There is nothing in Graham's notebooks to indicate her source. Graham 1973.
17 Graham 1998.
18 De Mille 1991, 296–7.
19 Taplin 2007, 119–23.
20 Cf. Nussbaum 1997 on the association between Medea and snakes.
21 Graham 1973, 163.
22 Interview in *Ballet Review*, quoted in De Mille 1991, 280.
23 Yaari 2003, 335 n. 68.
24 Graham 1998.
25 McDonald 2000; Reynolds 2000.
26 McDonald 2000, 117: 'Maria Callas made Cherubini's Medea her signature piece'. Cf. Kerrigan 1996, 102–3.
27 Syrmis 2012, 513–18; Ryan 1999.
28 On Pasolini's use of Romanian philosopher Eliade, see Kerrigan 1996, 103–10. Kerrigan does not mention Seneca among Pasolini's sources, but writes that Pasolini 'retrieves from behind Euripides' tragedy the Medea . . . [who is] the sorceress.'
29 This is religious language; Boyle 2014, 269 and 370. Costa 1973, 120 observes that '*hoc age* was the formula spoken at Roman sacrifices at the moment of killing the victim.'
30 Costa 1973, 159.

31 The section on Lavelli is abridged with permission from Slaney 2015, 249–55.

32 http://www.boutique.ina.fr/video/art-et-culture/arts-du-spectacle/RXF05005371/page-artistique-jean-louis-barrault-a-propos-de-medee.fr.html

33 '**MEDEA**: This day, bright day! / Day, you are here . . .! / Right now. / O just vengeance. / Time is on my side. / **JASON**: Kill me. Kill me! / You should want to kill me. Strike. Strike. / **MEDEA**: Are you asking for my pity? / Jason! It is done. / O my bitterness / I have nothing more to offer you. / Jason. / Ungrateful Jason, look. / Do you recognize your wife?'

34 According to David Whitton, 'His analysis of a play is based on a detailed study of the text but what he extracts from it is not literal meaning so much as its expressive rhythm: the interplay of strong and weak moments, the dynamic states of crescendo and decrescendo, the exchanges between soloist and Chorus.' Whitton (1987), 191.

35 The necromancy is reported, but this is still a form of (re-)enactment. *Oedipus* also contains a choral hymn to Bacchus which Hughes and Brook replaced with ecstatic chanting.

36 Schechner 1988 and 1985, and cf; Zeitlin 2004; Brook 1968; Artaud 2010 [1964]. The structuralist turn produced studies of Greek tragedy such as Vidal-Naquet 1981 [1972], Burkert 1983 [1972], and most pertinently Guépin 1968.

37 Quoted in Weber 1984, 125.

38 Translated by Ted Hughes. For this translation's performance history see Slaney 2009.

39 The full production is available online: https://www.youtube.com/watch?v=0_zpfJ528pA. Henry Stead and I were interviewed for the Open University's 'Classics Confidential' series: https://www.youtube.com/watch?v=phMl6RI1tKE.

40 Magelli is not the first to have associated Medea with volcanism. Isamu Noguchi, designer of Graham's *Cave*, likewise provided her with a 'volcanic pad' for her sunset-like descent, a black island which he glossed as 'the volcano, the house, birth . . . the way you go back to life.' Noguchi quoted in De Mille, 281.

Bibliography

Ahl, F. 2008. *Two faces of Oedipus: Sophocles' Oedipus Tyrannus and Seneca's Oedipus*. Ithaca, NY: Cornell University Press.

Akiyama, N. 2010. 'Corneille et ses pieces à machines'. *Dix-septième Siècle* 248.3, 403–17.

Arcellaschi, A. 1990. *Médée dans le théâtre latin d'Ennius à Sénèque*. Rome: École Française.

Artaud, A. 2010 [1964]. *The Theatre and its Double* (trans. V. Corti). Richmond: Oneworld.

Barton, C. 1993. *The Sorrows of the Ancient Romans: The Gladiator and the Monster*. Princeton, NJ: Princeton University Press.

Bartsch, S. 1994. *Actors in the Audience: Theatricality and Doublespeak from Nero to Hadrian*. Cambridge, MA: Harvard University Press.

Bartsch, S. 2006. *The Mirror of the Self: Sexuality, Self-knowledge and the Gaze in the Early Roman Empire*. Chicago, IL: Chicago University Press.

Bartsch, S. and Wray, D. 2009. 'Introduction' in Bartsch and Wray (eds) *Seneca and the Self*. Cambridge: Cambridge University Press, 3–19.

Beacham, R. 1991. *The Roman Theatre and its Audience*. London: Routledge.

Beacham, R. 1999. *Spectacle Entertainments of Early Imperial Rome*. New Haven, CT: Yale University Press.

Beard, M., North, J. and Price, S. 1998. *Religions of Rome*. Cambridge: Cambridge University Press.

Bexley, E. 2015. 'What is dramatic recitation?' *Mnemosyne* 68.5, 774–93.

Bexley, E. 2016. 'Recognition and the character of Seneca's Medea'. *The Cambridge Classical Journal* 62, 31–51.

Beye, C.R. 1982. *Epic and Romance in the Argonautica of Apollonius*. Carbondale: Southern Illinois University Press.

Bieber, M. 1971. *The History of the Greek and Roman Theatre*. Princeton, NJ: Princeton University Press.

Biet, C. 2013. 'A "Senecan" theatre of cruelty: Audience, citizens and chorus in French dramas of the late sixteenth and early seventeenth centuries' in Billings, Budelmann and Macintosh (eds) *Choruses, Ancient and Modern*. Oxford: Oxford University Press, 189–202.

Boardman, J. 1980. *The Greeks Overseas: Their Early Colonies and Trade* (3rd edn). London: Thames and Hudson.

Boyle, A.J. 1997. *Tragic Seneca: An Essay in the Theatrical Tradition*. London: Routledge.

Boyle, A.J. 2006. *An Introduction to Roman Tragedy*. London: Routledge.

Boyle, A.J. 2008. *Octavia: Attributed to Seneca*. Oxford: Oxford University Press.

Boyle, A.J. 2014. *Medea: Seneca. Edited with Introduction and Commentary*. Oxford: Oxford University Press.

Bray, R. (1951). *La formation de la doctrine classique en France*. Paris: Nizet.

Bremmer, J. 1997. 'Why did Medea kill her brother Apsyrtus?' in Clauss and Iles Johnston (eds) *Medea: Essays on Medea in Myth, Literature, Philosophy and Art*. Princeton, NJ: Princeton University Press, 83–100.

Brink, C.O. 1971. *Horace on Poetry: The Ars Poetica*. Cambridge: Cambridge University Press.

Brook, P. 1968. *The Empty Space*. London: McGibbon and Kee.

Brooks, P. 1984. *The Melodramatic Imagination: Balzac, Henry James, Melodrama, and the Mode of Excess*. New York: Columbia University Press.

Burkert, W. 1983 [1972]. *Homo Necans: The Anthropology of Ancient Greek Sacrificial Ritual and Myth* (trans. Bing). Berkeley: University of California Press.

Burnett, A.P. 1998. *Revenge in Attic and Later Tragedy*. Berkeley: University of California Press.

Butler, S. 2015. *The Ancient Phonograph*. New York: Zone Books.

Byre, C.S. 2002. *A Reading of Apollonius Rhodius' Argonautica: The Poetics of Uncertainty*. Lewiston, NY: Edwin Mellen.

Calder, W.M. 1976. 'Seneca: Tragedian of imperial Rome'. *The Classical Journal* 72.1, 1–11.

Clare, R.J. 2002. *The Path of the Argo: Language, Imagery and Narrative in the Argonautica of Apollonius Rhodius*. Cambridge: Cambridge University Press.

Clauss, J.J. 1997. 'Conquest of the Mephistophelian Nausicaa: Medea's role in Apollonius' redefinition of the epic hero' in Clauss and Iles Johnston (eds) *Medea: Essays on Medea in Myth, Literature, Philosophy and Art*. Princeton, NJ: Princeton University Press. 149–77.

Coleman, J. 1985. *Jean de La Péruse: Médée*. Exeter: Exeter University Press.

Coleman, M.K. 1990. 'Fatal charades: Roman executions staged as mythological enactments'. *Journal of Roman Studies* 80, 44–73.

Corey, F.C. 1990. 'Martha Graham's re-vision of Jocasta, Clytemnestra and Medea'. *Text and Performance Quarterly* 3, 204–17.

Corneille, P. 1987 [1660]. 'Les trois discours sur le poème dramatique' in *Oeuvres Complètes* (vol. 3). Paris: Éditions Gallimard.

Corrigan, K. 2013. *Virgo to Virago: Medea in the Silver Age*. Cambridge: Cambridge Scholars.

Costa, C.D.N. (ed.) 1973. *Seneca: Medea*. Oxford: Clarendon.

Couton, G. 1986. *Richelieu et le théâtre*. Lyon: Presses Universitaires de Lyon.

Csapo, E. and Slater, W.J. 1994. *The Context of Ancient Drama*. Ann Arbor: University of Michigan Press.

Davis, M.A. 1990. 'Ratis Audax: Valerius Flaccus' bold ship', in Boyle (ed.) *The Imperial Muse: Ramus Essays on Roman Literature*. Berwick: Aureal.

Davis, P.J. (2003). *Seneca: Thyestes*. London: Duckworth.

De Mille, A. 1991. *Martha: The Life and Work of Martha Graham*. London: Random House.

Dodson-Robinson, E. 2011. 'Performing the "unperformable" extispicy scene in Seneca's Oedipus'. *Didaskalia* 8.

Dougherty, C. 1993. *The Poetics of Colonization: From City to Text in Archaic Greece*. Oxford: Oxford University Press.

Duff, J.W. 1960. *A Literary History of Rome in the Silver Age: From Tiberius to Hadrian*. London: Benn.

Dupont, F. 1995. *Les Monstres de Sénèque: pour une dramaturgie de la tragédie romaine*. Paris: Belin.

Dupont, F. 2007. *Aristote ou le vampire du théâtre occidental*. Paris: Flammarion.

Eliot, T.S. 1951 [1927]. 'Seneca in Elizabethan Translation' in *Selected Essays*. London: Faber and Faber. 65–105.

Edwards, C. 1993. *The Politics of Immorality in Ancient Rome*. Cambridge: Cambridge University Press.

Edwards, C. 1997. 'Unspeakable professions: Public performance and prostitution in ancient Rome' in Hallett (ed.) *Roman Sexualities*. Princeton, NJ: Princeton University Press. 66–95.

Edwards, C. 2007. *Death in Ancient Rome*. New Haven, CT: Yale University Press.

Erasmo, M. 2004. *Roman Tragedy: Theatre to Theatricality*. Austin, TX: University of Texas.

Fantham, E. (ed.) 1982. *Seneca's Troades: A Literary Introduction with Text, Translation and Commentary*. Princeton, NJ: Princeton University Press.

Fantham, E. 2000. 'Production of Seneca's Trojan Women, ancient? and modern' in Harrison (ed.) *Seneca in Performance*. London: Duckworth. 13–26.

Fantham, E. 2002. 'Orator and/et actor' in Easterling and Hall (eds) *Greek and Roman Actors: Aspects of an Ancient Profession*. Cambridge: Cambridge University Press. 362–76.

Fischer-Lichte, E. 1999. 'Between text and cultural performance: Staging Greek tragedies in Germany'. *Theatre Survey* 40.1, 1–30.

Fitch, J.G. 1981. 'Sense-pauses and relative dating in Seneca, Sophocles and Shakespeare'. *American Journal of Philology* 102, 289–307.

Fitch, J.G. 2002. 'Medea' in *Seneca: Tragedies* (vol. 1). Cambridge, MA: Harvard University Press.

Fitch, J.G. and McElduff, S. 2002. 'Construction of the self in Senecan drama'. *Mnemosyne* 55, 18–40.

France, P. 1991. 'L'Hyperbole chez Racine' in *Racine: théâtre & poesie*. Leeds: Cairns. 23–36.

Freeman, E. 1984. 'Introduction' in *Jean Anouilh: Eurydice and Médée*. Oxford: Blackwell, vii–xlviii.

Fyfe, H. 1983. 'An analysis of Seneca's Medea' in Boyle (ed.) *Seneca Tragicus: Ramus Essays on Senecan Drama*. Berwick: Aureal, 77–93.

Gellrich, M. 1994. 'Socratic magic: Enchantment, irony and persuasion in Plato's dialogues'. *Classical World* 87, 275–307.

Gill, C. 1997. 'Passion as madness in Roman poetry' in Braund and Gill (eds) *The Passions in Roman Thought and Literature*. Cambridge: Cambridge University Press, 213–41.

Gill, C. 2009. 'Seneca and selfhood: Integration and disintegration' in Bartsch and Wray (eds) *Seneca and the Self*. Cambridge: Cambridge University Press, 65–83.

Gordon, R.L. and Simón, F.M. (eds) 2010. *Magical Practice in the Latin West: Papers from the International Conference held at the University of Zaragoza, 30 Sept–1 Oct 2005*. Leiden: Brill.

Graham, M. 1973. *The Notebooks of Martha Graham*. London: Harcourt Brace Jovanovich.

Graham, M. 1998. [Untitled interview] in *Martha Graham Dance Company* (VHS tape). New York: Nonesuch.

Graf, F. 1991. 'Gestures and conventions: The gestures of Roman actors and orators' in Bremmer and Roodenburg (eds) *A Cultural History of Gesture from Antiquity to the Present Day*. Oxford: Oxford University Press.

Griffin, M. 1976. *Seneca: A Philosopher in Politics*. Oxford: Clarendon.

Guastella, G. 2001. 'Virgo, Coniunx, Mater: The wrath of Seneca's Medea'. *Classical Antiquity* 20.2, 197–219.

Guépin, J-P. 1968. *The Tragic Paradox: Myth and Ritual in Greek Tragedy*. Amsterdam: Hakkert.

Gunderson, E. 2000. *Staging Masculinity: The Rhetoric of Performance in the Roman World*. Ann Arbor: University of Michigan.

Gunderson, E. 2017. 'Repetition'. *Ramus* 46, 118–34.

Hall, E. 2000. 'Medea on the eighteenth-century London stage' in Hall, Macintosh and Taplin (eds) *Medea in Performance 1500–2000*. Oxford: Legenda, 49–74.

Hall, E. and Harrop, S. (eds) 2010. *Theorising Performance: Greek Drama, Cultural History and Critical Practice*. London: Duckworth.

Hall, E., Macintosh, F. and Taplin, O. (eds) 2000. *Medea in Performance 1500–2000*. Oxford: Legenda.

Harris, W. 2004. *Restraining Rage: The Ideology of Anger Control in Classical Antiquity*. Cambridge, MA: Harvard University Press.

Harrison, G.W.M. (ed.) 2000. *Seneca in Performance*. London: Duckworth.

Heavey, K. 2015. *Early Modern Medea: Medea in English Literature, 1558–1668*. Basingstoke: Palgrave Macmillan.

Henderson, J. 1983. 'Poetic technique and rhetorical amplification: Seneca *Medea* 579–669' in Boyle (ed.) *Seneca Tragicus: Ramus Essays on Senecan Drama*. Berwick: Aureal, 94–113.

Henry, D. and Walker, B. 1967. 'Loss of identity: *Medea superest*? – a study of Seneca's Medea'. *Classical Philology* 62.3, 169–81.

Herington, J. 1966. 'Senecan tragedy'. *Arion* 5.4, 422–77.

Hersch, K. 2010. *The Roman Wedding: Ritual and Meaning in Antiquity*. Cambridge: Cambridge University Press.

Hill, T.D. 2004. *Ambitiosa Mors: Suicide and the Self in Roman Thought and Literature*. London: Routledge.

Hinds, S. 1993. 'Seneca's Ovidian Loci'. *Studi Italiani di Filologia Classica* 9, 5–63.

Hinds, S. 2011. 'Medea in Ovid: Scenes from the life of an intertextual heroine'. *Materiali e discussion per l'analisi dei testi classici* 30, 9–47.

Hine, H.M. 2000. *Seneca: Medea*. Warminster: Aris and Phillips.

Hobson, M. 1982. *The Object of Art: The Theory of Illusion in Eighteenth-Century France*. Cambridge: Cambridge University Press.

Hunter, R. 1993. *The Argonautica of Apollonius: Literary Studies*. Cambridge University Press.

Huskinson, J. 2005. 'The rivers of Roman Antioch' in Stafford and Herrin (eds) *Personification in the Greek World: From Antiquity to Byzantium*. Aldershot: Ashgate, 247–66.

Inwood, B. 2005. *Reading Seneca: Stoic Philosophy at Rome*. Oxford: Oxford University Press.

Jocelyn, H.D. 1967. *The Tragedies of Ennius: The Fragments*. Cambridge: Cambridge University Press.

Johnson, W.R. 1987. *Momentary Monsters: Lucan and His Heroes*. Ithaca, NY: Cornell University Press.

Johnson, W.R. 1988. 'Medea Nunc Sum: The close of Seneca's version' in Pucci (ed.) *Language and the Tragic Hero: Essays on Greek Tragedy in Honour of Gordon M. Kirkwood*. Atlanta, GA: Scholars Press, 85–101.

Jondorf, G. 1990. *French Renaissance Tragedy: The Dramatic Word*. Cambridge: Cambridge University Press.

Jones, J.M. 1990. *A Dictionary of Ancient Roman Coins*. London: Seaby.

Jones, L.W. and Morey, C.R. 1930–1. *The Miniatures of the Manuscripts of Terence Prior to the Thirteenth Century*. Princeton, NJ: Princeton University Press.

Karamanou, I. 2014. 'Otherness and exile: Euripides' production of 431 BCE' in Stuttard (ed.) *Looking at Medea: Essays and a Translation of Euripides' Tragedy*. London: Bloomsbury, 35–45.

Kelly, H.A. 1979. 'Tragedy and the performance of tragedy in late antiquity'. *Traditio* 35, 21–44.

Kemp, R. 2012. *Embodied Acting: What Neuroscience Tells Us about Performance*. London: Routledge.

Ker, J. 2009a. *The Deaths of Seneca*. Oxford: Oxford University Press.

Ker, J. 2009b. 'Seneca on self-examination: Rereading On Anger 3.36' in Bartsch and Wray (eds) *Seneca and the Self*. Cambridge: Cambridge University Press, 160–87.

Ker, J. and Winston, J. 2012. 'Introduction' in *Elizabethan Seneca: Three Tragedies*. London: Modern Humanities Research Association, 1–66.

Kerrigan, J. 1996. *Revenge Tragedy: Aeschylus to Armageddon*. Oxford: Clarendon.

Kohn, T.D. 2003. 'Who wrote Seneca's plays?' *Classical World* 96, 271–80.

Kohn, T.D. 2013. *The Dramaturgy of Senecan Tragedy*. Ann Arbor: University of Michigan Press.

Koortbojian 1995. *Myth, Meaning, and Memory on Roman Sarcophagi*. Berkeley: University of California Press.

Kragelund, P. 2016. *Roman Historical Drama: The Octavia in Antiquity and Beyond*. Oxford: Oxford University Press.

Lada-Richards, I. 2002. 'The subjectivity of Greek performance' in Easterling and Hall (eds) *Greek and Roman Actors: Aspects of an Ancient Profession*. Cambridge: Cambridge University Press.

Lada-Richards, I. 2003. 'Mobile statuary: Refractions of pantomime dancing from Callistratus to Emma Hamilton and Andrew Ducrow'. *International Journal of the Classical Tradition* 10.1, 3–37.

Lada-Richards, I. 2004. 'Mythōn eikōn: Pantomime dancing and the figurative arts in imperial and late antiquity'. *Arion* 12.2, 111–40.

Lada-Richards, I. 2007. *Silent Eloquence: Lucian and Pantomime Dancing*. London: Duckworth.

Lawall, G. 1979. 'Seneca's Medea: The elusive triumph of civilization' in Bowersock, Burkert and Putnam (eds) *Arktouros: Studies Presented to Bernard M.W. Knox on the Occasion of his 65th Birthday*. Berlin: De Gruyter

Lawrenson, T.E. (1986). *The French Stage and Playhouse in the XVIIth Century: A Study in the Advent of the Italian Order*. New York: AMS.

Lessing, G. 1973. 'Von den Lateinischen Trauerspielen welche unter dem Namen des Seneca bekannt sind' in Göpfert (ed.) *Lessing: Werke* (vol. 4). München: Hanser.

Lessing, G. 1984. *Laocoön* (trans. E.A. McCormick). Baltimore: Johns Hopkins University Press.

Littlewood, C.A.J. 2004. *Self-Representation and Illusion in Senecan Tragedy*. Oxford: Oxford University Press.

Llewellyn-Jones, L. 2005. 'Body language and the female role-player in Greek tragedy and Japanese Kabuki theatre' in Cairns (ed.) *Body Language in the Greek and Roman Worlds*. Swansea: Classical Press of Wales, 73–105.

Macintosh, F. 2000a. 'Introduction: The performer in performance' in Hall, Macintosh and Taplin (eds) *Medea in Performance 1500–2000*. Oxford: Legenda, 1–31.

Macintosh, F. 2000b. 'Medea transposed: Burlesque and gender on the mid-Victorian stage' in Hall, Macintosh and Taplin (eds) *Medea in Performance 1500–2000*. Oxford: Legenda, 75–99.

McDonald, M. 2000. 'Medea è mobile: The many faces of Medea in opera' in Hall, Macintosh and Taplin (eds) *Medea in Performance 1500–2000*. Oxford: Legenda, 100–18.

McGuire, D.T. 1997. *Acts of Silence: Civil War, Tyranny and Suicide in the Flavian Epics*. Hildesheim: Olms-Weidmann.

Mahelot, L. 1920. *Memoire* (ed. Lancaster). Paris.

Manuwald, G. 2013. 'Medea: Transformations of a Greek figure in Latin literature'. *Greece and Rome* 60.1, 114–35.

Marin, L. 1992. 'Théatrialité et pouvoir, magie, machination, machine: Médée de Corneille' in Lazzeri and Reynié (eds) *Le pouvoir de la raison d'etat*. Paris: Presses Universitaires de France.

Marshall, C.W. 2000. 'Location! Location! Location! Choral absence and dramatic space in Seneca's *Troades*' in Harrison (ed.) *Seneca in Performance*. London: Duckworth. 27–52.

Masters, J. 1992. *Poetry and Civil War in Lucan's Bellum Civile*. Cambridge: Cambridge University Press.

Mastronarde, D. 1970. 'Seneca's *Oedipus*: The drama in the word.' *TAPA* 101, 291–315.

Mayer, R. 2002. *Seneca: Phaedra*. London: Duckworth.

Mazouer, C. 2002. *Le théâtre français de la Renaissance*. Paris: Champion.

Meere, M. 2015. 'From the Catholic Mystery play to Calvinist tragedy, or the reinvention of French religious drama' in Earle and Fouto (eds) *The Reinvention of Theatre in Sixteenth-Century Europe*. London: Routledge.

Mendell, C.W. 1941. *Our Seneca*. New Haven, CT: Yale.

Miola, R. 1992. *Shakespeare and Classical Tragedy: The Influence of Seneca*. Oxford: Clarendon.

Mittman, B. 1984. *Spectators on the Paris Stage in the Seventeenth and Eighteenth Centuries*. Ann Arbor: University of Michigan Press.

Most, G. 1992. 'Disiecti membra poetae: The rhetoric of dismemberment in Neronian poetry' in Hexter and Selden (eds) *Innovations of Antiquity*. New York: Routledge.

Nikolaidis, A.G. 1985. 'Some observations on Ovid's lost Medea.' *Latomus* 44, 383–7.

Norland, H. 2009. *Neoclassical Tragedy in Elizabethan England*. Newark: University of Delaware.

Nussbaum, M. 1993. 'Poetry and the passions: Two Stoic views' in Brunschwig and Nussbaum (eds) *Passions and Perceptions: Studies in Hellenistic Philosophy of Mind*. Cambridge: Cambridge University Press.

Nussbaum, M. 1997. 'Serpents in the soul: A reading of Seneca's *Medea*' in Clauss and Iles Johnston (eds) *Medea: Essays on Medea in Myth, Literature, Philosophy and Art*. Princeton, NJ: Princeton University Press, 219–49.

Ogden, D. 1999. 'Binding spells: Curse tablets and voodoo dolls in the Greek and Roman worlds' in Flint et al. (eds) *Witchcraft and Magic in Europe: Ancient Greece and Rome*. London: Athlone, 1–90.

Ohlander, S. 1989. *Dramatic Suspense in Euripides' and Seneca's Medea*. New York: P. Lang.

Paule, M.T. 2017. *Canidia: Rome's First Witch*. London: Bloomsbury.

Perris, S. 2010. 'Performance reception and the "textual twist": Towards a theory of literary reception' in Hall and Harrop (eds) *Theorising Performance: Greek Drama, Cultural History and Critical Practice*. London: Duckworth.

Pratt, N.T. 1983. *Seneca's Drama*. Chapel Hill: University of South Carolina Press.

Pucci, P. 1980. *The Violence of Pity in Euripides' Medea*. Ithaca, NY: Cornell University Press.

Radt, S. (ed.) 1977. *Tragicorum Graecorum Fragmenta* (vol. 4). Göttingen: Vandenhoeck and Ruprecht.

Rawson, E. 1987. 'Discrimina Ordinum: The Lex Iulia Theatralis'. *Papers of the British School at Rome* 55, 83–114.

Reynolds, M. 2000. 'Performing Medea: Or, why Medea is a woman' in Hall, Macintosh and Taplin (eds) *Medea in Performance 1500–2000*. Oxford: Legenda, 119–43.

Robin, D. 1993. 'Film theory and the gendered voice in Seneca' in Rabinowitz and Richlin (eds) *Feminist Theory and the Classics*. New York: Routledge, 102–21.

Roller, D.W. 2006. *Through the Pillars of Herakles: Greco-Roman Exploration of the Atlantic*. New York: Routledge.

de Romilly, J. 1975. *Magic and Rhetoric in Ancient Greece*. Cambridge, MA: Harvard University Press.

Romm, J.S. 1992. *The Edges of the Earth in Ancient Thought: Geography, Exploration and Fiction*. Princeton, NJ: Princeton University Press.

Rosenmeyer, T.G. 1989. *Senecan Drama and Stoic Cosmology*. Berkeley: University of California Press.

Ryan, C.M. 1999. 'Salvaging the sacred: Female subjectivity in Pasolini's "Medea"'. *Italica* 76.2, 193–204.

Sandis, E. 2015. 'Palimpsestuous Phaedra: William Gager's additions to Seneca's tragedy for his 1592 production at Christ Church, Oxford' in Earle and Fouto (eds) *The Reinvention of Theatre in Sixteenth-Century Europe*. London: Routledge.

Scarry, E. 1985. *The Body in Pain: The Making and Unmaking of the World*. Oxford: Oxford University Press.

Schechner, R. 1985. *Between Theatre and Anthropology*. Pennsylvania: University of Pennsylvania Press, 49–76.

Schechner, R. 1988. *Performance Theory*. Routledge: New York.

Schiesaro, A. 1997. 'Passion, reason and knowledge in Seneca's tragedies' in Braund and Gill (eds) *The Passions in Roman Thought and Literature*. Cambridge: Cambridge University Press.

Schiesaro, A. 2003. *The Passions in Play: Thyestes and the Dynamics of Senecan Drama*. Cambridge: Cambridge University Press.

Schiesaro, A. 2009. 'Seneca and the denial of the self' in Bartsch and Wray (eds) *Seneca and the Self*. Cambridge: Cambridge University Press, 221–35.

Sear, F. 2005. *Roman Theatres: An Architectural Study*. Oxford: Oxford University Press.

Segal, C. 1982. 'Nomen sacrum: Medea and other names in Senecan tragedy'. *Maia* 34, 241–6.

Segal, C. 1984. 'Senecan baroque: The death of Hippolytus in Seneca, Ovid and Euripides'. *TAPA* 114, 311–25.

Segal, C. 1986. *Language and Desire in Seneca's Phaedra*. Princeton, NJ: Princeton University Press.

Seidensticker, B. 1969. *Die Gesprächsverdichtung in den Tragödien Senecas*. Heidelberg: Carl Winter Universitätsverlag.

Serafini, N. 2015. *La Dea Ecate nell' Antica Grecia: una protettrice dalla quale proteggersi*. Ariccia: Aracne Editrice.

Sherwin-White, A.N. 1966. *The Letters of Pliny: A Historical and Social Commentary*. Oxford: Clarendon.

Slaney, H. 2009. 'Liminal's Kosky's Hughes's Artaud's Seneca's Oedipus'. *New Voices in Classical Reception Studies* 4, 52–70.

Slaney, H. 2013a. 'The voyage of rediscovery: Consuming global space in Valerius' Argonautica' in Ziogas and Skempis (eds) *Geography, Topography, Landscape: Configurations of Space in Greek and Roman Epic*. Berlin: De Gruyter.

Slaney, H. 2013b. 'Seneca's chorus of one' in Billings, Budelmann and Macintosh (eds) *Choruses, Ancient and Modern*. Oxford: Oxford University Press.

Slaney, H. 2015. *The Senecan Aesthetic: A Performance History*. Oxford: Oxford University Press.

Slaney, H. 2016. 'Senecan Gothic' in Dodson-Robinson (ed.) *Brill's Companion to the Reception of Senecan Tragedy*. Leiden: Brill.

Smith, R.R.R. 1991. *Hellenistic Sculpture: A Handbook*. London: Thames and Hudson.

Sourvinou-Inwood, C. 1997. 'Medea at a shifting distance: Images and Euripidean tragedy' in Clauss and Iles Johnston (eds) *Medea: Essays on Medea in Myth, Literature, Philosophy and Art*. Princeton, NJ: Princeton University Press, 269–74.

Stafford, E. and Herrin, J. (eds) 2005. *Personification in the Greek World: From Antiquity to Byzantium*. Aldershot: Ashgate.

Stanley Spaeth, B. 2014. 'From goddess to hag: The Greek and Roman witch in classical literature' in Stratton and Kalleres (eds) *Daughters of Hecate: Women and Magic in the Ancient World*. Oxford: Oxford University Press.

Stapleton, M.L. and Austin, S.F. 1994. '"Shine it like a comet of revenge": Seneca, John Studley, and Shakespeare's Joan la Pucelle'. *Comparative Literature Studies* 31.3, 229–50.

Star, C. 2012. *The Empire of the Self: Self-Command and Political Speech in Seneca and Petronius*. Baltimore, MD: Johns Hopkins University Press.

Storm, W. 1998. *After Dionysus: A Theory of the Tragic*. Ithaca, NY: Cornell University Press.

Sutton, D.F. 1986. *Seneca on the Stage*. Leiden: Brill.

Syrmis, M. 2012. 'Pasolini's erotic gaze from "Medea" to "Salò"'. *Italica* 89.4, 510–31.

Taplin, O. 2007. *Pots and Plays: Interactions between Tragedy and Greek Vase-Painting of the Fourth Century BC*. Los Angeles: Getty Museum.

Tarrant, R.J. 1978. 'Senecan drama and its antecedents'. *Harvard Studies in Classical Philology* 82, 213–63.

Tarrant, R.J. (ed.) 1985. *Seneca's Thyestes*. Atlanta, GA: Scholars' Press.

Treggiari, S. 1991. *Roman Marriage: Iusti Coniuges from the time of Cicero to the Time of Ulpian*. Oxford: Clarendon.

Trinacty, C. 2014. *Senecan Tragedy and the Reception of Augustan Poetry*. Oxford: Oxford University Press.

Tsetskhladze, G.R. 2006. 'Revisiting Ancient Greek colonisation' in Tsetskhladze, G.R. (ed.) *Greek Colonisation: An Account of Greek Colonies and Other Settlements Overseas* (vol. 1). Leiden: Brill.

Turcan, R. 1998. *The Gods of Ancient Rome: Religion in Everyday Life from Archaic to Imperial Times* (trans. Nevill). Edinburgh: Edinburgh University Press.

Van Zyl Smit, B. 2014. 'Black Medeas' in Stuttard (ed.) *Looking at Medea: Essays and a Translation of Euripides' Tragedy*. London: Bloomsbury, 157–66.

Varner E.R. 2000. 'Grotesque vision: Seneca's tragedies and Neronian art' in Harrison (ed.) *Seneca in Performance*. London: Duckworth, 119–36.

Viala, A. 1997. *Le Théâtre en France des origines à nos jours*. Paris: PUF.

Vidal-Naquet, P. 1981 [1972]. 'Hunting and sacrifice in Aeschylus' Oresteia' in Vernant and Vidal-Naquet, *Tragedy and Myth in Ancient Greece* (trans. Lloyd). Brighton: Harvester. 150–74.

Webb. R. 2008. *Demons and Dancers: Performance in Late Antiquity*. Cambridge, MA: Harvard University Press.

Webb. R. 2009. *Ekphrasis, Imagination and Persuasion in Ancient Rhetorical Theory and Practice*. Farnham: Ashgate.

Weber, C. 1984 (ed. and trans.) *Heiner Müller: Hamletmachine and Other Texts for the Stage*. New York: Performing Arts Journal Publications.

Whitton, D. 1987. *Stage Directors in Modern France*. Manchester: Manchester University Press.

Williams, M.F. 1991. *Landscape in the Argonautica of Apollonius Rhodius*. Frankfurt: Peter Lang.

Wilson. E. 2014. *Seneca: A Life*. London: Penguin.

Winkler, J. 1985. *Auctor & Actor: A Narratological Reading of Apuleius' Golden Ass*. Berkeley: University of California Press.

Wray, D. 2009. 'Seneca and tragedy's reason' in Bartsch and Wray (eds) *Seneca and the Self*. Cambridge: Cambridge University Press, 237–54.

Wygant, A. 2007. *Medea, Magic and Modernity in France: Stages and Histories, 1553–1797*. Farnham: Ashgate.

Yaari, N. 2003. 'Myth into dance: Martha Graham's interpretation of the classical tradition'. *IJCT* 10.2, 221–42.

Young, G.K. 2001. *Rome's Eastern Trade: International Commerce and Imperial Policy 31 BC–AD 305*. New York: Routledge.

Zanobi, A. 2008. 'The influence of pantomime on Seneca's tragedies' in Hall and Wyles (eds) *New Directions in Ancient Pantomime*. Oxford: Oxford University Press, 227–57.

Zanobi, A. 2014. *Seneca's Tragedies and the Aesthetics of Pantomime*. London: Bloomsbury.

Zeitlin, F. 2004. 'Dionysus in 69' in Hall, Macintosh and Wrigley (eds) *Dionysus Since 69: Greek Tragedy at the Dawn of the Third Millennium*. Oxford: Oxford University Press, 49–76.

Zimmermann, B. 2008. 'Seneca and Pantomime' (trans. E. Hall) in Hall and Wyles (eds) *New Directions in Ancient Pantomime*. Oxford: Oxford University Press, 218–26.

Zwierlein, O. 1966. *Die Rezitationsdramen Senecas*. Meisenheim: Hain.

Index

Ingram Content Group UK Ltd.
Milton Keynes UK
UKHW020046240423
420349UK00031B/336